Wisdom to Wellness

Healing Your Emotional Sufferings so the
Physical Healing Can Follow

Wisdom to Wellness

Healing Your Emotional Sufferings so the
Physical Healing Can Follow

Maureen Minnehan Jones

BOOKS

Winchester, UK
Washington, USA

First published by O-Books, 2011

O Books is an imprint of John Hunt Publishing Ltd., The Bothy, Deershot Lodge, Park Lane, Ropley,
Hants, SO24 0BE, UK
office1@o-books.net
www.o-books.com

For distributor details and how to order please visit the 'Ordering' section on our website.

Text copyright: Maureen Minnehan Jones 2010

ISBN: 978 1 84694 399 7

A CIP catalogue record for this book is available from the British Library.

Design: Tom Davies

Printed in the UK by CPI Antony Rowe
Printed in the USA by Offset Paperback Mfrs, Inc

We operate a distinctive and ethical publishing philosophy in all
areas of its business, from its global network of authors to
production and worldwide distribution.

CONTENTS

Foreword   1

Introduction to the MO (Modus Operandi)
    Technique   3

Chapter 1: How We Keep Killing Ourselves and
    What Can We Do to Stop It   6

Chapter 2: Solving the Mystery with the
    MO Technique   12

Chapter 3: The Common Thread of Disease   23

Chapter 4: The Role of Chakras in
    Health and Healing   35

Chapter 5: Divine Connection
    Using the Infinity Sign   55

Chapter 6: How the MO Technique Works   57

Chapter 7: Steps to Releasing Emotional Sufferings
    with the MO Technique   62

Chapter 8: Learning the Lessons Our
    Bodies Can Teach Us   78

Chapter 9: What About Our Children   82

Chapter 10: AIDS/HIV   85

Chapter 11: Allergies   96

Chapter 12: Alzheimer's Disease   106

Chapter 13: Arthritis   118

Chapter 14: Cancer   128

Chapter 15: Breast Cancer   134

Chapter 16: Prostate Cancer   147

Chapter 17: Cholesterol Problems   154

Chapter 18: The Common Cold   164

Chapter 19: The Flu   173

Chapter 20: Fibromyalgia   184

Chapter 21: Heart Disease   193

Chapter 22: Hepatitis C   206
Chapter 23: ALS Disease   213
Chapter 24: Menopause   225
Chapter 25: Migraine Headaches   234
Chapter 26: Multiple Sclerosis   242
Chapter 27: Parkinson's Disease   249
Conclusion: The Opposite of Fear is Love   259
Expressions of Thanks   261
Endnotes   265
About the Creator of the MO Technique   272

Maureen Minnehan Jones's book Wisdom to Wellness is effectively a master-piece. Now, this strong statement needs explaining. But first, a disclaimer. My opinion is NOT based on my book Messages from the Body. Rather, it's based on the fact that Maureen has taken her profound wisdom and life experiences to pull together a remarkably effective healing system and a brilliantly presented interpretation of several of the disorders from my book.

Why is that important? It makes Wisdom to Wellness a manual for self-healing and for client-serving that can be virtually life-saving. It also provides a working model for how to understand both the emotional and soul determinants of disorders that underlie physical ailments. Its strength lies in providing a guiding example of how to go about healing them.

All of these things make Wisdom to Wellness an invaluable teaching device for people to work with — to free themselves from the shackles of the outcomes of their life's history. This major breakthrough for both physical and mental healers will have a huge impact on how we regard and approach physical disorders. It should be on every healer's desk and, indeed, in every home.

Michael J. Lincoln, PhD, author of *Messages from the Body* and forty other books

Maureen Minnehan Jones is trained in Western medicine and, with a broad understanding of healing in its deepest sense, offers a gold mine of important information in this important book. Using examples of celebrities and ordinary people, she skillfully takes us through a process of healing that offers hope and practical approaches to a wide variety of disease states. Simple and complex. Powerful and easy to practice. This book should be read by everyone who aspires to healing and health.

Kathleen Brehony, PhD, author of *Awakening at Midlife, Ordinary Grace, After the Darkest Hour,* and *Living A Connected Life*

Wisdom to Wellness is a healing catalyst that valiantly carries "the banner of truth." Written with compassionate comprehension, it offers a deep under-standing of the truth behind how disease is created. More than that, it provides a new paradigm for living a healthy and whole life—for all people. Wisdom to Wellness brings a dynamic resource for healing to anyone willing to receive the message. A must read!

Jennifer Tobias; author of *Live, Love and Earn: Creating Wealth While Working From Home* and *The Little Business That Wanted To Grow*

"Maureen's enlightening and heart-opening Wisdom to Wellness creates hope, understanding, and a clear path through the stress and fear of illness to true healing."

Lynn Telford-Sahl, M.A., *Intentional JOY: How to Turn Stress, Fear & Addiction into Freedom* (2009)

"In editing and revising Maureen's massively important work, we've learned to apply its principles to our own experiences. Maureen holds a vision of healing and love for everyone on our planet, and most importantly, she shows us how to achieve this vision, starting with ourselves. Her success in helping people heal from all kinds of diseases and conditions and stay healthy without drugs or surgery indicates that a paradigm shift is in order for the medical community. Wisdom to Wellness reflects positive action based on earnest research and well-tested experience. It's a book we're proud to endorse from a writing and a content point of view."

Barbara McNichol Editorial team

Dedication
This book is dedicated to Michael J. Lincoln, Ph.D.
Through his passionate work and wisdom, he has been an
inspiration to my life, goals, purpose, and
the creation of this book.

A Special Note to My Readers

Because of my belief system, I *thank* those in my family of origin rather than blaming them for any problems I've encountered. Let me explain why. Most parents do the best they can. We learn to parent from our own life experience, and we pass that experience down to our children the same way we would bequeath Aunt Edna's coffee table or Grandma's pumpkin pie recipe. A family's emotional suffering is handed down from generation to generation, and our souls decide if we pick them up.

It's my sincere belief that we came to this life school for experiences to further our soul consciousness through what I call *soul discoveries*. These discoveries help us accept total responsibility for *everything* that happens to us.

The most powerful force in life is *love*. I believe the discovery that's imperative to get from this book is to embrace self-love and know that you are a treasure. When you've mastered loving yourself, you have an excellent chance of healing on every level.

The opposite of self-love is fear. Many of us have an internal block wall holding a cyclic pattern of fear. The good news is that it can be released with the MO Technique described in this book. In these pages, I offer you a gift—the precious gift that sustains the body—self-love.

This book is not intended to be a replacement for good medical diagnosis and treatment. It's best to ask your physician if this self-healing method could be used with your treatment plan. Therefore, before attempting the MO (Modus Operandi) Technique, it is suggested that you seek the expertise of a trained physician for diagnosis, treatment, and guidance for using this particular therapeutic modality.

I recommend you read the chapters in sequential order, as each one builds on the information found in the preceding chapter. When discussing Dr. Lincoln's commentary on any given illness I selected sections that were relevant to the examples we were working on.

Thank you, Maureen Minnehan Jones, RN, GIP

Acknowledgments

I express my love and gratitude from the deepest part of my heart to everyone who loved and supported me through writing this book.

First and foremost, I would like to thank my husband, Jerry, for his ever-present love and encouragement. He has been there every step of the way. To my two special gifts: my daughter, Amber, and my son, Michael, for their unconditional love and for being with me through thick and thin.

Thanks to my dear new family—Phil and Baby Jack, Brenda, Shawn, Emma, and Cole—Anita, Luis, Nico and Mia—my second mom, Harriett—Doug, Terry, and Georgia. I thank you for your understanding, support, and love.

I am forever grateful to Maureen Van Tress for being my lifesaver and helping me heal. Thanks to Cheryl Canfield who helped facilitate my growth and healing. Thank you to Lynn Telford-Sahl, who not only helped me heal but has been my supportive, loving friend.

Thank you to all my family:

- Mom and my beloved father, Ray, who raised me to have strength and faith through all of life's tribulations.
- Rosie and her family for their support and seeing value in my technique.
- Carolyn, who is one of my great teachers, and her family for supporting me.
- Colleen for being my biggest fan and whose ongoing support has touched me deeply. Thanks to all of her family for using my technique.
- Joe and his family for believing in me and using my technique.

Thanks to Shayna Howitz, Jan Rien, and Deneen Drader and Lisa Jamison for sending me tons of clients and being there for me, and for all that they have done.

Thanks to all of my clients who, by coming to heal, have been my greatest teachers. Without them, this book would not be possible. *(Please note: I've changed their names and identifying characteristics to protect their privacy.)* Thank you to Richard Carey, Ph.D., for showing me my wisdom and value as a young nurse. Thanks to Susan Ezra and Terry Reed, my two fun and knowledgeable spiritual teachers. Also my gratitude to Shelly Thomas for her spiritual wisdom.

Many thanks to Gina Vance, who saw value in this technique and was my first paying client 12 years ago and to Susan Hunt for her creative input and giving this book its start.

I am indebted to Barbara McNichol and Peggy Henrikson of Barbara McNichol Editorial for their invaluable editorial service and insightful input.

Thanks to Kathleen Brehony for being my amazing personal coach who encouraged and shepherded me through this project. Also thanks to Juanell Teague and James Huggins for their kindness and insightfulness.

A special thank you to all my *champions* who gave so generously of their time, love, and support—Zeda Bertozzi, Janet Dyson, Anita Garza, Colleen Gingery, Robert Guardiola, Shayna Howitz, Gayle Jackson, Farrell Jackson, Kathy Jensen, Catherine Kelber, Brenda Kiely, Pat Kuhn, Terry Reed, Marilyn Rockey, Lynn Telford-Sahl, Michael Sosinsky, Paulette Spadini, Dee Stearman, Amber Tretheway, Gina Vance, and Jean Western.

Thank you to Lia Santucci for believing in me and John Quinones for his expertise and being a co-presenter in my seminars as well as the attendees who took time out of their busy lives. Thank you to my Dream Team, Jennifer Tobias and Jennifer Hill for your support and creative ideas.

Thank you to *The Oakdale Leader* for sharing my message in

several articles in our hometown newspaper. Thanks also to *Central Sierra Health Publication* for publicizing my message and supporting my mission. I am also grateful for the Oakdale Community Hospital, Valley-Sierra CAMFT, American Association of University Women, the American Holistic Nurses Association and Saint Joseph's Hospital in Stockton, California for allowing me to speak and present my work.

Thank you to Stan Meek for his artistic talent in creating the diagrams throughout the book.

I offer my sincere thanks to the amazing production team at O-Books who kept me on track and for the belief in my work and enthusiastic support and caring. Thank you for your commitment to publishing books that enlighten, enrich and bring positive energy to the world.

Love and hugs to my spirit guides who always amaze me. And thank you, God, for this amazing journey and guiding, protecting, and helping me through every crossroad.

Maureen

A Special "Thank You"

Nicole walked into my office with both hands clenched. A tall, slender 20 year old with long brown hair and a radiant smile. Nicole suffered from reflex sympathetic dystrophy (RSD). This had caused her right hand to be closed shut for the past three years and her left hand for the past month.

Nicole had seen several doctors, psychologists, a physical therapist, and a spiritual advisor which helped her on several levels. She'd even undergone medical procedures in hopes of reopening her hands. But her hands were still clenched. Understandably, she'd missed a lot in three years. Nicole couldn't dress herself, much less drive. She didn't date.

Just before each of her hands closed, she had two separate car accidents, which doctors believed could have something to do with her clenched fists. As Nicole read about clenched fists in a book I gave her called *Messages from the Body*, she laughed at the suggestion that her problem might have started in the womb. "Mom has always said that when we find what caused my hands to close, it would undoubtedly be her fault!" she explained.

Joking aside, when I asked her mother about her pregnancy with Nicole, she said, "I was a basket case. I was working with physically disabled children and I was terrified of having a physically disabled child."

Nicole laughed and waved her clenched fists. "Well, here I am, Mom!"

I suggested to Nicole that she have several sessions to release the fear that had actually started in the womb. She agreed, ready to try my MO Technique that forms the core of this book. Nicole and her parents left my office that day feeling at peace for the first time and believing everything would be okay.

I had seen Nicole on a Thursday; her left hand opened on Saturday, seventy two hours later. After five more sessions over several months, her right hand opened. Nicole was also getting help from other healers.

It took her 10 months more to detoxify at a pain clinic from the daily morphine her doctor had prescribed to relieve the pain in her hands. At the clinic she gained 90 pounds, had migraines, and couldn't tolerate sound, light, or scent. She stooped over and always wore sunglasses and a black hat, making her look much older than her 20 years as she went through this process.

Today, Nicole is now happily married and leads the life of a normal young woman. She understands that this has been her journey—and she wouldn't trade this clenched-fist experience for anything.

Nicole is undoubtedly one of the most courageous young women I've ever met. Through her and with her, I have learned patience, faith, and determination, and how to see the *bigger picture*. Because of her, I hung a sign in my office that reads *Everyone is My Teacher*. My heartfelt thanks to Nicole for being an important teacher to me.

Foreword

Maureen is like a world-class master chef. She has dedicatedly put all of her life experiences together in order to ascertain the primary ingredients of all dishes, and then she has gone on to discover and perfect her expertise so as to produce a unique gift with each contribution she makes to the person-in-a-situation.

She has integrated all of her life experiences and work into a coherent, innovative, wisdom-loaded understanding of what makes people tick.

And now she is putting out her mastery as a psychological/shamanistic/spiritual/medical genius into a totally transferable body of skills for the world to work with in healing people at a deeply and permanently effective level.

She does it in a thoroughly grounded and practical manner that makes what her mastery is composed of completely clear, so that you are able to apply it right along with her. She is a great teacher.

Perhaps the most outstanding characteristic of both Maureen and her system of healing is that she pulls *all* of the ingredients that go into effective corrective transformation together, as well as shares her recipe so that all can benefit.

To be more specific, I am referring to what she knows—how and why diseases develop, what emotional sufferings are, what The Common Thread is among all physical disorders, what a "signature emotional suffering" is, what a "unique emotional suffering" is, what Universal Soul Discoveries are, what our inherent Dynamic Natural Authentic (DNA) Power is, and how to use my discoveries regarding what underlies individual illnesses at the emotional and learning history levels.

She has generated a healing intervention system that she calls the *Modus Operandi Technique*. She explains how life experiences and soul intentions and discoveries affect energy systems, the chakras, and our imagery process to create our illnesses and to precipitate our healing.

She lays out the 12 steps of the MO system in concise and concrete terms, after which she explains how to utilize the infinity symbol to integrate and consolidate the MO effects. And she draws upon the spiritual wisdom of the world to prescribe a 40-day implanting system so the healing becomes permanent.

Finally, she presents a considerable number of "chef dishes" (illness interventions) to guide you in your work and to thoroughly flesh out your understanding and skill in applying the MO Technique.

All in all, this is a truly remarkable book of tremendous significance, effective applicability, and profound relevance. I have never encountered something so right on, releasing, and richly rewarding in the way of a healing system. *C'est magnifique!*

Michael J. Lincoln, Ph.D.

Heart-Centered Sacred Teacher

Author of *Messages from the Body* and 40 other books

Introduction to the MO
(Modus Operandi) Technique

"If I had my way, I'd make health catching instead of disease."
– Robert Green Ingersoll

When you ask people to identify the most important aspect of their lives, what do they say? You guessed it: their health and the health of their loved ones.

This book reflects an original concept in the connection between mind, body and soul wellness. The Modus Operandi (MO) Technique becomes the model for people to look compassionately inside themselves and take responsibility for their illnesses.

The focus of this book is not about the cure—rather it addresses the soul discoveries that illnesses present. These discoveries are the real gems that allow healing to take place on multiple levels. Once we know the emotional component of why and how an illness manifested, we can accept our wounds and issues with compassionate eyes and delete patterns that keep the wounds open. When we allow ourselves to open up to our soul consciousness, we can become our true selves—our true nature, which is whole and perfect.

Twelve years ago, the Modus Operandi (MO) Technique was my life saver. After surviving a devastating divorce, I found myself in an oncologist's office. He said, "You have megoblastic anemia, but your lab results indicate that we need to do a bone marrow biopsy to determine if you have cancer." Frankly, I already knew something was terribly wrong. My skin bruised easily. As an example, a friend came up behind me and patted me on the shoulder. The next day, perfect finger and thumb marks appeared right where he had touched me.

I'm not sure what possessed me, but I told the oncologist I would be back in 40 days. He made me sign a form that I was taking my life in my own hands. I had been using the MO Technique with my clients with success, but I was now given the ultimate test. I had been using Dr. Michael Lincoln's work, *Messages from the Body*, on others to help release the psychological meaning of disease out of the body with the MO Technique. I looked up my blood disorder in Dr. Lincoln's book, and the psychological meaning of the blood disorder spoke to me. I began the MO Technique on myself to release the emotional components and learn the soul discoveries of the blood disorder. After 40 days, I went back for another blood test. My blood work was normal and has been normal for the last 12 years. No matter what the blood disorder might have been, I knew my blood work couldn't be normal in 40 days without some kind of treatment.

Throughout my healing and working with my clients for the last 12 years, I have discovered how the emotional component that underlies physical disease can trigger disease. The Common Thread of *all* disease became clear. I saw how feeling powerless after my divorce—like I was dwelling at the bottom of the barrel—had collapsed my immune system. I was raised in an alcoholic environment with constant chaos, and I had built up anger in my body and carried immense amounts of resentment throughout my life. I did not love myself—and didn't even have the foggiest idea how to love myself. As I healed, I saw how my childhood programming and Modus Operandi played a major part in my disease. I understood that my disease presented my soul work and soul discoveries to me. In the end, this discovery would connect me with my true power. I understood that I could heal within—where my true spirit resides.

The MO Technique has become a powerful tool for under-standing how the emotional and soul determinates underlie physical ailments. A person's unique Modus Operandi pertains to how he or she operates in the world, which is determined by lifelong programming. By understanding our Modus Operandi, we can free ourselves from the shackles of our life history.

Disease is universal; the soul determinates—those factors that determine our individual soul discoveries or our soul intentions—pertain to everyone. The purpose of disease, then, is to create a connection that can globally unite us as one as we seek healing and health. The MO Technique helps guide the soul's truth back into every cell, helping us meet our life goals. By learning the "real message" the disease is telling us, we can learn to heal at a deep, permanent level and give ourselves the ultimate gift—the gift of health.

For me, developing the MO Technique has been quite a journey, with more life adventures and soul discoveries ahead. Today I look forward to experiencing them because I know my well-being will expand as each soul experience presents itself to me.

Chapter 1: How We Keep Killing Ourselves and What We Can Do to Stop It

"Houston, we have a problem."
– Apollo 13

This book raises probing questions meant to pierce your assumptions and change your paradigm. It starts with asking about the origin of life-threatening diseases and offers an effective, non-invasive technique that everyone can access. Details about the MO Technique are introduced in Chapter 2. But first, it's important to ask these four tough questions:

Have we been misguided?
What is the missing link?
How can we experience self-love?
How can we dismiss blame?

1. Have We Been Misguided?
Heart disease is the leading cause of death in the United States. In fact, cardiovascular heart disease accounts for nearly 50 percent of deaths in both the developed world and in developing countries. Indeed, according to Sean Henahan, author of *State of the Heart, The Future of Cardiology*, the risk of dying from heart disease is greater than AIDS and all forms of cancer combined.[1]

- How has this happened? Serious concerns emerge when we attempt to answer these critical questions that affect almost everyone:
- Why do we not have a cure for most diseases, especially the number one killer?

- Why are the causes of many diseases unknown?
- Have we been programmed to get rid of disease at the expense of other solutions within our control?

Broadcast celebrity Katie Couric, reporting for a *Stand Up To Cancer* fundraiser in 2008, stated that every *minute* someone dies of cancer.[2] People are dying, but do we know *why* and *how* cancer manifests in the body? Aren't those the billion-dollar questions— why and how?

Yes, we can take medications that interrupt the body's natural chemistry. We can have our organs cut out from our bodies, causing our other organs to work harder. But where has this led us? With this unnatural approach, these two top killers—heart disease and cancer—continue their deadly paths. As a result, the *truth* behind how disease is created remains untouched and unacknowledged. Until now . . .

2. What is the Missing Link?

What are we missing? In my research and working with clients for the last twelve years, I have discovered these two profound truths:

Love is the universal energy that sustains life.
Self-love is the energy that sustains the body.

If we don't have self-love, we are missing the biggest component of a healthy body. Self-love is its concrete foundation. And what happens when the foundation of a house is damaged or destroyed?

A house will eventually crumble if it's not fixed, right? Similarly, when the foundation of the body is lacking, its inner workings will eventually crumble. At the core of the body's foundation is the heart, the symbol of love. Therefore, doesn't it make sense that **self-love** is required to make it tick in harmony?

In societies that do not teach their people to love themselves, what happens? Self-love is absent. In fact, often we are taught that self-love may be selfish. But selfish behavior or being self-absorbed refers to when we put ourselves first without regard for others.

In contrast, when we make self-love our foundation, resentment and anger can't build because we take care of the "caretaker" first. Only by caring for ourselves first will we have the energy to nourish others with love—and do it joyfully.

We know that *self-love* strengthens the immune system and every organ in the body, especially the heart. Imagine what would happen if self-love prevailed in our society. Humans would rise to a whole new consciousness. And once we master self-love, **unconditional love** will follow—the greatest and most important discovery of this planet. Euphoria!

If everyone embraced self-love, would disease of the heart become a thing of the past? I believe so. Why? Because we would take care of ourselves and treat ourselves as a treasure first. This, in turn, provides the energy to nourish others with love and eventually create a loving society.

3. How Can We Experience Self-Love?

The wonderful thing is that once we experience self-love at the core of our being, we can compassionately look inside ourselves and take personal responsibility for our illnesses *without pushing any blame buttons*. The very act of blaming has put us back centuries in our quest to cure disease; we have made ourselves comfortable in this "old house". But this old house is musty and run-down; to build a "new house", we have to put blame aside and provide room for new structure and new knowledge. It's time to create a paradigm that works, right?

The word *blame* means to place responsibility for (an error, fault, etc.) on someone or something. The word *responsible* refers to one's ability to distinguish between right and wrong, and to think and act rationally.[3] Can we throw out the word *blame* and replace it with the word *accountability*? That is the concept of being responsible by acting rationally and being answerable for our behavior. We are expected to do this in every other area of our lives, so why not with disease?

4. How Can We Dismiss Blame?

Another way to dismiss blame is by acknowledging that the soul (one's spirit) is the only part of the body that goes on to the afterlife. At that point, the soul looks back and asks, "Did I accomplish what I set out to do on Planet Earth?" Because the soul is the only part that goes on, wouldn't our soul discoveries be the most important reason we reside on Planet Earth? Disease presents us with this critical reason, which is more completely addressed in Chapter 2.

Bruce Lipton, Ph.D., author of *The Biology of Belief*, stated, "Human Intelligence can only be fully understood when we include spirit ("energy") or what quantum-physics-savvy psychologists call the superconscious mind."[4]

I believe that when the superconscious mind, soul, or our spirit (where our truth resides) is understood, we will know our true power. But without connecting with our superconscious mind, we cannot nourish the core of who we really are—and therefore we cannot nourish the world. Once the soul or spirit is incorporated into healing (as happens with the MO Technique), we can heal our whole being—mind, body, and spirit—and prevent the killers that shorten our lives and steal our joy.

We've been told that lung cancer may be caused by smoking—another instance of blaming an outside source. But why do people smoke? According to Dr. Michael J. Lincoln in *Addictions and Cravings: Their Psychological Meaning,* the smoking habit often stems from feelings of self-rejection—in other words, it may actually be caused by feelings and judgments from within.[5] Smoking is a form of self-rejection and lack of self-love that can *lead* to heart disease. Therefore, it's best to start by looking within!

Tied to self-love is self-discovery, which leads us to mastery of our inner selves, rather than blaming outside sources. That's why I say it's time to throw out blame and declare, "I do not blame myself or anything else. Instead, I am responsible and accountable for me."

Heart Problems: #1 Killer

Dr. Michael Lincoln, also the author of *Messages from the Body*, wrote, "Anyone with artery problems is Joyless Joe or Jo. To them, life is one long problem to be solved . . . a very serious business, indeed. They have lost the ability to feel and express love, and they tend to be hard and bitter."[6]

It's highly probable that heart disease results from a failure to love oneself. Given the grave consequences of this failure, it's unfortunate that few people have strong role models for loving themselves. How many have actually been *taught* to love themselves? How many of us treat ourselves as a treasure, as one of the most precious gems in the world? When I spoke at the 2008 American Holistic Nurses Convention, I asked audience members to raise their hand if they loved themselves and treated themselves like one of the most precious gems in the world. Only one person raised her hand!

I recognize that self-love—acknowledging all our faults and failings—may be the most difficult kind of love to achieve. Yet it's this love that keeps our hearts and bodies healthy. When the body doesn't have any self-love, the foundation is absent and the heart weakens. A weakened heart weakens the whole body.

"Houston, We Have a Problem"

"Houston, we have a problem" was a life-threatening call from the spacecraft Apollo 13 alerting the space program's base in Houston of a life-threatening situation aboard the spacecraft. It's now humorously used to report a crisis. But Planet Earth, we really do have a problem, and this crisis is life threatening.

Because disease runs rampant and is often incurable, let's research how the emotional component is related to why and how disease manifests in the body. *After all, looking outside ourselves has just not worked very well.* Instead, let's look compassionately within and take responsibility for our diseases. Let's embrace disease as its soul discoveries. Let's understand the emotional and soul determinates of disorders that underlie physical ailments. Let's free ourselves from the shackles of our life histories.

In this book, you'll learn what a disease might be telling you. Once you understand the message of the illness, then the way it bubbles up in the body becomes clear. You see the world through how you think and feel, which determines how you operate. This is your MO or *modus operandi.*

Get ready to not only have a future that promises health, but to become aware of the plans laid down by your soul.

Chapter 2: Solving the Mystery with the MO Technique

"What is necessary to change a person is to change his awareness of himself."
– Abraham H. Maslow

If you're a fan of detective novels, you're undoubtedly familiar with the hard-boiled private eye searching for a criminal's MO, saying things like, "No question about it. That criminal's MO was all over that crime scene." MO in Latin is *modus operandi* and means a distinct pattern or method of operation.

MO Defined

Modus operandi (mo-dus op-er-an-di) as defined by the American Heritage Dictionary of the English Language (4th ed) means:

1. A method of operating or functioning
2. A person's manner of working

Patterned ways of approaching the world aren't reserved for criminals. Each of us has a unique way of operating. And because of that, it's impossible to lump everyone together and assume that what works for one will work for all. It's not a one-size-fits-all world.

That applies to techniques, as well. Think about all the ways you differ from others, your siblings included. Birth order makes a difference. Even if you have an identical twin, each of you is still unique. Your family circumstances and environment growing up influence how you operate in the world. Even the exact time, day, month, and year of your birth affects your upbringing.

But I think people's unique differences boil down to individual soul discoveries. An individual's soul reflects the higher self, the true power with which he or she is born. Your soul knows your life's purpose even when you don't. It presents you with soul discoveries, often through how the body functions. I call that the soul's MO or *modus operandi*.

We can regard diseases as wake-up calls. They signal us to listen to our souls so we can bring our personalities or egos in line with our authentic, divine natures. What did we sign up to learn in this school of life? Our bodies can tell us.

What are Soul Discoveries?

We have only one part of us that comes in and goes out into the afterlife, called "our spirit" or "our soul". The physical body gets left behind when we pass away.

But our Western way of treating disease treats the physical body and rarely addresses the soul. Doesn't it make sense that the soul needs more attention, especially when it comes to disease?

As I have worked with disease using the MO technique I have seen how disease shows us our soul intentions—a powerful, new, and exciting perspective. As Oprah Winfrey said on one of her TV programs, "The smallest change in perspective can transform a life. What tiny attitude adjustment might turn your world around?"

Are you ready to look at disease with a new perspective? My perspective refers to how you see, understand, and operate in the world, your *modus operandi*, which is why I named my technique the Modus Operandi (MO) Technique.

As a registered nurse, I have always been amazed that the sources of diseases are unknown. Do we have a cause or cure for diseases such as cancer, Lou Gehrig's, MS, or Parkinson's disease? Should the first billion-dollar question that's answered be *how does disease manifest in the body?*

For many years working in hospitals, I wanted to know why we get disease and how it manifests in the body, not just give a medication and hope it went away. That is why today I spend one to two hours in each client session. I want to figure out my patients' MO (*modus operandi*) and how it relates to their diseases. Now that I have worked with clients for over 12 years using the MO Technique, the mystery of disease has been solved for me and my happy clients.

According to my theory, our Modus Operandi comes from our programming. Our MO pertains to how each individual operates in the world based on programmed messages taken in from birth. Our MO—combined with what our soul came to learn—determines the risk we have of contracting a certain disease.

The Modus Operandi Theory

How and why disease develops in the body:

- Our programming from conception throughout life determines our Modus Operandi, the way we think and feel about ourselves, and the disease we might develop.
- Our programming is determined by first asking, "What did my soul sign up to learn or discover in this school of life?"
- Life goals are selected by a person's soul, which refers to individual agreements we decided to learn to fulfill our divine potential before coming into this world. At conception, we begin the journey of meeting those life goals. Our families and life experiences give us the opportunity to understand and achieve the goals we've selected.
- When we go off course and our life goals are not being met, the body reveals it in many ways. One way is through disease.

Not everyone has signed up for the same soul experience, which explains why a certain disease affects one person and not another. For example, this may be why former President Reagan developed Alzheimer's but Michael J. Fox developed Parkinson's. Think of it this way: Would you stick a kid who is ready to learn calculus in a class that teaches algebra? Of course not. So why assume that we all need to learn the same thing from our bodies? Have we all had the same life experiences? Did we all have the same parents who helped program us? No, of course not.

The body serves as the barometer of a person's *inner world*, which determines how we look at life and how the outside world affects us. Changing our programming starts by shifting our perspective. As Oprah said, just one tiny attitude adjustment can turn your world around.

How Our Programming and MO Sets Up Disease

Have you ever programmed an iPod or MP3 player? You can choose to load it with a whole CD or you can pick your favorite segments. Your choices will probably be different than mine. Yes, we might like some of the same songs, but our actual programming will be different.

Here's the tricky part. Sometimes these gadgets come with music on them, but they don't come with your favorites. So you shop online and download a few music files. Or you get out your favorite CDs and upload them first to your computer, then onto the MP3 player.

That's just like how we operate. We come into the world seemingly as blank slates ready to be programmed. Through our experiences, we add to that programming, overwrite it, and update it. But it's just easier (or less confrontational) to leave it alone. When we refuse to recognize our Modus Operandi and programming—or don't even know they're there—we tend to make the same mistakes over and over again. It's like a self-fulfilling prophecy. The mistakes of this self-fulfilling prophecy can cause us great pain. I refer to this great pain as our emotional sufferings.

How Emotional Sufferings Affect Us

Emotional sufferings are negative emotions stored in the cells and subconscious mind. These negative emotions get programmed throughout life and settle in to the body's cells or subconscious mind based on what our souls signed up to learn. As Candace Pert, PhD, stated, "Your body is your subconscious mind." (Sounds True CD—*Your Body Is Your Subconscious Mind*, 2000)

Emotional sufferings include abandonment, betrayal, feeling not good enough, powerlessness, anger/rage, and lack of self-love—to name just a few. These emotional sufferings relate to the underlying cause of disease. Just like we can choose the music we want, we can learn to consciously choose what emotions we want by feeling them, not repressing or suppressing them. We have the power to consciously choose to *not* hang on to negative emotions. We can even make releasing them out of the body a healthy habit.

Many people have lost sensitivity to what they're feeling; they experience emotional numbness a lot. But using the MO Technique, they can learn to feel again and choose what to feel all the time. I believe regulating our feelings and experiencing a greater array of emotions is the next frontier in human evolution.

I also believe that learning to love oneself is how to connect with ourselves and feel again. We learn how to program in self-love, replacing numbness with compassion and love, using the MO Technique.

Why must emotional sufferings be a part of our lives? Because we have an inner connection to our Source. For some, these sufferings are present in daily life. For others, they're buried deep inside. Each of us came to this Earth to connect with Source and become the energy of unconditional love. Betrayal, abandonment, hurt, sorrow, and all negative emotional sufferings will continue until we experience unconditional love universally. Disease will haunt our planet until everyone attains self-love.

However, once we have embedded self-love deep inside, we can move onto the consciousness of unconditional love. War, poverty, murders, rapes, molestations, and all the sorrows of the world will continue until our collective consciousness rises to that level. We humans *have* to suffer, often drastically, until life gets so painful that we seek help to understand ourselves and our purpose on earth.

I have listed several emotional sufferings that tend to be involved in each disease. Those that resonate with individuals are the ones they need to release. Because we're all unique, what may pertain to one individual may not apply to another.

Inherent in each disease are four aspects: a *signature emotional suffering*, a *unique emotional suffering*, a *Universal Soul Discovery*, and *triggers*. Let's look at these one by one.

What is Signature Emotional Suffering?

A handwritten signature is a well-accepted mark of one's identity. Similarly, the signature emotional suffering assigned to a disease is what identifies one disease from another. For instance, the multiple sclerosis signature is rigidity that may be programmed in with a feeling and by a phrase starting with "I have to". This MO causes the physical body to become rigid. Lou Gehrig's disease's signature is a *deep need for acceptance* that causes the physical body to deteriorate, become paralyzed, and ultimately die.

Do you see how the signature emotional suffering pictures outwardly how one feels deep inside? The physical body reflects what we think and feel, thus the disease indicates our true feelings, which may be different from what we show the world.

What is Unique Emotional Suffering?

Sometimes a disease will also have a unique emotional suffering, which is distinctive to an individual because each person is unique. It could be something like this: *"I'm not going to let you get to me. I don't care about you—you can't hurt me. Never again!"*

My client Diane, had adopted this attitude most of her life. She had been severely berated and undermined as a child. Repeating these sentences and feeling it helped protect her from the pain and also created isolation and alienation in her life. Diane divorced her husband when she was in her 20s and never had another love relationship. This attitude became her protection, but it actually kept others at a distance. Not surprisingly, she felt very alone.

Once she released this unique emotional suffering using the MO Technique and instilled her truth at the soul level, she lightened up. About to retire from her job, she finally believed it was okay to be happy for the first time in her life. Letting down this barrier gave her a glimpse of getting the love and support she so desperately wanted.

These unique emotional sufferings can cause great pain in life. With the MO Technique, they can be released out of cellular memory, and truth can be instilled at the soul level. In fact, our soul and the superconscious mind are ecstatic when the subconscious releases an untruth. Then the conscious mind (ego) can realign with the soul or spirit. The reprogramming provided by the MO Technique allows the body to experience the universal discovery its soul set out to find on this planet.

What is a Universal Soul Discovery?

A universal soul discovery pertains to all mankind and brings us together as one. In turn, each disease has a universal soul discovery. For instance, the universal soul discovery of AIDS is to teach tolerance and love of all (which you'll read about in the AIDS/HIV chapter).

Stated another way, when intolerance is present, conditional love, and non-acceptance (either parental or societal) are present, disease will exist. The intolerance of one person affects all of us. That means individuals with AIDS/HIV have come to teach the rest of us how to be tolerant of all people. That's what their souls wanted to bring to the world. Once this principle is understood, connecting everything through the wisdom of disease may provide the key to peace and unity on this planet.

What is a Trigger?

Specific kinds of attitudes and experiences—when unconscious and unhealed—create a background for the expression of a particular illness. Triggers in life cause these dormant potentialities to come to the surface and manifest in the body as symptoms and illness.

A trigger is an *adverse event* that puts an individual "over the top" and it erupts a symptom, condition or disease that pertains to the soul discovery the individual signed up to learn. (You'll see many different triggers in the case histories in the following chapters.)

Many of my clients are surprised that a certain adverse event could be connected to their disease. Because almost everyone experiences adverse events, it's easy to see why many people are affected by disease, yet the connection between the event and the disease often gets overlooked. However, once we understand the process of what sparks disease, we can chose how to react positively to the adverse event.

How Disease Gets Triggered in the Body

As part of the MO Technique, I use a term called *The Common Thread of Disease*. I gave it this name because it resides in everyone and connects us all. Understanding *The Common Thread of Disease* can help weave a tapestry of wholeness and wellness. What is it?

Although the experiences and attitudes of people who suffer

from arthritis, cancer, high blood pressure, and others differ, all disease encompasses four emotional sufferings. Together they make up *The Common Thread*. These four sufferings are:

1. Resentment
2. Anger that can turn into rage
3. Powerlessness
4. Lack of self-love

Developing disease requires an emotional substrate to create the perfect physical, psychological, and spiritual backdrop to be expressed. These four sufferings make up the emotional substrate.

What Sparks Disease?

Think of a volcano—a volcano is a place where lava, ash, and gases spew out of the interior of the earth onto the surface. This mixture simmers and simmers until one day, below the earth's surfaces, the gases can't escape easily. The trapped gas accumulates enough pressure to escape, setting up a powerful explosion when the gas breaks through the earth's crust.

We can relate this to our own bodies. In our lives, resentment builds and builds in the body from our negative experiences and if it's not released out of the body each time it comes up, it could eventually produce anger and rage. When a devastating event happens—loss of a loved one, divorce or breakup, financial struggles, problems with our children—anger may erupt like a volcano. This eruption can trigger the symptom, condition, or disease related to the particular soul discovery the person needs to experience. A diagnosis of a particular disease can follow as early as six months to a year later after the adverse event.

With this emotional eruption may come a feeling of powerlessness. Think about how you'd feel after a devastating divorce or loss of a dear loved one. The powerless victim-like feeling that results suppresses and even collapses the immune system. This system in turn becomes weak and allows a symptom, condition, or disease to erupt. It goes straight to the area of the body related to the soul discovery that the individual wanted to learn. It can especially undermine health if self-love, the foundation of the body, is absent. That's why it is important to address this emotional suffering in addition to the other three—collectively called The Common Thread.

Some may experience years of inner conflict and suppressed anger and grief before that disease trigger shows up. It's the adverse event that ignites the festering coals. Think back to the volcano. The foundation is absent (self-love). The lava builds (resentment) and festers and eventually it erupts (anger, rage) when there is too much pressure (the adverse event). The rocks that make up the volcano break through (powerlessness) and the lava explosion (disease) escapes to the surface. Six months to a year can pass after an adverse event for the disease to show up.

Example: Maura was diagnosed with vaginal cancer. What may have triggered the cancer cells to erupt? She bought a house and the house was appraised at 1900 square feet. A single teacher with two children, she wanted to refinance it. When they reappraised it, they said it had 1632 square feet and therefore less value. No one would admit any fault—the realty company or the appraiser—so she took it to the attorney general who told her she would have to get an attorney and fight the reappraised decision. She did not have the money and couldn't fight it. When she shared this story with me, she said she'd been angry for the previous eight months. I asked, "How do you feel about this situation?" She said, "I've been screwed—this is unfair. I'm so angry. There is no way out!" Knowing about the MO Theory, she instantly connected those thoughts to her disease and added, "No wonder I have vaginal cancer!"

Maura had been divorced for several years. She put her two children through college on her teacher's salary; her ex-husband did not help her in any way. Maura said she was very resentful that she had to do it all on her own but felt she could not do anything about it. According to the Modus Operandi Theory and The Common Thread of Disease, the resentment builds up throughout her life. Then, when she was treated unfairly again, the resentment turned into anger that made the cancer cells erupt. It went right to the area of the body that pertained to how Maura felt—screwed!

Maura did not have a solid foundation of self-love. She showed all of the ingredients of *The Common Thread of Disease*— resentment, anger/rage, powerlessness, and lack of self-love. Once we put the pieces of the puzzle together, she said, "Maureen, it's scary that my thoughts and this event may be connected to the cancer." I replied, "Maura, once we understand how and why the disease manifested emotionally in the body, we can then release it. That's not scary. It can be life-saving."

Thinking that disease can just show up out of the blue is frightening for many of us. For instance, those who haven't smoked and don't have cancer in the family are baffled how they may have developed lung cancer. But if we look at The Common Thread of Disease and the emotional and soul discoveries of lung cancer, and understand the emotional component of how and why it manifested, then we can release it. Any fear of disease coming "out of the blue" may be an obstacle that we can overcome. This information of how and why disease develops in the body from an emotional standpoint can help with all disease.

Chapter 3: The Common Thread of Disease

"All that we are is a result of what we have thought."
– Buddha

When you use the MO Technique, you deal with these three principles:

1. **You have self-love as the foundation of your body.**
2. **You are never a victim.** Feelings of powerlessness can be released with the MO Technique. Then once you instill your DNA (Dynamic Natural Authentic) Power at the soul level, you ask the right questions. Example: How do I solve this problem instead of thinking there is no way out?
3. **You know that anger and resentment must be released.** They're released out of your body *every time* they come up so they don't build and then erupt.

A healthy body has self-love as its foundation. It releases anger and resentment every time they come up so they don't build and ignite disease. It always keeps its personal power—never sinking into victim mode, and knowing there is a solution to every problem even if professional help is necessary to find the solution.

What Happens When We Instill Self-Love?

Lack of self-love affects our ability to give, and, especially, receive. Physiologically, the heart sends oxygenated blood to the body (giving) and brings back blood to be cleaned and re-oxygenated (receiving). We can't live without this vital cycle. This is also the cycle of self-love. If we don't have it, we may have difficulty knowing how it feels to receive or give, which creates an imbalance in the body. The heart regulates our whole system and represents *love*. For heart energy to work efficiently, we must have a balance of giving and receiving. When compassionate energy flows freely through the left (receiving) hand, it flows to the heart and nourishes it with love from self and others. Then the energy moves out of the heart and out the right (giving) hand so we can give love to others. When we instill self-love and practice it faithfully, we create the balance the heart needs to function properly.

Do you give too much and have a difficult time receiving from others? If so, this situation can create an imbalance and affect your health, perhaps causing heart problems or strokes. Sometimes, it's exactly the opposite. It's easier to take but painful to give. This also creates an imbalance and can harden your heart.

Imagine that self-love—the energy that sustains the body—is our "new house". This completely "new house" now has its foundation. Once we have self-love as our foundation, we can build upon that and keep our body healthy by learning how to keep our power and by releasing resentment and anger every time they come up. Lack of self-love includes self-rejection and self-betrayal, and feeling unaccepted, unworthy, abandoned, not good enough, and so on. The good news is that when you release these feelings, you can fall madly in love with yourself. Healthy self-love strengthens the immune system and every organ in your body—especially the heart.

- Learn how to instill self-love in Chapter 7.

Turning Powerlessness into DNA Power

DNA Power stands for Dynamic Natural Authentic Power—a power inherent in all of us and given to everyone by our Source. (To me, this Source is God, but for others it might be Allah, Supreme Being, or Universal Spirit.)

This is the incredible power that helps heal disease and keeps our bodies strong.

Taking responsibility for ourselves is the first step toward reclaiming this immense power. Feeling like a victim takes away our energy and collapses the immune system. In contrast, DNA Power becomes our strength and vitality; it energizes our mind, body, and spirit. Without it, we're like sitting ducks for attracting disease—just aim the loaded gun (a trigger event) and we don't have much chance to survive.

How can you claim this incredible DNA Power? By releasing powerlessness out of the subconscious and instilling your DNA Power at the soul level with the MO Technique. Once instilled, you program it into the conscious mind for 40 days, allowing yourself to vibrate at a higher consciousness. Because powerless feelings collapse the immune system, make sure you get out of the victim mode right away. How? By asking questions like, "How do I solve this problem?" and then coming up with viable solutions.

Doing this provides the feeling of inner control, which helps establish a place of safeness, security, self-confidence, and self-worth. Fear transforms into love for people who have this DNA Power.

Anyone who has symptoms, conditions, or disease has not claimed this super-power—the most amazing force and gift one can have. This DNA Power allows our natural energy to flow, awakens the divine within, and brings joy to the soul. It taps into that vast universal knowledge and reveals our individual truth.

A power struggle was born the first time we were told, "No!" Why? Because embedded deep in our human consciousness and cellular memory is a belief that, to survive, we must dominate as a victor. That in turn creates a victim consciousness: for every victor, there's a victim. Do you see how this fear-based need to dominate can trigger power struggles and violence in our world?

After the first "No!" we likely got a slap on the hand or the bottom—our first experience of violence. Of course, I agree that saying "No!" is necessary from time to time. For example, if a young child reaches for a knife or an electric plug, parents must clearly instruct the child not to touch it for safety reasons. But by being conscious in the moment rather than on parental autopilot, this "No" can be expressed firmly and clearly without being punitive and eliciting a power struggle. Rethinking how we raise children might help stop disease because their feelings of powerlessness and anger/rage haven't been triggered all their lives.

Actually, this raises a good question: If punishment could set up The Common Thread cycle, how can we raise children and still let them have their personal power?

Let's Find a Way

Imagine how the experiences of children would be different if adults said, "Let's find a way to make this work," instead of "No!" This negative message sets their cellular memory to register *"I can't"* rather than *"I can"*.

Try an experiment right now and say the words "I can't." Do you get a suffocating feeling in your throat, as I do? Now say the words, "I can!" Wow! That brings air into my lungs—I can take in a big breath and feel powerful.

We can learn much from other cultures like the Inuit of Greenland. Inuit children are treated like treasures. They are healthy, not spoiled, and turn out well without being punished growing up. The bond between child and parents is very strong. *This bond has been handed down generation after generation to ensure continuity.* Elder Inuit are regarded with great respect. The head man is an advisor, not a ruler. Men and women have always been considered equals. People are cherished, celebrated, and deeply involved in family and traditions. They assist each other and know that help will always be available when they need it, thus creating a strong social fabric. The Inuit are a connected, spiritual people, with Shamans to guide them on their spiritual path.

However, Inuit society is becoming Westernized.[1] Diseases such as diabetes, heart disease, and cancer that were previously unknown to the Inuit are now showing up. Researchers associate these changes with their new Western lifestyle. Western occupations, living conditions, and diet are replacing sacred Intuit fundamentals. This introduces resentment, anger/rage, powerlessness, and lack of self-love—The Common Thread of Disease—into the society.

Imagine how the experiences of children would be different as adults if they were not made to feel helpless, powerless, cheated, or ripped off in some way? I can!

To me, C-A-N stands for Create Another Norm—that is, to develop new beliefs and different rules to empower people rather than leave them feeling angry and resentful. Learning how to empower ourselves and use our DNA Power can help instill desired new beliefs.

Without our DNA Power, we might stay in jobs, marriages, or situations that don't bring happiness. Yet we endure them because we feel we have no other choice. Eventually, these choices lead to frustration and stress, which many people try to quench with addictions such as smoking, unhealthy food, alcohol, drugs, and sex.

Dr. Richard Gerber, author of *Vibrational Medicine*, wrote, "Many illnesses which are manifestations of chakra imbalances are the result of faulty data on old memory tapes which have been recorded and programmed into the unconscious mind during early portions of the individual's life."[2] Powerlessness and lack of self-love are really faulty data. They can be turned into correct and accurate information with the MO Technique.

- Learn how to release powerlessness and instill your DNA Power with the MO Technique in Chapter 7.

Anger
Now, feeling anger gets a bad rap, but consider it to be a healthy emotion in that anger tells us something is wrong and invites us to change. We know that everything around us affects our body's

energy. Resentment lowers its energy level, festers and can cause limitations. Anger really means there's a deep need inside that must be filled. I teach my clients how to see and understand that need and then fulfill it.

As I was going through my healing process after the divorce, I wrote a letter to my anger and had my anger write a letter back to me. In a surprising outcome for me, I made friends with my anger and learned to listen to it, then release it out of my body every time it came up so it did not build. My letter read like this:

Dear Anger:

I hate this tug of war inside me. You have ruined my marriage and I am so afraid and lonely. You make me very sad and this is so painful. I cry every day. Isn't it about time to stop? Let's put the PAST behind us and go FORWARD.

I know I can use you sensibly and I pray for that daily. I know I need this kick in the pants. You have made me feel strength I've always had.

Thank you for helping me stop beating myself up and for hating myself because I know I'm really not that person. I am only reacting.

I am a good person, and you are helping me find strength and peace of mind. Being alone is okay and I know I have the ability to love myself again.

Love, Maureen

Here's the letter that "Anger" wrote back to me.

Dear Maureen,

If I was out to get you, don't you think you would have been divorced years ago? I was your ONLY and natural defense. I have no brain or great harm. YOU gave me the power. I live off your fears but I die from your peace of mind.

I don't want to hurt you. You're a good person. You have to let go of me and use me sensibly—I do serve a purpose.

Maybe if we try listening to each other and talking to each other, we can find a way to exist in peace without hurting each other. You have to deal with whatever is inside you that brought you here. Okay?

Work with me—we'll get through this. You must remember, you and your faith have more power than I do.

Love, Anger

Anger really means there's a deep need inside that must be fulfilled. I teach my clients how to see and understand that need and then fulfill it. For example, Marsha was angry with her boss and we talked about her feelings.

"My boss doesn't pay attention to what I say and doesn't think my ideas are important," she told me when she was feeling relaxed and at her *soul level—a deep level where she could see inner truth about herself.*

"What is the need that you need fulfilled when you're angry at your boss?" I asked.

"Acknowledgment that I'm intelligent, have good opinions, and I am of value."

"While you're at your soul level—your truth—do you believe you are intelligent? Do you have good opinions of yourself? Are you of value?"

"Yes!"

"Give that to yourself," I said with encouragement. Using the MO Technique, I had her fill her body with the energy that reflected a deep understanding, of knowing her value, intelligence, and good opinions.

I taught Marsha that anger needs to be *felt* but then be released out of the body *every time* it comes up. Then the area where she released it she fills that area back in with a loving energy. Then she needs to ask herself, "What do I need?" Whatever it is, she gives it to herself and fills her body up with that energy every time she releases anger or resentment.

Marsha clearly saw that *this time* her anger stemmed from needing to be valued. Once she found her truth, she could release the anger and practice fulfilling her need to feel valued deep inside every time she felt this with her boss.

How did she actually do that? With my help, she completed the first seven steps of the MO Technique (described in Chapter 7).

I had Marsha *feel* the anger at her boss. I then had her image the anger. She imaged it as a black ball, and she felt the energy of the black ball in her abdomen. She imaged the black ball bouncing out of her abdomen. She filled that area back in with a loving energy.

I then asked Marsha to imagine going to her soul level, tapping into her spirit or higher self. While Marsha was at the soul level I asked her how she would feel if she valued herself, knew she had good opinions and was intelligent. She said, "I would feel great, happy and content."

I then asked her if she put feeling great, happy and contented into a ball of energy, what color it would be. She said, "Pink."

I said, "Put that pink ball of energy under your feet and fill every cell with the pink energy. While you are filling it up, say to yourself, 'I am of value, I have good opinions, and I am intelligent. This makes me feel great, happy, and contented.' Feel the *euphoria* of knowing and feeling who you are now." (It is so important to feel the joy of your affirmation—really feel the euphoria—knowing that from this moment forward your life and your new consciousness will now reflect that affirmation.)

Once the body is filled up—leave that pink euphoric energy in your body, but in your "mind's eye" send that pink energy to everyone in the world. Then allow it to come back and envelop your whole auric field. (The aura consists of seven major layers of energy that surround the physical body.)

Sending the good energy out to the world and then bringing it back allows the body to both give and receive, which is crucial for balance in the body. It also sends the energy and consciousness of wanting and allowing everyone in the world to have it too. Having it come back and envelop the auric field sets up the template of positive energy for the physical body.

At that deep level, Marsha recited her affirmation out loud. *"From this moment forward I make all decisions based on knowing that I am of value, intelligent, and have good opinions. This makes me feel happy and content."* Saying it out loud at the soul level takes it to the core of her being and reprograms her subconscious mind.

Her need may be different every time; sometimes she may need love or understanding when she is angry.

Her affirmation for 40 days would be:

1. I release anger out of my body every time it comes up. I fill that area back in with a loving energy. Then I ask myself, "What do I need?" and I fulfill my deep need inside.
2. I now know I am of value, I have good opinions, and I am intelligent. I feel great, happy and contented.

She will say these two affirmations for 40 days to reprogram the conscious mind. There may be a different affirmation the next time she is angry and releases it.

Anger needs to be *felt* and then released out of the body *every time* it comes up, even if it's 100 times a day. The deep need needs to be fulfilled each time also. This can be accomplished using the MO Technique.

After my difficult divorce, I started releasing anger out of my body whenever it came up. I imagined it as a huge black bowling ball. I'd see this heavy energy moving out of my solar plexus and watch it roll down the bowling alley, knocking down all the pins, getting a strike! After years of practice releasing anger from cellular memory, that big black bowling ball transformed into a feather. I've learned to step back, understand, and fulfill the deep need inside me that causes the anger. As a result, my physical body feels energetically lighter and my emotional body is softer and more loving.

When feeling and releasing anger becomes a habit, anger does not build up in the body. You get to fulfill your needs each time you are angry. Anger then becomes happiness because it is a catalyst for us to change whatever is not working in our lives. We can delete it from our hard drive and fulfill what we need, which is pure bliss.

- Learn how to release anger with the MO Technique in Chapter 7.

Resentment

Resentment is an emotion that gets built up in the body when we feel that we are powerless. It can fester and eventually trigger anger. The anger, in turn, can erupt a symptom, condition, or disease.

How does resentment build up? One way is if we don't have self-love as our foundation and we give-give-give and don't get our own needs met. Neglecting our own needs may produce feelings of resentment and powerlessness. Resentment understandably builds for women who nurture everyone else but don't get their own needs met often enough. Men endure resentment, too. For example, they may get passed over at work and not get the promotion they think they deserve. As time goes by, this inner feeling may become toxic and turn into anger and explode if triggered by a devastating event.

In this society, many of us have designed our lives so that we are constantly overworked. The American Dream seems to be more about how much we accumulate than how well we live.

This worldview means we never have enough time or money to live the way we think we should.

My clients say things such as: "There isn't enough of me to go around," or "There's never enough time for *me*." Naturally, resentment builds up in our bodies over time because we can't meet the demands we've set for ourselves. How we handle demands from relationships and work determines our well-being. Any resentment can fester and eat away at the body until, finally, disease shows up.

Recognizing our resentment, *feeling it*, then releasing it every time it comes up can prevent anger/rage. We learn how to keep our power and not become victims. We learn how to recognize our needs and give what we need to ourselves.

Likewise, if we have self-love as our foundation, we will give ourselves what we need if we get passed over at work. At the base of feeling resentful that we got passed over may be a need to feel valued. So we give that to ourselves and know that we are valuable. Once we become that energy, we will attract it from the outside world.

The body doesn't lie; it sends us memos constantly.

We learn our soul discoveries through all of our trials and tribulations in life. If we look at it from this perspective, we can move on and let go of being resentful, which only harms ourselves and sets the body up for disease.

- Learn how to release resentment and stay on top of your own needs in Chapter 7.

Releasing The Common Thread

The MO Technique guides you to release The Common Thread out of cellular memory first. Once you release The Common Thread of Disease and replace it with a solid foundation, then you can work on and release the signature cause of each particular illness.

If we were taught how to release resentment every time it came up and fulfill our need inside, it might not build into anger and rage, and there would be much less hostility and violence. Better still, if authentic self-love were practiced on a global level, we would treat ourselves and others like the treasures we are; resentment and anger wouldn't build up in the body at all. Then each individual would have DNA Power and take personal responsibility. No one would need to be submissive or to dominate others. If we were taught to love ourselves at the core, we would have much less fear. Do you see that disease feeds on fear but can't live in a body that loves itself unconditionally? Releasing The Common Thread underlying disease and learning how to make our emotions work for us becomes the template, or blueprint, to empower us all.

Chapter 4: The Role of Chakras in Health and Healing

"To meet the challenge of the future, our imagination must be bold, but it must be balanced by wisdom."
– David Sarnoff

Traditional medicine has not incorporated the concept of chakras into treating disease, which I believe is one of the missing links. *Chakra* is a Sanskrit word meaning "wheels" because chakras are like spinning wheels of energy of color and light. This knowledge was first described by the yogic tradition of ancient India. Most traditional methods of healing do not work with the chakras. With the MO Technique, the chakras are balanced and cleansed then reprogrammed and a template for healthy energy is set up.

The main chakra system consists of seven spinning wheels of energy that radiate out into the energy field surrounding the body. These spinning wheels also take in energy from the outside world and distribute it to the blood, major glands, organs, and nerve centers. In effect, they help specific parts of the body function properly.

Our thoughts and feelings directly affect the chakra system. In fact, our thoughts, feelings, and attitudes can decrease or even fully block a chakra's energy flow to specific areas of the body, depending on the degree of our difficulties or obstacles in life and the way we handle and look at life's tribulations. For example, if we've been hurt over and over in our relationships, our MO might be based on the belief that "love is a poisoned apple", so we shut down energy or life force to the heart chakra. After years of this habitual pattern, the heart cannot receive the life force energy it needs. This energy deprivation creates an abnormal energy flow, which, over time, can result in a physical illness such as heart disease. Emotional sufferings such as hard-heartedness may create a severe blockage of energy in this chakra, causing the heart to malfunction. An individual's soul discovery may be to learn compassion.

Dr. Gerber wrote, "The development of compassion and empathic feelings for others is one of the first steps on the path toward opening the heart chakra and developing higher consciousness. When these elements are lacking in the personality, one can be sure that some blockage in the heart chakra exists."[1] Maybe this is one reason heart disease is the number one killer in Western society—because the concept of chakras has been deemed "new age" nonsense and hasn't been addressed in traditional medicine.

Keeping your chakras healthy depends on keeping your thoughts and emotions healthy. You can protect your chakras from the negative energy from the outside world by first being aware of the negative energy that may be directed toward you.

When I am around negativity, I envision a white protective light around myself with the intention that the negativity cannot enter my energy field. Then I can listen and have empathy without taking on another's negative emotions, thus allowing my energy field and chakras to remain healthy.

Functions of the Chakras
Chakras not only help our bodies function properly, they also relate to our soul consciousness. Emotional sufferings, power-lessness, resentment, anger/rage, and self-negation can affect all chakras.

Let's look at this missing link in traditional healing and examine the functions of each chakra and how their dysfunctions (and their related emotional sufferings) can result in physical problems or diseases.

The First, or Root Chakra holds root family issues. For instance, if the soul discovery is learning to support oneself — not only monetarily but physically, mentally, and spiritually — dysfunction of the root chakra might manifest as back pain. The back represents the support system of the body. When this chakra malfunctions, it might be because we weren't supported by the main people in our lives, especially those in our family. Our MO may be a result of not learning to support ourselves in every way. Therefore, we must become the energy of support to ourselves to attract support from the outside world. Without it, we will continue to attract lack of support, which calls attention to this issue until we release that particular emotional suffering. If back pain tells us to support ourselves, the energy of non-support can be released using the MO Technique. This, in turn, may help release the pain itself. Once support is instilled at the soul level, our soul discovery becomes not only to learn to support ourselves but also to allow and attract support from others.

Additional physical problems connected to root chakra dysfunction include sciatica, immune-related diseases, rectal tumors, and varicose veins. Anything to do with the base of the spine, legs, bones, feet, rectum, and immune system is part of root chakra consciousness.

The emotional sufferings of the root chakra are not feeling safe, not being able to stand up for oneself or move forward in life, fear of not being able to take care of oneself, lacking support, and feeling insecure or helpless.

Example: June, a 25-year-old, beautiful, fit blonde had lower back pain and had tried many modalities to get relief without success. Using the MO Technique, she imaged lack of support and saw a picture of her mom and dad always fighting. I said, "Find the energy of that picture of your mom and dad fighting in your body." She said, "It's in my lower back." I had her imagine releasing the snapshot of her mom and dad fighting out of her back. She did, and then threw it away. Then I told her to instill a loving energy back in the area where she released it. I then asked, "How did this make you feel when your parents were fighting?" She said, "It was scary, and I felt helpless." I asked, "How old were you?" She said she was five. I had her envision herself as this child and asked her what she would say to her young self right now if the child were standing in front of her. She envisioned herself as five, standing in front of her, and said to her child, "You are safe, and I will always be here to protect you and make you safe." I asked how the five year old felt now. June said she was smiling and happy.

I then asked my client, "If you put feeling safe and protected and always supporting yourself into a ball of energy, what color would it be?" She said, "White." I then asked her to fill her body with that white energy and say to herself, "I am safe and protected. I am always there for and support myself, and I can discern who can be there for me and support me." I asked her to really feel the euphoria of it and become it as she filled her body up. I asked her to leave that energy in her body but, out of her mind's eye, to send that positive energy to everyone in the world—then allow it to come back and envelop her whole auric field.

June's affirmation for 40 days was: "I am safe and protected. I am always there to support myself. I can discern who can be there for me and support me, and I allow that."

We then discussed that one of her soul discoveries was to become the energy of self-support and to always be there for herself and support herself in every way. Once she mastered that, she could then attract support from the outside world. In her session, she released The Common Thread of Disease and lack of support. Before she left our session, June said the pain in her back was gone.

Greg Braden, author of *Walking Between the Worlds*, wrote, "You must become that which you choose to have in your life.

You must become trust to have trust in your life. You must become your worth and feel union to experience worth and heal separation in your life."[2]

With the MO Technique, you release what your illness is messaging for you to heal, fill your body with the positive energy you've been lacking, and become that energy. In June's case, she filled her body with the energy of support and became the energy of support. You can feel the union by *feeling* and instilling the euphoric energy of what you want to heal. The secret is to release the energy out of your body which is holding you back or creating illness and become the energy of who you want to be and what you want to attract in your life.

Because of a mirroring process, we attract the same energy we carry inside. If we can see it, we can heal it. Once it's mastered and cleared inside, we no longer embody that energy so it no longer attracts that particular energy from the outside world.

A great example of this happens in relationships. Often people who divorce and remarry end up with the same type of partner—a new husband or wife has the same energy as the ex and it's usually more pronounced. This indicates that when we don't heal and change our energy, we attract the same thing over and over until we *do* change. The lesson even gets a little more intense each time, eventually forcing a need to heal and change.

It would be a lot easier, of course, to be fully aware of those soul discoveries from the start. If it weren't for our spiritual growth and free choice, we might forget the goals our soul wants to accomplish. So we set off on the adventure of life to figure them out. More than once, I've felt like Dorothy from *The Wizard of Oz*, hoping a great wizard would rescue me and tell me what I came to learn. But it was only when I rediscovered my soul's truth that I could walk down the right path. After all, the soul never forgets; it keeps us on the path of enlightenment by sending us soul discoveries.

The emotional sufferings of the first chakra requires learning the soul discovery of self-support—coping with life's demands, feeling safe, and standing up for oneself.

The Second, or Sacral Chakra relates to relationships and creativity. This chakra is the seat of procreation. Our MO may include having major problems in our relationships or not expressing creativity, which indicates dysfunction of the sexual chakra. This can manifest in the body as pelvic, bladder, ovary, uterus, or male organ problems. Sexual dysfunction can range from impotence to just not having the desire for sex. A person with second chakra imbalances might also suffer from hip, large intestine, appendix, or lower vertebrae problems.

Emotional sufferings of the sexual chakra include rejecting oneself, feeling that one doesn't measure up or is unworthy, having a lack of trust, feeling shame for one's feminine or masculine self, having a lack of confidence and anxiety about one's competence, and feeling isolated, disconnected, or abandoned. For men, having to be the "man" of the house at a very young age might create dysfunction in this chakra. For women, having to be the "mom" at a young age may create dysfunction of this chakra. Not taking an active part in creating one's future because of mistrust might create hip problems.

Example: This case history looks at the emotional sufferings of fibroids, which also involve the uterus and the sexual chakra.

Shannon, 50, came to me wanting to heal her fibroids and avoid surgery. She and her ex-husband were battling over issues with their divorce at the time. She said she always felt "stupid" compared to him, and she wanted to feel confident through these divorce dealings. But underneath, she felt she'd just get taken advantage of again because she didn't "have what it takes."

The psychological meaning of fibroids according to Dr.

Lincoln is: "'She-rejection.' They are caught up in rejection of their femininity, sexuality, womanhood, and or motherhood. They are manifesting accumulated or unexpressed guilt, shame, inner confusion, or past hurts and abuse that they attribute to their being female."[3] Any tumor or growth represents a form of self-rejection. With fibroids, it may reflect a resistance to do the creative feminine purpose a woman has came on earth to do. What message do fibroids carry? A need to regain her feminine power and do her creative work.

I explained to Shannon that the emotional cause of fibroids was rejection of womanhood. They can also form after a painful experience with a loved one. I suggested she look into doing her creative work. Using the MO Technique, she released her feelings of self-rejection, powerlessness, resentment, anger/rage, and lack of self-love. She also wanted to release abandonment and the hurt that stemmed from her divorce, which she did in another session. She saw the hurt as a broken heart and released that negative energy out of her chest. She saw her heart mended and whole at the soul level and instilled the positive energy. For abandonment, she imaged an empty wooden box in her back. She imaged the box lifting off of her back, then smashed it and sent it off in a horse trailer to be taken to the dump. At the soul level, she imaged not abandoning herself in any way as a beautiful lavender light. She filled her body with the positive energy. She also signed up for a class to pursue her dream of writing plays. After her second session, Shannon's fibroids couldn't be detected and she didn't have to undergo surgery.

Before fibroids form, the symptoms usually include heavy bleeding, bleeding between periods, painful periods, or fullness in the pelvic area. The emotional sufferings of these early symptoms can be released with the MO Technique and the emotional component of fibroids may not form.

> The emotional sufferings of the second chakra requires learning the soul discovery of connection—trusting oneself, being able to connect and bond with self and others, believing in oneself, being confident and competent and doing creative soul work.

The Forgiveness Ball of Energy

When clients are ready to forgive those who have caused them pain, I have them do a forgiveness exercise. I have them imagine filling their heart up with pink loving energy. Then, out of their mind's eye, I have them send that pink ball of love to the mind's eye and heart of the person they want to forgive. As they are sending it, I have them say, "I forgive you, and I forgive me," until they feel a release. Once they feel a release, I have them just relax and be with the feeling of compassion for themselves and the other person. When I have used this technique with my clients, I see a gold energy (forgiveness) come in on their aura printout, which I discuss in the Chapter 7, Steps to Releasing Emotional Sufferings with the MO Technique.

The Third, or Solar Plexus Chakra provides a means for projecting our power out into the world. To keep this chakra healthy requires having our DNA Power. Our MO may include being critical of ourselves and others, having low self-esteem, feeling alone, depriving ourselves, experiencing a lack of joy, expecting betrayal or non-acceptance, or being over-responsible and self-defeating. It can include the "why me?" or "poor me" syndromes and the feeling that we actually deserved and somehow asked for our misery. These emotional tendencies prevent us from using our power effectively by not allowing us to achieve a powerful position in the world. When we overcome these, we can allow our soul to achieve its purpose.

These emotional sufferings could manifest as arthritis, ulcers, pancreatitis, indigestion, anorexia or bulimia, hepatitis or liver dysfunction, or adrenal malfunction. Any problem with the abdomen, stomach, gallbladder, upper intestines, spleen, kidney, pancreas, adrenals, or middle spine might be the body's wake-up call to release these emotional sufferings.

Resentment, anger, and rage are stored in the liver, which connects with the third chakra. When this chakra malfunctions, digestion and purification of the liver is affected, and the body may become toxic. The pancreas may malfunction because the person lacks sweetness in life. This feeling at a deep level can trigger diabetes. When the negative energy affects the adrenals, the body becomes fatigued and the immune system weakens, enabling disease to attack anywhere in the body.

The third chakra (solar plexus) is the seat of personal power. Because it's located in the abdomen, it provides energy for digestion and purification.

If the emotional sufferings of this chakra are not released, we might feel a need to either dominate other people or be submissive and powerless. This can lead to problems in any of the organs mentioned above.

Example: Jane, a 40-year-old client, very thin, had been to several doctors and had an array of tests done but everything came back negative. She had severe stomach problems and was losing weight, and her stomach hurt every time she ate or drank. She could barely sit in the chair and talk to me she felt so nauseated and weak. I asked her if any adverse event had happened in the last six months to a year. She told me in the previous year her mother had been diagnosed with pancreatic cancer and had passed away three months later. Both of her grandmothers passed away just before her mom. She said the doctors didn't catch her mother's cancer in time, and now she felt they may not catch it if she had cancer.

Jane's dad had died in a car accident when she was four years old. She said, "Maureen, I have nobody, and I'm all alone. When

I get sick, everything falls apart—no one knows how to carry out the responsibilities at home. I keep everything going. In order to exist, I have to keep proving myself, and I'm exhausted." Jane was feeling alone and over-responsible. She didn't have self-love as her foundation, and she had much resentment, anger, and extreme fear that her doctors would not be able to find out what was wrong with her. This showed up as severe stomach problems. As Jane released her emotional sufferings and regained her DNA Power, she became peaceful. The MO Technique was new for Jane, but she said the peacefulness she felt would help her be able to calm down and look at her life with a different perspective. After the session, she immediately drank some water and affirmed that the pain had lessened incredibly. The soul discovery of the third chakra is regaining our personal power.

This chakra discovery begins with the mastering of loving oneself—the foundation of all healing. The Common Thread gets released in the first MO Technique session. Then the client works on the emotional sufferings of a particular disease in the follow-up sessions. Thus the chakra discoveries are multi-layered—that is, you must first learn to love yourself and establish your DNA Power before you can begin to feel confident and worthy.

> The emotional sufferings of the third chakra requires learning the soul discovery of empowerment—being confident and demonstrating personal power in the world.

The Fourth, or Heart Chakra is how we receive love and give love to the world. The heart chakra can be burdened with numerous emotional sufferings that sap one's joy and life force. Grief, self-rejection, and lack of self-nurturing may be stored here. The individual's MO may be feeling abandoned, disconnected, undeserving of love, unsuccessful, or afraid of failure—all of which will negatively affect the heart chakra. So will co-dependency or feeling overly responsible. These emotional sufferings can manifest as problems with the heart and circulatory system, lungs, breasts, ribs or diaphragm, and thymus gland. They might show up as asthma, allergies, or mid-back pain.

Example: John, a 65-year-old fit male, came in with an arrhythmia and was under a doctor's care. He explained that every once in awhile his heart would just start beating irregularly and very violently, even though he was on medication for this problem. As I interviewed him, he said he felt his mother was never emotionally there for him. He said his father was a violent man. He felt he was shoved to the sidelines when he was around seven years old. He became a juvenile delinquent and felt he always had to fend for himself. He was sent to the military at 17 and became a "self-made" person. He was married once for five years but said of this experience, "Home was where the hurt was—it was never peaceful or loving." For the rest of his life, he has been in and out of relationships, not wanting to commit or become attached. When I interviewed him and we looked at his love life, he decided he has never had a steady love state with the women in his life. I then asked him, "Do you have a steady love state with yourself?" He answered, "I never really thought about that."

In *Messages from the Body*, Dr. Lincoln writes that the psychological meaning of arrhythmia is as follows:

> False alarms—they are a self-made person who believes that they are all they've got. They have felt cut off from the universe and the environment all their life, and that they therefore have to handle everything on their own hook, unassisted. This activates moments where things are getting out of control and beyond their coping capabilities. This brings on anxiety attacks and the resulting palpitations. It is

the result of never having received love and merging as a child. Fluttering infatuations—they have a fundamental inconsistency in their love nature—it comes and goes and *they can't maintain a steady love state,* input, or relationship. It reflects the instability of the nature of the close relationships in their family.[4]

John related to all of the above. Using the MO Technique, he released "not having a steady love state with himself." He imaged a woman, his first love (which surprised him), and felt the love state in his genitals. As he was releasing it, he said, "I wondered what was wrong with me when we broke up." He imaged the picture out of his body and instilled a beautiful loving energy. At the soul level he saw very clearly that love comes from within. John knew this on a conscious level but when he tapped into his spirit or higher self he saw his value and worth at a very deep level. He said, "God is love and God and I are one." He felt very peaceful and in harmony with himself.

He instilled loving himself at his core and treating himself as a treasure. He released the powerlessness and instilled his DNA Power. He learned to feel the anger and resentment and then release them. When he asked, "What do I need?" he said it was to feel valuable and he instilled that energy.

After his healing session, we discussed that one of his soul discoveries was to love himself steadily and unconditionally.

His 40-day affirmations were:

1. I now have a steady love state with myself mentally, emotionally, physically, and spiritually, and I love myself unconditionally.
2. I am loveable and valuable, and love myself exactly for who I am, and who I am is constantly changing for the better. I am the vibration of infinite harmony and treat myself and all with gratitude and love.

3. I am powerful and radiate God's quiet divine power to the whole world and within myself.
4. I feel my anger then release the anger and resentment every time it comes up. Then I ask, "What do I need?" and fulfill my deep need inside, which today was that I am valuable.

Once John masters having a steady love state with himself, he can then attract the same in his relationships. This was John's soul discovery and when he *masters* it, his heart may respond by being steady and in sync. Once he becomes "steady love", this will also radiate out into the world, and he could possibly have what he has been searching for all his life—love.

> The emotional sufferings of the fourth chakra means learning the soul discovery of self-love—deeply loving oneself at the core of one's being, and being able to give and receive love and create beautiful relationships.

The Fifth, or Throat Chakra. This chakra relates to how we express ourselves and communicate in the world. To keep the throat chakra healthy requires communicating in an empowering way. Emotional sufferings of this chakra and our MO may include being judgmental or irresponsible, suppressing what we want to say (or feeling guilt or shame after saying it), or being unable to express how we feel. Fearing any type of failure or misfortune can cause neck problems; we can't "stick out our necks" due to fear.

Other emotional sufferings that affect the throat chakra may result from being abused, fearing the worst in every situation, or buying into the "but not for me" syndrome. The "but not for me" syndrome applies to those who believe others have what it takes to be successful but they themselves never will achieve that. This can also manifest as the "when is it going to be my turn?" syndrome, which can result in thyroid problems.

One famous woman who has thyroid problems appeared to have it all—prestige, money, beautiful relationships, and a booming career. I was very curious why she developed thyroid problems. I read that she decided to take a week off to heal her thyroid and have no contact with her business world or friends. She said when she took time for herself she lost business associates and friends because she was not available and took time out from her grueling schedule to take care of herself. Perhaps she was feeling "when is it going to be my turn to relax?" When it comes to the emotional cause of disease, someone's outward appearance may not match what they are really feeling inside. That is why it is so important to understand our MO and programming and the emotional and soul determinates of disease.

The emotional disturbances of the fifth chakra could manifest physically as a sore throat, teeth or gum difficulties, TMJ (a jaw problem), or throat, mouth, neck, hypothalamus, and thyroid or parathyroid problems.

Example: Nancy, a petite blonde with blue eyes, was diagnosed with stage III lymphoma of the neck. Nancy, an only child, was raised in a perfectionist household. She was afraid of her mom and became a people pleaser so she would not get hit. She was never allowed to voice her opinions. She said, "Because of the way my mom treated me, I always felt like there was something bad inside me and that I was inadequate. I have always had a 'what's the use' feeling as I could never please her. I never felt it was okay to be who I am."

Lymphoma's psychological origin, according to Dr. Michael Lincoln, is as follows: "Unable to forgive and forget. The individual is sitting on deep-seated resentment and resignation. They have always been running on empty with insufficient equipment. The individual has a growing feeling of 'What's the use?' along with abiding anger about their whole situation. They have always had to suffer silently. They feel that they have always come up a day late and a dollar short because of some inherent evil. They therefore have not felt the right to request or require much, much less complain about or explain their situation. It is a result of a shame-inducing family who conveyed to them that they can expect nothing but the worst."[5]

I worked with Nancy for more than seven months to help her release her childhood emotional sufferings. Through our sessions, Nancy tapped into her true spirit and now loves who she is. She learned how to speak her truth in an empowering way, which has allowed her to master the emotions of the throat chakra.

What may have been the trigger that erupted the cancer? She said she was very stressed about all the paperwork she had to do as a speech therapist. It took away from time she could spend focused on the children. She explained, "That really sucked the joy out of going to work for me. I would walk into the office every morning, look at my pile in my in-box and feel as if the life force was literally being sucked out of me." She had diarrhea every Sunday night for two or three years and it wouldn't go away until Wednesday afternoon, when she felt the weekend was on the way. She felt trapped into working for the school district until she was able to move out of state. The pay scale and benefits lured her into the feeling that she had to stay and earn the most she could for retirement.

As she released her emotional sufferings, her life became manageable and filled with joy. She and her husband moved out of state, and she now enjoys agility training with her dogs—her passion. She healed without chemotherapy or radiation.

She wrote this note to me:

I began appointments with Maureen after I was diagnosed

49

with stage III lymphoma. Through her MO Technique, Maureen helped me understand how illness can be a wake-up call in life. With her guidance, I learned how various issues and emotions allow disease to develop in the body. I also learned how to deal with these issues and emotions so that the disease could leave my body. After seven months, my CT scan and PET scan were normal, as is all of my blood work. I will be eternally grateful for the learning and healing that I've experienced with Maureen's help.

> The emotional sufferings of the fifth chakra requires learning the soul discovery of communication—being able to communicate in an empowering way without shame or guilt.

The Sixth, or Brow Chakra, is the "mind's eye", or how we "see" the world. It includes the brain, eyes and ears, nose, pituitary gland, pineal gland, and nervous system. Emotional sufferings of the brow chakra and MO of the individual may include lack of faith in the universe, lack of control or fear of external control, feeling abandoned, difficulty seeing, not wanting to hear, feeling unprotected, fearing the future, not being the "master of one's own ship", and believing that they are the only one who can handle a situation. A person with a brow chakra imbalance might be the "family hoist" who takes on the world's problems with little recognition for doing so. These emotional sufferings might manifest in the physical body as brain tumors, eye problems, hearing problems, seizures, strokes, neurological disturbances, and difficulties of the spine.

Example: Sara, a 50-year-old school teacher, had a benign pituitary tumor removed. After her surgery, one of her friends suggested that she see me. I discussed with her that a dysfunction of the pituitary can be from not being the "master of your own ship", as the pituitary is the conductor gland. She related to that immediately. She said, "The school blames us for not having our kids at a certain level. It's very frustrating; I don't feel like I can do anything about it, so I don't feel like I'm the master of my own ship." She continued, "We get very little recognition for the hard work we do, and I feel that I have to do it all with little help."

With the MO Technique, Sara released not being the "master of her own ship." She imaged a pirate ship with skull and cross-bones on it. She found the energy of that image in her head. She released it out and put a loving energy back in. At the soul level she saw clearly she could only do her best with what she had to work with and that allowed her to be the master of her ship. She quit beating herself up for not measuring up to others' standards. She connected with her spirit or soul and forgave herself for not meeting all the children's needs, and she felt at peace. She said to herself, "My spirit is special and has many gifts." She told me that everyone at school wanted to know what changed for her because her attitude was one of peace and contentment. She knew at her soul level that she was doing the best she could and that she could only control her thoughts. She said, "The funny thing is, once I tapped into my true self and was at peace with myself—peacefulness came from the outside world."

One of the soul discoveries of migraine headaches is to heal abandonment and this relates to the sixth chakra. When abandonment is one of our soul discoveries and we release it with the MO Technique, we learn first to not abandon ourselves, which is one of our soul discoveries to work on. When this is instilled at the soul level and reprogrammed on the conscious level for 40 days, then we have a choice when abandonment shows up in our life. But *we* must change first. I tell my clients that the big test comes *after* they release abandonment or whatever they are releasing. Just as in school, we get tested to see if we've learned the lesson. When the soul discovery shows up again, I instruct them to notice how they handled it and be very compassionate with themselves as they just observe. Did they react the same way or differently? After we pass a few tests and have the awareness that it's one of our soul discoveries, we can keep practicing not abandoning ourselves. Eventually, we may see it coming a mile away and not "go there".

> The emotional sufferings of the sixth chakra requires having faith and trust in the universe, which means letting go of the ego and connecting with soul consciousness.

The Seventh, or Crown Chakra is how we relate to our Creator. Emotional sufferings of this chakra include feeling separated from our Creator. The MO may be "everything rides on me", "I can never be good enough", and "the buck stops here", feeling ultimately responsible for everything. We may believe we can't cope with life or have an inability to forgive. These attitudes and feelings tend to physically manifest in the muscular system, skin, nervous system, and skeletal system. They may create problems such as depression, exhaustion, extreme sensitivities, skin disorders, and what we might call the "dark night of the soul".

> The emotional sufferings of this chakra requires learning the soul discovery of connection—using one's divine energy and accomplishing one's soul work, which is a personal gift to the world.

Example: A 35-year-old woman who had a red eye went to her physician, who prescribed an antibiotic. She took the antibiotic for 45 days without relief. Then she came to me and her eye healed in one session. Her gracious note to me stated that she saw a difference the very next day, and in four days, her eye had completely healed.

She used the MO Technique to release The Common Thread and, during the session, she was also able to *see* what her soul came to do. The next day, she signed up for a class to start the process of finding her purpose.

An antibiotic didn't help the eye because her eye was telling her one of her soul discoveries, which was to see and start working on her life purpose. When her medication did not work, she looked below the surface of the illness to find relief.

Balancing the Chakras

I have one client who would leave our sessions with her chakras in balance, but after she had a medical procedure of any kind, she'd return with her chakra out of balance in the area that had been worked on. I recommend balancing the chakras every day, and especially after a hospital visit or trip to the doctor. It takes only a few minutes, but they're minutes extremely well spent.

Chakra balancing is not as abstract and mysterious as it would seem. It's simple to do—and crucial for optimum health. Balancing the chakras involves cleansing the auric field, which allows the chakra to then spin in the right direction and in a balanced fashion. It draws in energy to help retain health.

The model of treating disease with medication creates a situation in which it may be necessary to take drugs for life. If you stop taking the drug, and your symptoms return it may be because the underlying problem was not corrected.

Look at the results in our world. We have an overly medicated society, caught in a vicious cycle of prescriptions and office visits, because most often the *underlying causes of disease are not being addressed*. Yes, modern medicine can produce "miracles", but people still become ill and will continue to do so until they deal with their unique MO, programming, and emotional sufferings. The concept of chakras and their healing lessons compose a big piece of the puzzle missing in Western medicine. This might be the 21st century's cutting-edge "medicine" that takes the world to a higher consciousness of physical, emotional, and spiritual health.

All of the emotional sufferings of the chakras can be released with the MO Technique. An individual's symptoms, condition, or illness is the road map to see exactly which one their soul signed up for.

Prevention of disease starts with embracing and then releasing the emotional sufferings of symptoms—for example, releasing symptoms of a cold may prevent more serious lung disease. If every time people went to a physician for a problem they also released the emotional sufferings, they may prevent further problems.

For in-depth information about chakras, my two favorite books are *Anatomy of the Spirit* by Caroline Myss and *Vibrational Medicine* by Dr. Richard Gerber. Dozens of books on the chakras written by expert physicians and healers are available. I recommend taking advantage of this crucial knowledge for your own health and healing.

Chapter 5: Divine Connection
Using the Infinity Sign

"Belief Code 1: Experiments show that the focus of our attention changes reality itself and suggest that we live in an interactive universe."
– Gregg Braden

The infinity sign—the symbol for cosmic consciousness—looks like the number 8 lying on its side. Using this sign is a part of the MO Technique that breaks down barriers between ourselves and our Source. These barriers must be dissolved for us to instill the positive thoughts, feelings, and attitudes that allow our soul consciousness to operate and heal our bodies.

When working with clients to align, harmonize, and balance the body's energy, I gently swing a pendulum in a figure 8—the infinity symbol—over their chakras. This moves energy, helping create an electromagnetic balance in their bodies. It also helps align the right and left side of the brain, allowing them to use both sides equally. This motion breaks down the block wall of fear so the person can go deep into the soul consciousness. I get clients to imagine going deep inside to their soul level or tap into their spirit where their truth resides and positive energy gets instilled.

My clients are logically able to see what needs to be healed (represented by the left brain) and release negative aspects out of their subconscious. Then they intuitively access the information of the higher self, their soul consciousness (represented by the right brain), and they find a resolution and instill that positive energy. This part of the MO Technique helps them tap into their own soul wisdom where they can transform their emotional sufferings into peace, joy, and harmony.

After drawing a figure 8 eight times over a client with my pendulum, I stop at the crown chakra. I focus my intention on connecting with the Divine Source and instruct my client to do the same. Doing this helps dissolve the block wall of fear and divine energy pours through the crown chakra, infusing every cell of the body with unconditional love.

Because of this unconditional love, individuals can "see" who they are at the soul level, from which they instill their truth. This also brings into balance the receptive nature of the feminine (associated with the left side of the body) and the dominant nature of the masculine (associated with the right side of the body). More than that, tapping into the superconscious perspective can impart a positive meaning to something that might have seemed negative to the conscious mind.

This part of the MO Technique aligns the body so it can tap into the soul consciousness. The infinity sign allows us to tap into our spirit. *This is where our spirit integrates with our humanness and we can experience a shift in perspective at a very deep level.*

For further explanation of how the infinity sign affects the block wall of fear, read Sherry Anshara's *The Age of Inheritance: The Activation of the 13 Chakras.*[1]

Chapter 6: How the MO Technique Works

"We cannot teach people anything, we can only help them to find it within themselves."
– Galileo Galilei

By becoming aware of our emotional sufferings and the patterns of our MO that keep our wounds open, and by learning how they manifest, we can free ourselves and create the healthy lives for which we yearn.

We have negative and positive emotions for contrast and for growth and learning. We now can choose how long we want to hold on to negative emotions, and with the MO Technique, move them out on demand. Then we can renew and accumulate positive energy, which is important for health.

Outside sources and environmental influences such as diet, bacteria, viruses, pollens, and pollutants operate as triggers for an already aimed and loaded gun. Physical symptoms may arise from our emotional sufferings, which are negative thoughts that have shaped our lives from repeated experiences and may have been repressed from our awareness.

At every moment of life, our bodies are becoming what we think about, which is largely determined by how we are programmed. But we can't just think our way into healing—we must also feel our way into it. Thought has little power until we put emotion into it. Our thoughts plus an intense euphoric feeling can move healing energy to create the kind of health and mental state we desire.

The MO Technique takes focused energy with feeling and reprograms the body back to the soul consciousness. The MO Technique reprograms the subconscious, superconscious, and conscious minds—*and all this together makes the lasting change.* Like many healers suggest in their work, we can actually change the body back to its original blueprint—which is what the MO Technique can do.

MO Technique Wipes Out Harmful Programming

The other day, my computer crashed. I turned it on . . . nothing. I hit the keyboard. Again, nothing. I talked nicely to it . . . right, nothing! Being the super computer whiz that I am, I quickly called the repair guy. He had to wipe out the hard drive and reload the operating system. As he explained what he was doing, I realized it was just like using the MO Technique I developed.

Remember, all we are in this world is energy—both good and bad. Although energy cannot be created or destroyed (according to Einstein), it can be transformed . . . just like my hard drive. When we have bad programming, we have to wipe out the hard drive and reprogram it with something that works—our new blueprint for fulfillment.

Energy Fields and the MO Technique

The MO Technique reprograms the subconscious, superconscious, and conscious minds through four elements: (1) healing energy to balance the chakras, (2) imagery to release emotional sufferings that underpin disease, (3) positive energy instilled back into the body to reprogram the superconscious, and (4) affirmations to reprogram the conscious mind. These elements reflect Einstein's formula $E=MC^2$—that is, everything is made of energy that can neither be created nor destroyed but can be shaped into whatever we desire.

As described in Chapter 3, every living thing is surrounded by an energy that also includes the individual. This surrounding energy is called the aura. This aura stores information as energy from our past, present, and future. It carries, stores, and receives information 24 hours a day and provides the key to our physical, mental, and spiritual state. The aura energy can be compared to the electrical currents of cell phones and unseen waves of energy transmission. Western alternative energy healers have known this for decades; Asian cultures have known it for thousands of years. Wouldn't it be exciting for traditional medicine to get on board?

Imagery and the MO Technique

Because the *human brain recognizes no difference between an image of reality and a visualized image,* we can change the cell programming to whatever we want by using focused energy. That's how we can come closer to our original blueprint—what our soul intended us to be before our programming got in the way. The MO Technique uses imagery to release the negative emotion because the brain knows no difference between an image of reality and a visualized image. The negative trapped energy of the image is actually released out of the body. At the soul level, the focused energy that's used to fill the body up changes the cell programming in a positive way. *Changing the energy of our body is one of the keys to wellness.*

Here's an important consideration about imagery. Many people tell me they don't think they can use imagery effectively. My imagery teachers, Terry and Sue, said, "If you know how to worry, then you know how to image." In effect, humans image all the time, only we don't call it that. We process our thoughts, imagine outcomes and scenarios, stew about the pictures we create, and daydream about the things we want. All too often, what we image frightens us, causing stress and more fear.

Yet we can use imagery to help us release old patterns and messages that no longer serve us. As Einstein once said, "Imagination is more important than knowledge." Without imagination, we would not have cars to drive or movies to watch. We wouldn't have cell phones to answer, books to read, or paintings to hang on our walls.

Here are several ideas for images people use to release specific emotions.

- Rage—Imagine the energy of a gorilla, find it in your body, then set the gorilla free and watch it run out of sight.
- Powerlessness—Imagine an anvil, find the energy of the anvil in your body then image it out and throw it in the ocean and let it sink.
- Lack of trust—Imagine a wooden board and find the energy in your body, then remove the board and throw it away.
- Fear of rejection—Imagine a red ball with a face on it, find the energy of it in your body then take it in your hands and toss it out of your body.
- Incompetence—Imagine a child or infant (yourself), find the energy in your body then place him/her in God's hands.
- Betrayal—Imagine the energy of a wolf, find it in your body then see the energy get sucked into a vacuum.
- Competence anxiety—Imagine the energy of a helpless bird, find the energy of it in your body then let the bird fly away.
- Self-doubt—Imagine an orange ball wrapped in a package, find the energy in your body then send it downstream.
- Lack of self-love—Imagine a black ball, find the energy in your body, image it out and then toss it into the ocean.
- Non-support—Imagine a dozen tennis balls, find the energy in your body then hit each of them out of your body and over the fence.
- Abandonment—Imagine a blanket, find the energy in your body and let it blow away.
- Trapped feeling—Imagine lying in a mummy case, then unlock the case and imagine stepping out.
- Anger/rage—Imagine fire, find the energy of it in your body then witness Archangel Michael dousing the fire and

replacing it with a loving light.

- Inability to cope—Imagine a tornado, find the energy of it in your body then let it spin away outside of your body.
- Over-responsibility—Imagine a gold crown, find the energy of it in your body, image it out and then set it on a nearby shelf.
- Guilt—Imagine a dark blue color, find the energy of it in your body then imagine putting it in a box and let the angels take it away.
- Not trusting the process of life—Imagine a bucking horse, find the energy of it in your body, image it out and then see it run into the sunset.
- An adverse event prior to diagnosis—Create an image of the event as a snapshot. Find the energy of the picture in your body. Tear up the picture and let the wind blow it away.

These are simply suggestions that can create a bridge between the body and the mind. No matter what image you choose, it's right for you and never wrong. *After releasing the image out of the body, a beautiful loving energy is instilled to replace the old energy.*

Chapter 7: Steps to Releasing Emotional Sufferings with the MO Technique

"What is necessary to change a person is to change his awareness of himself."
– Abraham H. Maslow

This chapter includes an explanation of the 12 steps of releasing the emotional sufferings with the MO Technique that you can take yourself as well as the 10 steps that I take in working with my clients and guiding them through the Modus Operandi process.

The 12 steps of the MO Technique are simple, practical, and non-threatening, with no side effects! You get to release all that is not serving you—and treat yourself like a treasure, a precious gem. If you follow them carefully, you're on your way to loving yourself. We must feel all of our emotions, whether negative or positive, as they are all vital for our survival. The MO Technique allows you to feel all emotions and process them, bring repressed or suppressed emotions to the forefront, and release those that no longer serve you. You create your own reality.

Step 1: Identify the Emotional Suffering

Identify and write down the emotional sufferings of the disease that pertains to you. The Common Thread of Disease is the foundation from which to start. These emotional sufferings are lack of self-love, powerlessness, anger, and resentment. Read through steps 1 to12 first, then read the instructions for releasing The Common Thread following the 12 steps. You'll be doing steps 1 through 7, then following these instructions.

Step 2: Identify the Adverse Event

Did an adverse event happen six months to one year prior to the diagnosis of your disease or condition? Was there a death or a loss of some sort? Did a child leave for college? Was there a job loss or a job change? Was there an event that made you very angry and left you feeling powerless? Identify and write down this adverse event.

Step 3: The Grounding Procedure

Imagine your feet firmly planted on the ground. See yourself as a big, stable oak tree, with the roots of the tree extending deep into Mother Earth and out in every direction. Stay in this position until you feel stable and grounded. Imagine drawing positive energy from Mother Earth through these roots to your toes. Imagine this energy running from the tips of your toes all the way to the top of your head. Imagine connecting to the universal energy and allowing that energy to flow naturally through your body with the intention of letting all negativity flow through it and out of your body.

Step 4: Cleansing and Balancing the Chakras

This step removes debris from your aura. To clear the auric debris, begin at the root chakra (See Diagram1: The Seven Chakras). Lie on your back and imagine a spinning wheel rotating counterclockwise over the root chakra. Imagine any and all negativity stored in the chakra whirling out into the universe. Take your time with this. Remember to breathe.

Now imagine a spinning wheel rotating clockwise over and through the root chakra, restoring positive energy or white light to this chakra. See it filling up like a balloon to the perfect size until it feels balanced and light. Repeat this cleansing and balancing procedure for each chakra.

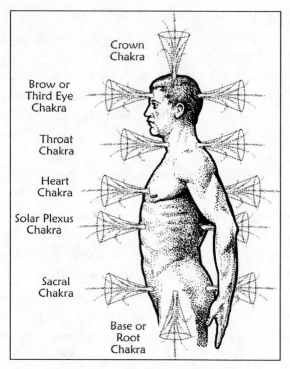

Diagram 1: The Seven Chakras

Step 5: The Infinity Sign

The infinity sign or the number 8 removes the block wall of fear, as previously explained. Imagine a figure 8 over your seven chakras. Actually trace it with your hand or in your imagination over the seven chakras. Do this eight times. On the eighth cycle, imagine energy shooting out of the top of your head, connecting with the universal divine energy. Then imagine the divine energy coming back through the top of your head all the way down to the tips of your toes, filling every cell of your body with unconditional love. (I imagine white loving light filling every cell of my body.)

Step 6: The Relaxation Procedure

Sit in a quiet spot. Relax your body from the top of your head to the tips of your toes. Take in a deep breath, breathing in what you need and exhaling and letting go of everything you don't need. Do this several times. Starting at the top of the head, allow the muscles in your scalp to relax. Let your brow soften and smooth out. Allow all of the muscles around your eyes to relax. Let your cheeks, lips, tongue, and jaw relax.

Allow those feelings of relaxation to run down into your neck, letting all the muscles in your neck relax. Then let the relaxation run down into your shoulders as your shoulders become limp and relaxed. Allow the relaxation to travel down into the upper arms, elbows, forearms, and all the way down into the hands and fingers. Let all tension simply flow out your hands and fingers.

Allow all the muscles around the heart and down into the lungs and through the whole chest area to relax. Pause. Now allow the relaxation to travel down into the ribs, relaxing the whole rib area. Pause. Then allow the relaxation to travel down into the abdomen, allowing the abdomen and all the abdominal organs to become soft and relaxed. Pause.

Wrap that relaxation around to the back, allowing it to travel all the way down the spine. Once you get to the bottom of the spine, let the relaxation travel down into the pelvis and the buttocks, allowing the pelvic organs and the whole area to relax. Pause.

Then allow the relaxation to travel down into the upper legs, allowing the quadriceps and the hamstrings muscles to relax. Then let the relaxation travel down into your knees, your lower legs, your calf muscles. Allow it to travel all the way down into the feet and toes, letting any bit of remaining tension flow out your feet and toes.

Step 7: Preparing for the Imagery

Once you've reached a glorious state of relaxation, go to a place in your imagination where you feel safe. This place may be real or imagined, familiar or not. I like going to the ocean in my mind's eye; others may travel to a meadow, a stream, or a favorite room. Simply let your imagination take you there.

Once you feel safe and relaxed, you will begin the focused imagery. You'll imagine the emotional suffering out of your body. (Keep this in mind: The event that triggered your disease or condition can be imagined and released out of the body in the same way you release the emotional suffering in this exercise.)

Step 8: The Imagery
Identify the specific emotional suffering that pertains to you. Try not to analyze the image. Rather go with the first image that comes to mind, whether it makes sense or not. That first thing could be an object, a person, a plant, a color, an old memory — anything that comes up.

Scan your body to see where the energy of the image is being held. It could be an ache, a heaviness, or a feeling in your body. To release the emotional suffering you've identified, you can use a vacuum cleaner, an eraser, a leaf blower — whatever tool you like. Some clients tie balloons to their emotional suffering and let them fly out of their bodies. Others imagine pushing their sufferings off a cliff, mountain, or building. Whatever works! Once you've released this image out of the body, use your imagination to instill a loving energy or light in the area where you just released the emotional suffering.

Step 9: The Soul Level
Imagine going to a deeper level — the soul level — and look at what was released in a positive way. *Tap into your spirit or higher self.* This level is where your truth resides. From your truth, describe what you would look and feel like if you did not have this emotional suffering. (For instance, what would you feel and look like if you treated yourself as a treasure, as one of the most precious gems in the world? You may say, "I would be happy, smiling, strong, confident, and radiant.") Put that positive

description into a ball of energy and give it a color. Then put that ball of energy underfoot and bring that white or colored energy up through the bottom of your feet all the way to the top of your head. Fill every cell of your body with this energy. Take your time, breathe, and feel the positive energy and emotions that you are instilling as you fill your body. *The effectiveness of this technique comes from really feeling the euphoria of what you are instilling as if you already have it.* While keeping that energy in your body, visualize sending that white or colored energy through your mind's eye to everyone in the world. Then allow it to come back and envelop your complete auric field.

> "The tendency to ignore our emotions is *oldthink,* a remnant of the still-reigning paradigm that keeps us focused on the material level of health, the physicality of it. But the emotions are a key element in self-care because they allow us to enter into the bodymind's conversation. By getting in touch with our emotions both by listening to them and by directing them through the psychosomatic network, we can gain access to healing wisdom that is everyone's biological right."[1]

Step 10: Instill the Affirmation

In your own words and at the deep level, instill a positive affirmation. Say the affirmation out loud. For instance, if you have released the lack of self-love, say, "From this moment forward, I make all decisions based on the truth that I am love itself, I am a treasure, I am a precious gem." Take this affirmation in and affirm it at the deepest level possible. Repeat this procedure with every emotional suffering one at a time.

Step 11: Return from the Imagery

Go back to the special place you identified earlier and just relax.

When you are ready, come back to this time and place feeling refreshed, safe, and wonderful. If lying down, sit up on the side of the bed until you feel stable. When you feel stable, stand up and ground yourself again, using the same grounding process you used in Step 3.

Step 12: The 40-Day Affirmation

Write down the affirmation that you instilled. Read the affirmation out loud every day for 40 days in a row. *(Put the affirmation somewhere where you will see it. If you miss a day, it's important to start over and repeat it for 40 days in a row.)* This 40-day process reprograms the conscious mind and makes it a habit. Ideally it would be best to release one emotional suffering, work on it for 40 days, then go on to the next one.

As you progress through the 40 days, notice what comes up in your thoughts and your body. It may be beneficial to journal your feelings throughout this time. Write down all events presented to you. Notice and record how you look at these events in a new light.

Do you have different insights now? Do you react differently?

Once you know that each emotional suffering is one of your soul discoveries, you will likely see it coming ahead of time. Then you can consciously choose what to do.

With focused effort and practice, these 12 steps will help you to create the life you've always wanted.

What's different about this modality? It reprograms all three minds. It releases the negative out of the subconscious, the body, instills the positive back into the soul consciousness, or superconscious, then reprograms the conscious mind by reciting the affirmation for 40 days and makes it a habit. It provides a working model for how to understand the emotional and soul determinates of disorders that underlie physical ailments and provides a guiding example on how to release them. It explains how life experiences and soul intentions or discoveries affect energy systems, or the chakras, and proposes an imagery process to precipitate healing. It uses the infinity sign to integrate and consolidate the MO effects. Then a 40-day implanting system is the client's homework so the healing becomes permanent. It teaches the power of self-love, which may induce euphoria!

How to Release The Common Thread of Disease
Steps to Release Lack of Self–Love

Follow steps 1 through 7 of the MO Technique, and then proceed to the steps below.

1. Step 8: Imagine the lack of self-love; find in your body the energy of the image that you come up with and release it out of the body.

2. Once the image is released out of the body, fill that area of the body with a loving energy.

3. Step 9: Imagine going to a deeper level, the soul level, or tapping into your spirit or higher self. Describe how you would feel and look if you treated yourself as a treasure, as one of the most precious gems in the world.

4. Put that positive description into a ball of energy and give it a color.

5. Put that colored ball of energy under your feet and imagine it filling every cell of your body—feel the *euphoria* of your description as you fill your body up with the new positive energy. Say to yourself as you fill your body up— "I am a treasure, a precious gem" or your description in your own words.

6. Once filled up, leave that energy in your body, and out of your mind's eye send that colored energy to everyone in

the world. (I envision the world and encase the whole world with the energy, and I imagine sending the energy to everyone in the world. I have clients that envision sending the energy to the countries one by one. Do what feels right for you.) Then allow it to come back and envelop your complete auric field.

7. Step 10: Say your affirmation out loud. "From this moment forward I make all decisions based on the truth that I am a treasure, I am a precious gem, I am love itself." (Use your own positive words and make it right for you.)

8. Do Steps 11 and 12 of the MO Technique.

Steps to Release Powerlessness

To release powerlessness, do the same procedure as releasing lack of self-love, only imagine powerlessness. At the soul level, fill your body up with your DNA Power.

Your affirmation would be something like: "From this moment forward, I make all decisions based on the truth that I have my personal power. I send that power out to the world with ease and then I help empower others." Say this affirmation for 40 days.

Steps to Release Anger and Resentment

Anger and resentment are a different procedure. Follow steps 1 through 7.

1. Step 8: Feel the anger and then imagine a picture of the anger or the resentment. Find the energy of the image or picture in your body and release it out of the body.

2. Fill that area of the body with a loving energy.

3. Step 9: Image going to the soul level or tapping into your spirit or higher self. From your truth or spirit, feel the anger. Then ask yourself, "When I am angry what do I need?" It may be to feel valued, loved, respected, under-stood, or a variety of things. (Make sure it's what you

need—not, for example, "I'm angry because my husband doesn't pay enough attention to me." I would then ask, but what do you need? It usually means you need to feel valued.)

4. Put what you need into a positive ball of energy and give it to yourself. If your soul discovery is to value yourself— you become the energy of that value you want to attract. Fill your body up with the energy and feel the euphoria of valuing yourself. Send the energy out to the world and then let it come back and envelop your whole auric field.

5. Step 10: Say your affirmation out loud. It can be something like: "I feel my anger or resentment then release the anger or resentment out of my body *every time* it comes up. I fill that area with a loving energy, then I ask myself what I need and fulfill my own need deep inside."

6. Follow steps 11 and 12.

The 10 Steps I Follow with Clients

Let me describe the steps and details of how I work with my clients when they do the MO Technique.

1. I create a printout of a client's seven-chakra energy system using the WinAura program. (This step requires the Win-Aura machine and is optional.)

2. I conduct an in-depth interview to find the client's way of operating in the world (MO) and discuss his/her specific health challenge. I ask what adverse event triggered the disease to erupt.

3. We highlight and share information relevant to the client's disease, referring to Dr. Lincoln's book *Messages from the Body*.

4. From this information, we determine the emotional sufferings and what needs to be released out of cellular memory.

5. I do energy work and chakra balancing and use the infinity sign to release the client's block wall of fear.

6. I help the client do a relaxation technique to prepare for a guided imagery session.

7. I guide the client in using imagery to release images of emotional sufferings from his or her body.

8. I have the client image the soul level before instilling the truth back into the cellular memory and generate corrective affirmations.

9. I create another Win Aura printout showing the client's changed energy. (optional)

10. After discussing the session, I get the client to compose and commit to repeating affirmations for 40 days, thus instilling the messages on the conscious level. We also discuss challenges that will likely come up and how to handle them.

Let me explain each of these steps in detail.

Step 1

I use the Win Aura machine before and after the session so clients can see the change in their energy fields once they do the work of healing themselves. This is what I've learned from using this machine:

- The color gold is the energy of forgiveness. I see this energy enter the client's auric field when a client forgives himself and others.

- The color blue appears when communication comes into the body. The body is saying, "Ahhh! You're finally feeling me and communicating with me."

- Violet energy is a "knowing" energy. This energy represents the client's truth instilled at the soul level when they have a "knowing".

- Green/yellow signifies that the client is in a healing state.
- Turquoise comes in when the individual brings in compassionate energy.
- Aquamarine is peaceful energy.
- Blue/white comes in when an actual healing comes into the body. (Blue is communication and white is divine healing energy.)
- White light represents the energy of truth and divine healing energy.

People who have mostly white light in their auras appear to be angel-like. I've had a few of these rare individuals as clients. They live at a high vibration and have a "knowingness" about them.

Step 2

The next step is an in-depth interview with the client to learn more about his or her MO. I ask questions such as these:

- What have you done up to now to address your disease?
- What was your childhood like?
- What are you attracting in your life that you'd like to stop attracting?

I allow plenty of time so I can listen carefully to the answers and, together, we get to the emotional root cause of the disease that houses their soul discoveries.

To determine an event that could have triggered the disease, I ask questions such as these:

- Did a loss or anything traumatic happen six months to a year before your diagnosis?
- Was there a death of a loved one?
- Did a child leave home for college or a job?

- Was there a job loss or a job change?
- Have you recently gone through a divorce?

Usually an adverse or traumatic event has triggered the disease within the past six months to a year. When clients think about possible trigger events, they're usually surprised because it never occurred to them that it would affect them physically. The event itself also needs to be released out of cellular memory using the MO Technique.

Step 3

Next, I get an overview of their backgrounds and how they were raised to determine their unique MO. As clients read about the message their disease is trying to convey in *Messages from the Body*, I ask them to highlight words or sentences that pertain to them.

Step 4

Once the client has highlighted several words or sentences, we discuss them in detail with the goal of reaching the emotional root cause of the disease. Inevitably, it stems from their childhood programming. We analyze the words and sentences to determine what emotional sufferings may exist. Then we make a list of the emotional sufferings as well as identify a trigger event.

Step 5

Once we've decided which emotional sufferings need to be released, the treatment begins. The client lies on his/her back on a massage table. I complete the energy work and chakra balancing, using the infinity sign to release the block wall of fear.

Step 6

I direct a brief relaxation exercise toward all the muscles from top of the head to the tips of the toes. Then I ask the client to take a few deep breaths, taking in what's needed on the inhale and letting go of what isn't needed on the exhale.

Step 7

We begin the guided imagery. I ask the client to go to a safe, comfortable, and relaxed place in his or her mind—real or imagined, familiar or not. I have the person imagine the previously discussed emotional sufferings—not to analyze them but to go with the first thing that comes to mind, whether it makes sense or not. That "first thing" could be a person, an object, a plant, a color, an old memory—anything that comes up. Then I ask the person to scan his or her body to see where the energy of the image is being held. Many clients feel that energy as an ache, pain, heaviness, or other feeling in their body. Everyone I've worked with has identified a place where that energy hangs out in the body.

To image out—or release—the emotional sufferings identified, the client can vacuum them, erase them, or blow them away, perhaps using the imagined actions listed earlier.

As a reminder, some tie balloons to their emotional sufferings and let them fly out of their bodies; others push their sufferings off a cliff, mountain, or building. Whatever works!

Step 8

Once an emotional suffering has been imaged out of the body, I ask the client to fill that space with a loving energy or light. It's important to fill the gap where it's been stored and replace it with positive, loving energy. It's like having a sizable splinter in your finger. After you remove it, you clean the area and apply an antibiotic cream. This gap-filling technique does the same thing internally.

At this point, I get the client to imagine going to a deeper level—the soul level—their spirit or higher self—and look at what was released in a positive way. He or she does this by imaging it into a ball of positive energy, putting that ball of energy underfoot, and allowing that energy to fill every cell in the body—feeling the euphoria as though he or she already is what's being instilled. While keeping that energy in the body, the person visualizes sending it through the mind's eye to everyone in the world then allows it to come back and envelop and embrace his or her complete auric field. Sending the energy out and allowing it to come back helps people connect with the world and learn how to receive the energy back. After all, the body needs a balance of energy going out and coming back in continuously. This recreates a positive template for the body.

Choosing the right words, the client then instills a positive affirmation at this deep level. From this moment forward, that person strives to make all decisions based on the powerful positive emotion that's been instilled.

After all emotional sufferings have been released and statements of personal truth have been instilled, I gently ask the client to come back to the present, feeling relaxed, safe, and refreshed. Once back to this reality, I ask him or her to become grounded again. (Frequently, clients can manage to release three emotional sufferings and the trigger event in each session. Ideally, it would be best to release one, work on it for 40 days, then go on to the next one. But because this technique is not yet covered by health insurance, the cost of treatment is out of pocket, so clients want to cover more ground in fewer sessions.)

Step 9

I print out a new chart of the client's energy so we can see what chakra has been affected and what energy needs changing for healing to happen. The printout shows any noticeable changes in the aura or energy of chakra(s) that housed the emotional suffering(s). It's visible proof! (This step uses the Win-Aura machine and is optional)

Step 10

I then instruct the client to write out the corrective affirmations to be instilled at the conscious level every day for 40 days.

We end by discussing what happened in the session and handling any outstanding questions. At this point, I warn my clients that they may be tested to see if they react differently now than in the past. For instance, if they released the emotional suffering of "betrayal", the next time a type of betrayal comes up, they'll likely see it coming and can consciously choose what to do.

Remember, the subconscious mind stores conscious experiences. It also reveals messages of our self-worth and stores negative programming as emotional blocks. The soul level (superconscious mind) sees from a higher perspective and understands things when the conscious mind does not. Therefore, it can see our soul truth and hold knowledge of solutions to our problems. It alters the negatively programmed "tapes" so we can see and hold the truth about who we are. This reprogramming of all three minds is the key to making desired changes last.

Certified Addiction Counselor Lynn Telford-Sahl (MA in psychology with holistic specialization and author of *The Greatest Change of All* and *Intentional Joy: How to Turn Stress, Fear & Addiction into Freedom*) experienced her MO Technique session this way: "I felt energized and joyful after my session with Maureen. As I worked with the positive images over the next 40 days, I was able to sustain what we'd accomplished. This is big news. So often after a healing session, the effects dwindle over time. I continue to have fun with the positive images and do so during my meditation."

Chapter 8: Learning the Lessons
Our Bodies Can Teach Us

"The body has its own way of knowing that has little to do with logic, and much to do with truth, little to do with control, and much to do with acceptance, little to do with division and analysis, and much to do with union."
— Marilyn Sewell

A few months ago, I was driving along California Highway 108 near my home, minding my own business, probably day dreaming about what I would cook for dinner, when I spotted unusual, tall, skinny green trees in the distance.

Now, I've traveled this road thousands of times and I'd never noticed these trees before. There's no way they just sprouted up!

The next day, I was sitting at my computer looking out the window, getting loads of work done, I'm sure, when I saw two of these same trees in my neighbor's yard. I've lived in this house for three years and stared out that window hundreds of times, but I'd never noticed these trees before. Weird. I started noticing these trees everywhere.

That got me wondering: Why am I seeing these trees everywhere I go? Isn't that how it is? We can be oblivious to things until we take conscious note of them, then we'll see them all the time.

It's that way with our body lessons. Once we see that our body is trying to tell us something, we start to see the signals all the time.

> If we understand our MO and the message of our symptoms, we can release them at the symptom stage and they are likely then to not turn into full-blown diseases.

Often when we go to a physician concerned about our symptom, condition, or disease, we don't get exposed to the underlying message of the disease. For instance, if you get pneumonia, the message is that you may not be able to breathe in life with ease, which is what the lungs help us do. You may realize that your MO is not letting yourself out or letting others in easily. Your lungs may become congested because of the emotional component which is not breathing and flowing with life. This may happen when a loved one dies or you go through a devastating event that puts you over the top. You want to look at an event that might have triggered the pneumonia by asking yourself, "Is there an adverse event that has happened in my life in the last 12 months when I felt powerless and angry and I just couldn't breathe with life?" This MO can lead to many other lung-related diseases. Using the MO Technique, you can release not being able to breathe with life and learn to flow easily with life which is the underlying message of the lungs.

By learning the soul discovery of each symptom, condition, or disease, life can become incredibly magical because we know what our soul intended. We just keep improving and reaching toward self-mastery.

Be aware that medication and any new miracle drug may be masking the soul discoveries of disease. Certainly using medicine alone has not provided us with the information we need to heal disease, although it still provides benefits, including relief from acute pain. But what if health care practitioners *worked together* to give patients information about the message of the symptom, condition, or disease? Yes, finding out the truth may be more difficult than swallowing a pill. Perhaps if the MO Technique came in pill form, it would be prescribed a lot!

We Don't Always Like What We Hear

On a visit to our home, our young grandson was running around the play park and wanting to climb just a little too high for his grandpa's liking. That meant Papa had to scold him. If you knew my husband, you would know the scolding went something like this: "Now, Cole, don't climb so high or you'll get hurt!"

When he heard that, Cole sat down and held his hands over his ears, crying, "My ears! My ears!" As a nurse, mother, and grandmother, I naturally began quizzing him. "Do your ears hurt? Is it an earache? Are you sick?"

"No. I don't like what I'm hearing!" he cried.

Yep, we often just don't want to hear things. We don't want to face the tough issues because it's easier not to—like Scarlet O'Hara in *Gone with the Wind*, who declared "I'll think about it tomorrow" . . . or never. That seems easier than dealing with our MO and our programming.

Everything is a clue to the puzzle of life, including every symptom, condition, or disease we may develop. I believe knowing our Modus Operandi can unlock any self-imposed limitations. Through disease, symptoms, and conditions, the wise body lets us know what we feel deep inside—even if we don't want people to see that truth, ourselves included.

Each time a disease appears, the body is actually asking us to surrender the old (unhealthy) aspects of the self and embrace the new. Changing our MO or letting go of old patterns that don't serve us and then rebirthing ourselves is a natural cycle. And once we heal the discoveries of our soul, we can move on to a universal soul consciousness.

> The universal soul discovery of each disease implies we are all one. It implies that this planet can change for the greater good when the consciousness of each individual changes.

Love Doesn't Mask Lessons Ready to Be Learned

Remember, the opposite of fear is love—the most powerful "drug" available. Love never masks the soul discoveries we came to learn.

The body is wise, and through it, the soul helps us confront issues we're missing. One of those issues may end up as a disease.

Both Western medicine and our society tend to be left-brain dominant, filtering information through logical, proven evidence. Yet contradictions abound. For example, estrogen therapy has been touted as good, then bad. Many pills have been taken off the market because they cause severe side effects.

I believe that, intuitively, we know what's right and what *isn't* right for us—if we can learn to tap into our inner wisdom and see beyond any smokescreens. That's why we need access to our intuition to find truth that's "outside the box". When the right and left hemispheres of the brain are in balance, we can think logically and do our research while also using our intuition to make decisions. The MO Technique enhances both, making thinking logically *as well as* thinking creatively the norm. That's when we enter the realm of "infinite" possibilities!

Our body is a metaphor for our life story. Let's change it to a love story. Let's love ourselves and treat ourselves like we are treasured and precious. If we love ourselves first, then the next step of generating unconditional love becomes the most crucial discovery of the planet. Imagine it! Remember, if we can imagine it—it can happen.

Chapter 9: What About Our Children?

"It's never too late to have a happy childhood."
– Tom Robbins

When I was a nurse, the only departments I didn't work in were pediatrics and labor and delivery, although I took training in both. I simply couldn't work there because, when I think of children who are sick, tears well up, and I get a lump in my throat and heaviness in my heart. If we as a society can prevent children from getting sick, it would definitely be euphoria for me.

Why do children become ill?
Let me share these three theories:

- **They teach us to see what is important in life.** As one of the most powerful forces on our planet, children have come to teach us. Many times, ill children show the people around them that life is a precious gift to be treasured. What happens when we know of or have a sick child? Every other worry seems insignificant.

- **They may not be getting their emotional needs met.** For instance, Dr. Michael Lincoln states in *Messages from the Body* that the psychological root cause of colic is like a Red Alert for children. "They are picking up mental irritation, impatience, annoyance, emotional upset, and tension from their parents and/or their surroundings, and it is alarming and upsetting them. They are becoming irritable, angry, and impatient with everything as a result. They feel like they are in a 'bed of prickles.'"[1] Yes, children pick up on what's going on around them and react to it. The Common Thread of Disease addressed earlier includes anger-resentment, feelings of powerlessness, and lack of self-love. With colic, these factors can all show up at a young age.

- **They're experiencing growth of their soul, which comes out of disease.** Indeed, disease tells us exactly what soul discovery we signed up for. Therefore, children may become ill for reasons of their own soul growth. This may start in the womb, even in the circumstance in which the child was conceived, and continue throughout the pregnancy. The fetus can pick up on the parents' emotions, what's happening in the outside world, and the parents' reaction to the events.

When a child gets sick, what questions should we ask?

- What is the psychological meaning of the disease the child has?
- What are the emotional and soul determinates of the disease the child has?
- Are there dynamics in the family contributing to the child's disease?
- How can they be changed?
- Are the child's emotional needs being met?
- Does the child feel loved, safe, and protected?
- Is the psychological origin of the disease based on an emotion that's been handed down from generation to generation?

What can be done to prevent the setup of disease in children?

Talking and communicating your loving feelings to your unborn baby makes the baby feel loved, safe, and protected.

Parenting errors usually occur at the subconscious or unconscious level. If you look at the psychological meaning and the emotional and soul determinates of every disease and understand how it relates to your child, you can do something about it. However, if you don't know how the disease develops in the first place, then you have no framework to work from. Teaching children self-love and treating them as treasures right off the bat is the answer.

What dreams for the future can we envision?

My dream is that everyone who has a child takes an oath to treat the child like a treasure. If we can imagine it—and see it "big"— then it can happen. Dreams do come true! I can see the future now. All children are treated like treasures, which they *are* you know! They are taught self-love and deeply loved. Authentic self-love is practiced on a global level. Resentment and anger doesn't build. We feel powerful because we love ourselves deeply. Disease doesn't exist; it can't live in a society where people love themselves unconditionally.

Chapter 10: AIDS/HIV

"Try to be like the turtle—at ease in your own shell."
– Bill Copeland

AIDS/HIV – The Virus and the Disease

The Human Immunodeficiency Virus (HIV) is one of several retroviruses that infect and destroy helper T cells in the body's bloodstream. When the body has a great reduction in the number of T cells, Acquired ImmunoDeficiency Syndrome (AIDS) results. This attack greatly weakens the immune system and leaves the body defenseless against disease.

The Soul Discovery of AIDS/HIV

The soul discovery of AIDS/HIV is to learn tolerance. This means attaining not only sexual acceptance but self-love, which encompasses tolerance of every aspect of themselves.

When intolerance, conditional love, and non-acceptance are present (either parental or societal), disease often results. This result only reinforces the childhood programming that one is not acceptable or worthy, and this deepens the intolerance of oneself. Like attracts like. When one's soul discovery is to learn to be tolerant of oneself, that energy attracts reinforcing events and people as well as diseases of intolerance into one's life. Because of that, it's safe to say that negative and intolerant cultural views of homosexuality and the way that AIDS/HIV is contracted have actually promoted this disease. For example, the intolerance of one person affects all of us. This is why understanding that self-love is the foundation of the body is crucial. Once this principle is understood, connecting everything through disease provides one of the keys to peace and unity on this planet.

I believe that when humans have mastered the Universal Soul Discovery of tolerance of all, the soul discovery of AIDS/HIV, these understandings have the potential to prevent and eradicate AIDS/HIV from our world. In fact, everyone can play a role in dealing with this disease. I believe humankind may have attracted this to teach us not only tolerance and love of ourselves but tolerance and love of humanity. This includes all races, heterosexuals and homosexuals, rich and poor, educated and uneducated—not just those who meet society's mainstream standards.

The intolerance is especially true in Africa where AIDS and HIV are at epidemic levels. In many parts of Africa, as elsewhere in the world, the epidemic is aggravated by social and economic inequalities between men and women. Women and girls commonly face discrimination in terms of access to education, employment, credit, health care, land, and inheritance. These factors can all put women in a position where they are particularly vulnerable to HIV infection. In sub-Saharan Africa, around 59 percent of those living with HIV are female. In many African countries, sexual relationships are dominated by men, meaning that women cannot always practice safe sex, even when they know the risks involved.[1]

Some women infected with HIV report more than one risk factor, highlighting the overlap in risk factors, such as inequality in relationships, socioeconomic stresses, substance abuse, and psychological issues. For example, in the North Carolina study of HIV infection in black women, the participants most commonly reported that their reasons for risky behavior were financial dependence on male partners, feeling invincible, and low self-esteem coupled with the need to feel loved by a male figure, and alcohol and drug use.[2]

Still, the main theme of AIDS/HIV, whether it's in Africa or the United States, or with heterosexual or homosexual individuals, is intolerance, which is the soul discovery of AIDS/HIV individuals and is programmed in at a very young age. Intolerance of oneself collapses the immune system, allowing the virus to attack.

The MO of AIDS/HIV

The MO of AIDS/HIV sufferers reflects an emotional commonality, which is a failure to accept oneself, or intolerance of oneself. This self-rejection creates a deep and desperate feeling of being unworthy, or not good enough. In turn, the feeling produces an auto-allergic reaction, or self-attack. Any virus can attack when a futile feeling saps a person's strength. HIV infection then causes the progressive loss of immune cells called helper T (or CD4) cells, which help other immune cells to function.

When the virus penetrates the body, it takes up residence in the helper T white blood cells. Normally, these white blood cells protect the body from infection. It could be that the person's low self-acceptance is being mirrored in the falling white blood cell count. Perhaps these helper T cells won't protect or *help* the individual because of the programmed thought pattern of self-negation. The unworthy feeling may have had its origin in childhood, when it was embedded into the subconscious mind. The subconscious doesn't reason; it just accepts what it's given as truth. The person may not feel worthy of protection, which may lead to activities such as drug abuse or unprotected, high-risk sexual encounters. These activities then trigger the old, familiar feeling that they aren't worthy, and the cycle becomes vicious. An individual who doesn't feel deserving usually won't ask for help and therefore creates a situation of self-sabotage. The individual feels defenseless and despairing, denying personal needs in a cycle of self-destruction.

As the virus continues to grow, it can damage or kill the helper T cells, weakening the immune system and leaving the individual vulnerable to AIDS, for which there has been little *help*. Because the individuals who contract this disease may have a lack of self-love and self-acceptance, their heart chakras have likely become blocked or seriously imbalanced over time.

The Universal Soul Discovery of AIDS/HIV
To embrace tolerance of all humanity.

Although the disease has taken on plague-like proportions and many who contract it are homosexuals, not everyone with AIDS is homosexual and not every homosexual has AIDS. As I offer the following thoughts on this subject, I also attempt to bring physical and emotional healing of this disease into the mainstream of society.

AIDS, like all diseases, exists to bring us a soul discovery. Not everyone signed up for this particular lesson, but many did. Because it arrived mainly under the umbrella of "alternative lifestyle", it often gets dismissed as punishment for deviant behavior.

In addition, it's not easy to pass the HIV virus from one person to another. It's not transmitted through food or the air, nor is it transmitted by sharing eating utensils or bathroom facilities or kissing or hugging. Usual means of transmittal include:

- Unprotected sexual intercourse (either vaginal or anal) with someone who is HIV infected
- Unprotected oral sex with someone who is HIV infected
- Sharing needles or syringes with someone who is HIV infected
- Infection during pregnancy, childbirth, or breast feeding (mother to infant transmission)

Unprotected high-risk sexual encounters and the use of intra-venous drugs for recreation tell the tale of self-rejection, most likely compounded by guilt. A buildup of these emotions along with feelings of resentment and powerlessness may eventually erupt in anger or rage.

The Emotional Sufferings of AIDS/ HIV

- Signature Emotional Suffering—Intolerance or non-acceptance of oneself
- Feeling it's not okay to be who you are
- Feeling undeserving
- Feeling not good enough
- Sexual guilt and shame
- Unique emotional suffering
- The Common Thread—lack of self-love, resentment, anger/rage, powerlessness

Our society has struggled with issues of sexuality, forcing men and women to hide or repress their preferences and shaming them if they don't. When either parental or societal tolerance and unconditional love and acceptance are absent, "dis-ease" reigns. When even one person walks through life with shame, guilt, anger, and denial, it affects us all.

Energetically, we are connected to everyone and all of life. Because we are connected to all of life, whatever we believe and whatever we do has an influence on the whole. The term "We Are All One" or "All Is One" is now becoming mainstream. We understand that we're all a part of the holographic principle—in which every piece of the hologram contains the information of the whole.

Of course, many gay men and women live happy, healthy lives free of this disease. Perhaps they were loved and accepted by their families, their friends, and, *most importantly*, themselves. This also may be why many individuals live with HIV for years but don't express the disease of AIDS. I believe it's a matter of what you signed up for in this life—your soul discoveries.

Complicating the emotional issues around HIV is the often-present matter of addiction, usually to drugs or sex. It's difficult to know which comes first—the low self-esteem or the addiction.

But the consequences can be desperation, deprivation, over-indulgence, disease, and perhaps a long road of misery. Despite the fact that medications are dispensed freely and sex is a marketing tool in our society, society frowns on addiction, thus adding another nail to the coffin of self-esteem for people suffering from AIDS.

Let's not miss the message that disease brings us—that is, let's not limit our tolerance, love, and acceptance to those who meet society's standards. Until we learn compassion and under-standing both for ourselves and others, we will likely retain a world of intolerance, conditional love, and lack of acceptance. We will remain at the mercy of illness and our own ignorance.

I hope the following case history increases the sunshine of compassion and understanding. It involves a homosexual man, but 70 percent of newly diagnosed AIDS/HIV patients in the United States are heterosexual African American women.[3] The soul discovery for all is acceptance of oneself.

Dr. Lincoln's psychological meaning of AIDS/HIV is this:

I don't deserve to exist. They have a strong belief in their not being good enough, in their not deserving to manifest their selfhood. The result is auto-allergy, self-intolerance, self-hatred and the operation of self-destructive programs. They simply cannot love and accept themselves fully as who they are, and they are systematically denying their own needs. They have a real need to become real, and to pay attention to how they live their life and who they in fact are. They are convinced that no one gives a damn, and they therefore feel ultimately hopeless, vulnerable, defenseless and despairing. They also suffer from sexual guilt arising from self-gratification and indulgence. Underneath it all is an extreme deep-seated rage at themselves, the world and the Cosmos.[4]

Louise Hay's mental cause is "Feeling defenseless and hopeless.

Nobody cares. A strong belief in not being good enough. Denial of self, Sexual guilt."[5]

This case history shows how Derek was set up or programmed for his soul discovery of tolerance of self.

Case History

Derek, a gay man of 45, has been HIV positive for 14 years. During this time, his health has fluctuated. He has lost and gained weight, and he has struggled with the flu, fatigue, and depression. After our first session, his T-cell count improved, increasing from 411 to 448 (a normal T-cell count is between 500-1500).

A recovering alcoholic, Derek had been sober for several years and was active in the recovery community. He had long since learned that alcoholism was a symptom of larger, underlying problems. Despite the internal work he had done, his depression persisted. His doctor attempted to find a working balance between the antidepressants and his HIV medication. Derek said he wasn't sure if he was over-medicated or under-medicated. As he began having trouble in his relationships, anxiety took over his life. A bright, funny, and generous man, Derek increasingly became sad and withdrawn.

At our first session, Derek spoke of the strained relationship between his parents, even before he was born, which told me that Derek's rejection may have begun in the womb. His father drank excessively and his mother smoked, signs they were both rejecting themselves. Neither parent had a healthy lifestyle, either physically or emotionally.

As a child, Derek had always felt different from his peers. He never quite fit in. He also revealed he'd been repeatedly molested and has carried sexual guilt ever since. He never thought he was good enough, and as a result, he sabotaged any successes in his life. As he attempted to numb his pain, he became an alcoholic. He first attempted suicide at the age of 17.

During our first session using the MO Technique, Derek worked on releasing his self-rejection, his feelings of not being good enough, and his belief that it wasn't okay to be who he was. The results of this session showed up immediately in his improved T-cell count.

At our second session, Derek worked on releasing his feeling of being defenseless, his belief that nobody cared, and his feelings of power-lessness, anger/rage, and deprivation. I suspected, however, that Derek had reservations about his healing. I wasn't sure he wanted to heal completely because it would dramatically change his existence and his way of thinking. It would also mean Derek might have to go back to work; then his life would no longer be a roller coaster of medical and emotional crises. He had seen his healing begin, and I sensed it scared him.

Healing Regression

In fact, this reaction isn't uncommon, especially for clients who state they have a pattern of self-sabotage or intolerance of themselves. In the clinical world, it's called "healing regression"—one step forward and three steps backwards.

Those who suffer have often become attached to their pain. It defines who they are and becomes an odd sort of comfort zone. When such people come to a healing session and have doubt in the back of their minds about whether they really want to heal, the pull of the familiar can remain stronger than the desire for help. Remember the crux of HIV infection: *the helper T cells quit working because the individual does not feel deserving of help.* To heal, one must believe it is possible and deserved, and one must let go of the familiar suffering.

Often in the process of emotional healing, clients engage in dysfunctional and/or primitive behaviors, feelings, thoughts, and reactions. This means they're "going along with" the healing process, and they've begun to "peel the layers of the onion", or regress to the wounds of their twenties then move back to their youth wounds. They're returning to old behaviors in reaction to the healing and replaying them as they go through the process, but eventually they heal and go on. Sometimes it's difficult to convince them they're not "falling apart" but rather "falling together".

Dive Bombing

The healing process also can precipitate what's referred to as "dive bombing". The individual begins spiraling downward as his or her life spins rapidly out of control. Stated another way, if you're dive bombing, you're going about your daily routine but you feel like you could "lose it" at any time. You start spiraling faster and faster until you hit bottom, increasing in speed like a plane that goes down to drop a bomb. You then bring what you have learned to the situation and release yourself from all of the damage.

Dive bombing for me was hitting bottom. This became my turning point to put me on the path of being emotionally healthy. Knowing two things brought me through the crisis: (1) that this can be a normal process to achieve emotional healing, and (2) that I was on the way to a breakthrough.

Although, this phenomenon is common in individuals doing healing work, it's a frightening occurrence—the breakdown on the way to the breakthrough. However, it's crucial for those in this healing crisis to stay with it. They bring new capabilities to bear on the original wounding situation and release themselves from the damage that devolved out of it. This takes great courage, determination, and intention.

Unfortunately, Derek didn't come back for another session. He continued to struggle with his anxiety and depression, as well as his medications.

Derek's Win Aura Printout

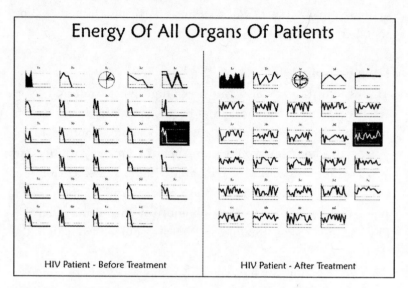

Diagram 2: Derek's Win Aura Printout

The Win Aura System I use in my practice prints out a page of the energy of every organ in the client's body. I print out this page before and after the healing session. Above is Derek's before and after printout of his first session. The first box shows the heart chakra. It had little energy before the treatment, but after he instilled self-love, the heart chakra energy filled in completely.

The energy of the brain is the third box on the top line. Before, Derek had one quadrant of the brain that lit up with energy; after, all four quadrants lit up with energy. (The MO Technique uses both sides of the brain.)

The last box on the first line is the energy of the body's balance. Before treatment, Derek's body was out of balance, and after treatment, it came into balance.

The energy of the organs in Derek's body was almost flat-lined. After treatment, the energy of every organ improved dramatically. This may be one reason Derek's T cells improved.

I have used this machine for 12 years, and I've had few clients whose heart chakra energy is filled in. When this energy is depleted, physical disease can develop, which may be another reason heart disease is the number one killer.

Keeping your chakras healthy depends on keeping your thoughts and emotions healthy. With the Win Aura System, they can see how it affects the energy of all their organs.

Emotions can be passed down not only from parents to children but from former generations. Researching *emotional generational links* will help us be more cognitive of how disease and emotions are interrelated. Teaching this can help people look at what happens from conception on and determine exactly what disease an individual is at risk to develop.

I look forward to the day when love of self and others rules. I believe that when we as humans have mastered the Universal Soul Discovery of tolerance—the soul discovery of AIDS/HIV— these understandings have the potential to prevent and eradicate HIV/AIDS from our world. This disease teaches tolerance of all. These wonderful souls who have AIDS/HIV have come to teach us all tolerance. As a student, I want to get an A on this assignment.

Chapter 11: Allergies

"Self-acceptance is my refusal to be in an adversarial relationship to myself."
– Nathaniel Branden

The Disease
Allergies are exaggerated or abnormal immune system reactions to substances or situations harmless to most people.

The Soul Discovery of Allergies
Allergies may result from an individual's programmed rejection of something in the environment. The body sends the message to overreact or "counterattack" instead of interacting and cooperating.

With allergies, the immune system mistakenly believes that a substance is harmful and attacks. Histamine is then released to attack the allergen, causing related symptoms. A natural substance, histamine protects our health. When it's released, it's saying that something is wrong. When the soul discovery of the allergy is learned, the allergic reaction can be released.

An allergic reaction may be triggered when the individual is threatened by, at odds with, or irritated by something or someone in his or her life. The allergy presents the individual with a particular soul discovery. Symptoms of allergies, such as sneezing, runny nose, itchy and watery eyes, are also symptoms of grief. Often these individuals hold an incredible amount of stored grief. This grief is probably related to unresolved problems or irritants from childhood, and an allergic reaction may be triggered when a similar irritating event occurs. The underlying reasons for allergies must be acknowledged, not covered up with medication, to eliminate the reactions.

People who suffer from allergies may not have received the

love they needed as a child. For these individuals, there is an actual inner crying and longing for a mother's love or someone close. The inner crying may show up as symptoms of allergies.

Symptoms of Allergies

- **Sneezing**: If a person sneezes a lot with an allergy, it may result from a non-deserving feeling, which triggers grief in the body and in turn activates the sneezing.
- **Itchy, watery eyes**: The individual may be trying not to see what is happening or may be unable to see the truth. Usually inner crying causes itchy, watery eyes.
- **Runny nose**: This symptom may signify suppressed grief which may be from deprivation in childhood, which gets triggered when a similar event happens. The runny nose attempts to release the suppressed grief from the body.
- **Breathing difficulties**: Asthma and other breathing difficulties offer the message of being unable to take in life fully. The person may hold feelings of low self-worth which in turns leads to avoiding life and not feeling safe.

All of these symptoms may be caused by suppressed grief from a loss, which brings about congestion and problems of the respiratory tract. Grief can be stored in the body, and it needs to be felt but released when loss or deprivation of any degree is experienced.

The Universal Soul Discovery of Allergies
To teach cooperation and acceptance of all.

The Universal Soul Discovery of allergies is to take in life fully, cooperating with and establishing total acceptance of self and others. If we continue to use allergy medication and not learn the soul discovery of the irritant, the allergy will remain and allergic reactions may become more severe.

For example, let's consider my former allergy to milk. Milk is one way we are fed and nurtured as babies. When I was three weeks old, my mom tried several combinations to find milk I could tolerate. She never did find one I could use without also being on a cold medication.

When an infant has an allergy to milk, the parents need to know that the ability to receive nurturance and self-acceptance are likely soul discoveries that the baby signed up to learn. Then they will know that *this baby needs to be nurtured and taught self-acceptance*. If I had known this was the soul discovery of a milk allergy, I wouldn't have had to wait until I ended up with a blood disorder and a painful divorce to *start* nurturing and accepting myself.

Diseases and allergies run rampant because we're not taught underlying causes of painful events. We have to get hit with a bigger stick for us to "get it".

The Soul Discoveries of Common Food Allergies
Common food allergies or aversions are milk, eggs, wheat, soy, seafood, and nuts.

- **Milk:** Milk is our first form of physical nurturance, usually accompanied by emotional nurturance. The soul discovery of people who are allergic to or have an aversion to milk is to nurture and accept themselves.
- **Eggs:** An egg is a reproductive body from which young hatch. Individuals who are allergic to eggs may carry resentment and rejection of the feminine, which can lead to a pattern of rejecting their creativity or success in the world. The soul discovery here is to accept one's feminine aspects.
- **Wheat:** Wheat is the chief ingredient in bread, which in many cultures is the mainstay of life. A wheat allergy signifies that the affected individuals' soul discovery is to learn to support themselves. Once they support themselves

on the inside, they will receive support from the outside world. This support may then help them produce what they want in life.

- **Soy:** Soy nuts yield valuable oil used in food, medicine, fuel, and manufacturing. Allergic individuals' soul discovery is to learn they are valuable.
- **Seafood:** Fish oils that contain omega-3 fatty acids are said to help prevent coronary artery disease. Individuals with an aversion or allergy to seafood are concerned about their love-lines, fearing abandonment and rejecting themselves. On the unconscious level, they may avoid intimacy and not believe they are "up to snuff". The soul discovery of their seafood allergy is to be there for themselves at all times and to embody self-love.
- **Peanuts:** People who have a peanut allergy may avoid love and intimacy and be self-rejecting. They may come from a severely rejecting family, and they may believe they don't deserve to be loved. The peanut allergy soul discovery is to heal the programming of rejection and love themselves unconditionally. Sadly, 1.5 million Americans have peanut allergies.

Case History 1

One of my clients, Sara, was severely allergic to peanuts. She had been raised in a family that was harshly and overtly rejecting. Her mother married quite young and was married for only six months when Sara was conceived. Her mom constantly berated her husband, Sara's father, and told Sara he was a loser. She would also tell Sara she was a lot like her father, which made Sara feel like a loser. After her mother divorced and remarried, she had three children in her second marriage and, according to Sara, treated them like royalty while Sara became "the ugly stepsister".

Sara's self-rejection from this programming and her lack of nurturance she felt from her mother were the underlying causes of her peanut allergy. The peanut allergy is the trigger that provided a message from her body to heal this devastating emotional programming and begin to love herself.

The Soul Discovery of Bee Stings

Bees make honey and live in colonies. An allergy to bee stings relates to an intense desire to keep oneself around the old colony. In other words, the person is programmed not to leave the nest and become successful in the world. These individuals may lack sweetness in their lives. *They tend to feel that if they seek their own destiny, they are betraying the family, or "the colony".* In turn, they reject who they are and have come to be. Looking at the soul discovery of bee stings, it may be easy to see why some people have a severe allergy to bee stings while others are hardly affected by them.

Case History 2

After my divorce, I moved into a home beside an orchard, where I'd run for my daily exercise. One day as I was running, a swarm of bees attacked, stinging me all over my head. I was in severe pain. At that time, I was wallowing in self-pity and severe self-rejection from the divorce. The bee stings "told" me to start accepting myself. I needed to go on with my life purpose. Because I had been studying Dr. Lincoln's work, the next day, I released the "keep them around the old homestead" programming. I signed up for a class and set out on my destiny's path and continued on it without feeling as if I would betray the family.

When the bees stung me, I felt cut off from my Divine Source, which is exactly how I felt after the divorce. Rather than dismissing the bee stings as a freak accident, I fortunately understood their message.

According to Dr. Lincoln, the psychological meaning of bee stings is as follows: "'How dare I?' It is reflective of guilty self-attack for

'having the nerve' to step out on their own direction of self-manifes-
tation, essence-expression and/or destiny development in violation
of their intense 'keep them around the old homestead' programming.
They experience it as a betrayal and as a destructive attack on their
family at the subconscious level."[1]

The "keep them around the old homestead" programming is
common, but because it's at the subconscious level, many people
don't know they have it. When I figure out my clients' MO, often
this programming comes up, so I help them release it. Once it's
released, they're free to pursue and accomplish their destiny without
feeling as if they're betraying their family.

The Soul Discoveries of Airborne Particles

Environmental allergens are dust mites, mold, animal dander,
and pollen from grass, ragweed, and trees.

- **Dust:** Individuals allergic to dust may avoid looking
  below the surface of things. Specifically, they may avoid
  looking at themselves and the truth of their life essence.
  The soul discovery is to not reject themselves but rather be
  their true selves.
- **Mold:** These allergic individuals may feel rejected from
  the start and feel unwanted. Common reasons for feeling
  rejected include being the wrong gender, being an
  unexpected baby, or being born when the family's circumstances were not right for having a new baby. The soul
  discovery of mold is to know their true being and love
  themselves.
- **Animal Dander:** Everyone who has a cat, dog, or other pet
  knows that this relationship is a commitment. Our four-
  legged friends must be cared for, and in many families,
  often become like our children. If a person is allergic to a
  cat, it may mean the soul discovery of accepting their
  feminine side. If allergic to a dog, it may mean acceptance

of the masculine. If allergic to animal dander, it may be the soul discovery of learning to commit. When individuals can't commit to themselves, it's a form of rejection.

- **Lawn Grass**: When I see grass-covered land, I think of lushness, abundance, and a grounding effect. Those allergic to grass may deny themselves the abundance of life. Their soul discovery is to nurture and protect themselves, grow, and allow abundance into their lives.
- **Ragweed:** This plant is considered a weed, which is usually unwanted. Those allergic to ragweed may feel they are not wanted. Of course, this leads to more feelings of rejection. The soul discovery of ragweed is to accept themselves.
- **Trees:** The tree signifies life, as in the "Tree of Life" and symbolizes individual growth. Those allergic to trees may be rejecting of life and they may have a fear of partaking in life. Their soul discovery is to learn and grow and find their passion in life.

Soul Discovery of Antibiotics

- **Antibiotics:** These drugs inhibit or kill microorganisms. Individuals who are allergic to antibiotics may have a deep distrust of the universe, forbidding and destroying any help. They may also be self-destructive. The soul discovery then is to learn to trust the universe and be able to ask for help when needed, and of course, embrace self-love.

Soul Discoveries of Chemicals

- **Cosmetics:** Cosmetic products are used throughout the world to make people, most often women, more attractive to others. People allergic to cosmetics may avoid their sexuality and passion because they feel they lack what it takes to be acceptable. The soul discovery is to accept themselves unconditionally.

- **Laundry Detergent:** Detergent is a cleaning agent. Those allergic to detergent may feel contaminated emotionally or dirty or bad inside in some way. The soul discovery then is to tap into their true spirit of love and feel self-acceptance.

The Emotional Sufferings of Allergies

- Signature emotional suffering—Self-rejection
- Grief
- Feeling a lack of trust
- Feeling a lack of support
- Unique emotional suffering
- The Common Thread—lack of self-love, resentment, anger/rage, powerlessness

These soul discoveries explain why some individuals are allergic to certain things while others are not. Do you see how *self-rejection* is the main theme of all allergen soul discoveries? After all, an allergy is a self-attack, or rejection of the self. When self-rejection and the soul discovery of each allergy is learned and released out of the body with the MO Technique, the allergy can disappear.

Louise Hay, author of *Heal Your Body,* wrote that allergies may be due to "denying our own power."[2] When we are no longer manipulated or irritated by outside forces, we can become powerful within. She also wrote that allergies may signify an aversion to another person. Many individuals and relationships mirror what we need to heal. So if someone irritates us, it's critical to find out why. For instance, it used to irritate me that a friend acted selfishly. I had to face the part of me that is selfish, what's called the "shadow". An excellent reference to help understand this concept is *The Dark Side of the Light Chasers* by

Debbie Ford. After reading this book, I started regarding people in an entirely different way. Now, when something irritates me about someone else, I question what *I* need to heal in a compassionate, loving way so I don't reject myself. I think, "That person reflects to me something I can heal, a soul discovery that will make me healthier and stronger."

All relationships create situations from which we can learn and grow. If we use this perspective to look at irritants in our lives, our relationships can become more accepting and loving. We can stop blaming others for something inside us we need to see, understand, and heal.

If your doctor says you're allergic to dust or dander or pollen, know that those things may be the triggers but not the underlying emotional cause of allergies. Certainly, the problem runs deeper than whatever is floating in the air at the moment. In *Allergies and Aversions,* Dr. Lincoln explains the psychological meaning of many allergies and aversions.[3] If you want permanent relief, you must release the emotional root cause and learn the soul discovery of each allergen, not just eliminate the trigger. This can be done using the MO Technique.

Case History 3

While I was married to my first husband, my allergies were so bad, I was afraid to go to a restaurant for dinner. I was a sneezing machine. How irritating for others to listen to me incessantly blowing my nose while trying to enjoy their angel hair pasta.

When we traveled, I would take my own sheets, fearing I would have a severe reaction to hotel laundry. I thought I was allergic to MSG and fabric softeners, but test results for these substances showed otherwise. I consulted a specialist who found no proof of allergies either, despite my difficulty in breathing. It's fair to say that I lived on an allergy medicine for quite a while.

By the time my marriage ended, I felt utterly powerless and had no self-worth. I was extremely angry and distrustful, not just of marriage, but of the Universe itself. It was hard to breathe with life.

Since childhood, I had felt unlovable, and throughout my life I had continually rejected and betrayed myself. So, of course, I attracted situations that magnified these tendencies and mirrored them back to me. They were screaming to be healed.

Once I released the allergy-causing emotional sufferings out of my cellular memory and took in self-love and acceptance at my super-conscious level, the symptoms disappeared. I could live without medicine. I stopped traveling with my own sheets. And I could go out to dinner without offending anyone.

Chapter 12: Alzheimer's Disease

"We live and grow by new knowledge."
– Thomas A. Edison

The Disease

Alzheimer's is a degenerative disease of the brain characterized by loss of memory and mental functioning and often including personality changes.

The Soul Discovery of Alzheimer's Disease

By the time Alzheimer's develops, the body may have cried out for 60 years or more with many other ailments that have been treated either by medication, surgery, or other forms of traditional medicine. The individual may not have realized what the body was trying to say with each symptom, condition, disease, or broken bone.

If people believe they're being "beaten up" by life for no reason, or if they've found little meaning or purpose in life, they may feel helpless and hopeless, become depressed, and just give up. The soul discovery of Alzheimer's disease is to *remember* the essence of our true spirit.

Dr. Lincoln, in *Messages from the Body*, stated that Alzheimer's disease is a form of succumbing to the confusion some people feel about what their lives have been or become. He believes they've been demoralized by having their competence and confidence undermined in childhood. There is distrust and disgust with the Universe and they feel angry, helpless and hopeless.[1] Louise Hay, author of *Heal Your Body*, wrote that Alzheimer's results from refusing to deal with the world as it is, and thus being overcome by hopelessness, helplessness, and anger.[2]

Individuals suffering from this disease may have been emotionally abandoned in childhood. Perhaps the undermining of their competence and confidence was combined with non-acceptance by their families. This non-acceptance could haunt them throughout life, setting up The Common Thread of Disease.

On a physical level, the habitual hopeless, helpless feelings throughout life can actually create chemical and neurological changes. Blockages may form and affect the brain's nerve impulses at the cellular level to a point where the brain loses its ability to store and recall memories. Eventually, brain cells may deteriorate, causing memory failure, personality changes, and inability to function in daily life. All of these characterize Alzheimer's disease.

The Universal Soul Discovery of Alzheimer's Disease
To remember our true selves.

We may come into this life and forget who we are, thus the universal soul discovery of Alzheimer's disease is to remember our true selves. From our life events, including disease, we can gain knowledge, experience, and spiritual maturity. As this book describes, we can tap into the innate wisdom of our souls at any time and become our authentic selves.

The Emotional Sufferings of Alzheimer's Disease

- Signature emotional suffering: Confusion due to forgetting one's true self
- Having their confidence and competence undermined
- Feeling helpless and hopeless
- Feeling unaccepted
- Feeling abandoned
- Being a private person who can't let themselves out or others in—the "portable plexiglass phone booth" syndrome
- Emotionally distant

- Unique emotional suffering
- The Common Thread—lack of self-love, powerlessness, anger and resentment

The MO of Alzheimer's Disease

It may seem contradictory, but I've observed that many children who are undermined at a young age grow up to become highly successful. How, then, do such people end up with Alzheimer's disease?

Perhaps as they become older, they keep striving to be good enough in their parents' eyes. However, unless they begin to feel self-love at their core, they won't obtain what they desperately need from the outside world. This constant seeking of acceptance from the outside may compel them to keep creating situations in which they hope they'll finally be accepted.

Although they may be outwardly successful, Alzheimer's sufferers may have difficulty feeling accepted and satisfied because their soul discovery is to *accept themselves*. But external acceptance is a temporary fix. Eventually, they may sink into a hopeless and helpless state, which could then cause the brain to deteriorate. This can especially happen at retirement if they believe they no longer have opportunities to prove themselves worthy and successful.

Alzheimer's disease soul discoveries may start at birth or early childhood, not at retirement age. A commonality exists in the MO and programming of Alzheimer's patients. At end stage of Alzheimer's disease, the client appears to be in a "portable plexi-glass phone booth" and *they can't let themselves out or let others in*—they are in their own "private world". This may have been their MO throughout their life.

Many of these individuals are reported to be highly private people. Reagan was said to be a private man, yet he became a movie star, governor, and president. These types of professions may keep others at bay and can be unconsciously chosen by the individual that has difficulty getting close to others. One of Reagan's children said his father never hugged him until after he'd developed Alzheimer's. These people may lack the intimacy in their life that they crave, but they just don't know how to let themselves out or let others in, which is one of their soul discoveries. This is usually due to their childhood programming.

Many times throughout life, they probably felt hopeless and helpless because of this unconscious programming, which may create brain impulses at the cellular level to cause nerve cells to become tangled and form plaque. Due to this plaque, the brain eventually loses its ability to store and recall memories. Eventually these sufferers sink into a hopeless, helpless state, which could then trigger the brain to shut out life completely. Constant seeking of acceptance from the outside world may compel those with Alzheimer's to keep creating situations in which they hope to finally be accepted.

Once I researched this pattern in Alzheimer's disease, I understood that I am a very private person. Thus I released the patterns and MO of Alzheimer's with the MO Technique. I am now enjoying the true intimacy that I've craved all my life. By accepting myself, letting myself out, and letting others in, I can truly be happy. I am giving it my all by working on truly connecting in hopes of preventing this devastating disease for myself.

For the last 12 years, I've used Dr. Lincoln's *Messages from the Body* to explain the psychological or emotional root cause of illnesses. I have my clients read the emotional root cause, and I have them highlight what pertains to them. Not every client would resonate with all of the aspects, but I've found that the emotional root cause is right on for most of my clients.

Reagan had the following illnesses, starting at birth and throughout his life. What were the soul discoveries of the illnesses, and how could the MO Technique have helped? At age four and again at age 36, he contracted viral pneumonia. Dr.

Lincoln described the psychological meaning of pneumonia as:

> . . . emotional abandonment at a very early age, to which they reacted with becoming a "self-made person" with a portable plexiglass phone booth around them that effectively isolates the person from others. They also have the experience that they have to handle the whole of life single-handed, with no help from any friends. Or in other words, they can't let people in or let themselves out. They are fearful and anxious to the point that they are overcome with desperation and futility feelings. They are struggling with confusion inducing conflict that there is failure to maintain immunity to negative ideas.[3]

I myself had pneumonia at a very young age and throughout my life, and the emotional root cause of pneumonia speaks to me. When I tell people I could have been a candidate for Alzheimer's, they say it's scary. What's more frightening to me is to one day have no memory because I didn't have a clue how Alzheimer's sparks in my body. Now at least I believe I have a chance to stop this devastating disease.

This doesn't mean if you've had pneumonia you will develop Alzheimer's, but the illness presents an opportunity to look at what the soul discoveries are and see if they resonate with you. The following diseases or conditions do not cause Alzheimer's but rather provide an opportunity to consider their soul discoveries. If we release the soul discoveries of the first disease or illness we encounter, we may not have to go on to others. This is why it's so important to understand the soul determinates that underlie physical ailments. When we incorporate this piece of the puzzle into Western medicine, we'll have a chance at the "cure". Euphoria!

Dr. Lincoln also described the emotional root of lung problems:

[These] people have a real inability to take in life and don't feel worthy of living life fully. They have a fear of the Universe, they lack cosmic and community conjugal contact. They are alone, sad, and non-belonging, with no sense of acceptance or approval. They are a product of a withholding and non-accepting family. They are heavily into competence-anxiety, self-distrust, and self-inhibition . . . .[4]

Prevention Using the MO Technique

By using the MO Technique clients with pneumonia would release their feelings of abandonment and learn how to connect with their Source, themselves and others to allow their support. They learn to love themselves, retrieve their power and release their anger and resentment every time it came up. They learn how to take in life energy and flow with all of life.

Besides pneumonia, many illnesses and surgeries plagued Reagan. In 1949, Reagan was hospitalized for seven weeks because he broke his right thigh in six places playing ball in a charity tournament. Broken bones are known to signify profound inner conflicting the depths of one's being. According to Dr. Lincoln the right thigh represents difficulty coping.

...There is a paralysis of action, fear of the future at present. They have major conflicts regarding how they go about manifesting their strength and providing themselves support. They have considerable difficulty accepting commitments in the world and giving support to friends, co-workers and colleagues. They also distrust and don't know how to relate to fellow workers and fellow travelers at large. They were systematically undermined in childhood. The are unlovable, and they vulnerability, intimacy and sexually avoidant. They were systematically confidence undermined.[5]

On July 18, 1985, he had surgery to remove colon cancer. Dr.

Lincoln described the psychological meaning of colon cancer this way:

> They are not happy with their life or with the world around them. They are in effect terrified of the universe due to being attacked from conception on. They have a deep-seated conviction that they deserve all of the insult. They are severely closed-minded with a very poor ability to learn life's lessons. They literally can't let go of yesterday's wastes, so their digestion gets backed up and so does their hatred.[6]

Louise Hay wrote that colon cancer reflects "deep longstanding resentment. Deep secret or grief eating away at self. Carrying hatreds. 'What's the use?' and colon is holding on to the past. Fear of letting go."[7]

Using the MO Technique at the pneumonia stage, the anger, resentment and hatred (part of The Common Thread of the MO Technique) would be addressed and released. If there were any adverse symptoms in the colon before the colon cancer, any "what's the use?" feelings and *hopelessness* could be released at that point.

Not too long after his colon surgery, Reagan underwent cryotherapy for two basal cell carcinomas—skin cancer on his nose. Louise Hay wrote that the nose represents self-recognition.[8] Dr. Lincoln described the the psychological meaning of nose problems this way:

> . . . [T]hey are deeply disappointed, disillusioned, despairing and/or feeling powerless. Their experiences have resulted in their not trusting themselves, and they systematically avoid power as a result. They never know when someone is going to pull a fast one. They are prone to humiliation and shame, and they tend to feel any honors they receive are for little achievement. They are lacking in self-pride and are also

sexually ashamed and inhibited because of having been subjected to a confidence undermining.[9]

Reagan then had prostate surgery on Jan 5, 1987. Here's what Dr. Lincoln wrote about the the psychological meaning of prostate problems:

> . . . Due to changes in their life such as divorce, aging, or illness, there are intense feelings of frustration, and uselessness. They are self-contained and lonely with a lot of deprivation, grief, and depression. There is a significant amount of fatigue, along with a breaking down and/or a certain giving up. They feel they just don't cut it at being a male. Now it is coming to roost in the symbolic center of masculine sexuality. *They are afraid that their purpose in being here is already over.* They are having great difficulty expressing or releasing these negative and corrosive emotions. It also came as a result of being thrust into the masculine role by their mother, who wanted them to be the man in their life or at least a man she could be proud of. They also modeled themselves after their patriarchal father.[10]

With the MO Technique feelings of uselessness, male shame, grief, and giving up would be addressed and released. Because Alzheimer's disease may develop from a sense of hopelessness and helplessness, it is especially significant to release the giving up and uselessness.

The body communicates to us through our ailments what we need to heal emotionally. When the underlying causes are not addressed and released, the body continues to communicate and the process can keep escalating.

For Reagan, in 1987, a heart arrhythmia was diagnosed. According to Dr. Lincoln, this signifies that —

. . . they are a *self-made person* who believes that they are all they have got. They have felt cut off from the environment and from the Universe all their life, and that therefore they have to handle everything on their own hook, unassisted. This activates moments where things are getting out of control and *beyond their coping capabilities*. They bring on anxiety attacks and the resulting heart palpitations. It is resultant of never having received love and merging as a child. They have a fundamental inconsistency in their love nature—it comes and goes and they can't maintain a steady love state, input, or relationship. It reflects the instability of the nature of the close relationships in their family, which were fleeting and chaotic.[11]

Reagan then developed "Dupuytren's contracture" of the left hand, which was diagnosed and operated on in January, 1989. This condition is an abnormal thickening of tough tissue underneath the skin of the palm and fingers, causing fingers to curl. His left ring finger was affected in this way.

Dr. Lincoln described the psychological meaning of the left palm as follows:

. . . [T]hey are experiencing conflicts around vulnerability, feelings and relationships with practical management issues. They are *inadequate to the cause of handling life's demands on the day-to-day level.* [12]

Ring finger problems refer to concerns around personal significance and issues connecting with the Creator. These concerns show up as an inability to flow with life. Left ring-finger problems reflect self-manifestation issues and are involved in conflicts around ethical issues, spiritual concerns, "letting love in", and deprivation-grief reactions in relationships.

Reagan also had hearing loss plus nearsightedness. Dr.

Lincoln's psychological meaning of these two conditions are:

> Hearing: [T]hey are backing away from vulnerability and involvement with the social environment because they feel it is too irrelevant, painful, and/or dangerous . . . are a "sealed unit" who is self-determined and a self-made person. Their family blamed them when anything went wrong and, in result, they developed the "urban hermit" lifestyle. Right ear hearing loss . . . disengagement from the world around them on the grounds that it hurts too much to be vulnerable to the processes going on out there. Left ear hearing problems . . . pulling into their core and putting a wall around themselves to prevent any further invasion or violations of their self-system.[13]
>
> Nearsightedness: . . . [T]hey have a fear of the future and they don't trust what is ahead or the process of life. They are chronically fearful and troubled by inadequacy feelings. They feel unlovable and so they don't reach out or project to the future because it is so threatening. They are past-fixated and they fully expect things to be as they always have been.[14]

Louise Hay also equated nearsightedness with fear of the future.[15]

Our physical body may cry out for 60 years or more with many other disease before Alzheimer's sets in. Knowing and releasing the psychological meaning of each disease is crucial. The MO Technique provides the knowledge of the psychological meaning of disease and the method to release the emotional sufferings.

Reagan received another body message when, in 2001, he fell and broke his hip. Because our hips physically move us forward in life, a broken hip reveals a fear of moving forward, reflected by thoughts that the future holds little promise. Another broken bone signified a further breakdown of his foundation. He had a need to assert his own authority and structure, which he could no longer do because his mind had deteriorated.

At the time of his broken hip, he'd had Alzheimer's for seven years. It makes sense that he would have felt a loss of hope for the future.

In the end, Reagan succumbed to aspiration pneumonia, *among the most common causes of death for people with advanced Alzheimer's disease.*

I'd always thought of this man as a big-hearted humanitarian whose love showed through by his warm and fatherly approach. Reading his biography and studying his diseases, I learned that he may have been a saddened man who just wanted to be loved, supported, and accepted.

Alzheimer's Effect on the Soul's Purpose

Our souls have a knowing. At times, when we aren't meeting our goals or understanding our soul discoveries, the brain acts up in the form of a headache or concussion—or anything from a brain tumor to a tragic disease such as Alzheimer's. It's best to understand this issue and be able to release it at the earliest headache stage.

Dysfunction of the brain may suggest serious conflicts may exist between an individual's goals and his or her divine intent according to Dr. Lincoln. The brain operates within the sixth chakra. If a person's individual thoughts and mental activities become unclear or confused, dysfunction of this chakra may develop. When the energy of the sixth chakra is blocked for an extended time, it may cause the nerve cells in the brain to become tangled and form the plaque that triggers Alzheimer's. This chakra is the "mind's eye", or what is sometimes called the "third eye". If we're not "seeing" what we want to accomplish in life, the life energy that keeps this chakra healthy may be decreased, causing dysfunction of the physical body.

The seventh chakra, or crown chakra, according to Caroline

Myss, "influences the major body systems: the central nervous system, the muscular system, and the skin. The seventh chakra is the entry point for the human life force, which pours endlessly into the human body."[16]

This chakra is our connection with the divine and our life's purpose. We can keep this chakra healthy by tapping into our soul's wisdom to determine our purpose on this earth as soon as we are able to use the MO Technique. Then the trick becomes following up on it—accomplishing it no matter what others might feel or think about it.

Once we accept ourselves and instill self-love at the soul level, it is ours; no one can take it away. I see many people who've worked all their lives develop Alzheimer's when they retire. This may indicate they've not been able to see or accomplish their soul's purpose; on an unconscious level, they feel helpless, hopeless, and without direction. Or perhaps they've worked at careers that *did* fulfill a life purpose but they don't realize they have other purposes to fulfill. If they believed their work *was* their life and now it's over, hopelessness can set in.

It is predicted that one in eight over 65 and 50 percent of those over 85 will get the disease. In 2011, 10,000 baby boomers will turn 65 every single day. That means over the next four decades the number of Alzheimer's cases could triple.

The body and mind don't deteriorate if they're deeply loved, which is our only real job on this planet. I believe we are here to grow spiritually and learn our soul discoveries. This process starts at birth and doesn't not stop at 60, retirement, or any particular age. Understanding our MO and incorporating the emotional component into healing is critical for us to get a handle on this devastating disease.

Chapter 13: Arthritis

"You are never a victim. When we blame, we give away our power."
– Greg Anderson

The Disease

Arthritis is a chronic disease marked by inflammation of the joints, which causes pain and stiffness.

The Soul Discovery of Arthritis

Arthritis soul discovery is to learn to connect with oneself, which is reflected in the symptoms expressed in the body. Arthritis affects the joints, the body's connectors that allow it to move freely and easily.

Arthritis may originate with *self-criticism,* which creates an inflamed or angry feeling that may trigger the disease. An individual's critical attitudes and beliefs may get mirrored in the body as it becomes less and less mobile. Inflammation is the body's normal response to injury, in which the affected area becomes hot, red, and painful. Habitually finding fault or rejecting oneself is akin to self-injury. This emotional wound creates subconscious anger and resentment, which in turn becomes the hot, red pain that plagues people with arthritis.

The self-rejection also causes a feeling of powerlessness that can build to subconscious rage, which explodes as an inflamed joint in fingers, hands, knees, hips, or spine. Although arthritis has a universal soul discovery, each affected joint has a unique soul discovery as well.

The Universal Soul Discovery of Arthritis
To learn to connect with ourselves and with others in the world.

The universal soul discovery of arthritis is to accept and connect with oneself. Self-acceptance not only creates harmonious connections within the body, but it supports and enhances one's connection to others.

I've seen dozens of people who have difficulty connecting with themselves. I was one of them. It may stem from when you feel that there is something inherently wrong with you; then you don't learn to be understanding, compassionate, and self-loving. My mother has severe arthritis; her mother was wheelchair-bound because of arthritis; some of my sisters also have it. By learning to connect with myself and trust myself, I've been able to prevent this generational disease to date.

The Soul Discoveries of Specific Joints

- **Fingers**—These can point the blame, but as people point an index finger at someone else, three fingers are pointing back at themselves. When finger joints are inflamed, the soul discovery is to not blame and criticize themselves or others, but instead, to let go of control. The soul discovery is to be more flexible and allow themselves to bend with the process of life.
- **Hands**—Hands are used to handle and hang on to things. The left hand is our receiving hand; the right hand our giving hand. Perhaps individuals who have arthritis that affects the hands need to connect with themselves and learn to give and receive in balance. The soul discovery may be to let go of a clutching or gripping way of life, become flexible, trust themselves and let go of control to free themselves emotionally.
- **Knees**—They support us and enable us to bend. The soul discovery of people with arthritis in the knees is to be spontaneous—to flow and bend with all of life with ease.
- **Ankles**—They bear the weight of the human body.

Individuals with arthritis in the ankles are being encouraged to let go of being overly responsible and carrying others' "weight". They often believe they should be concerned with everyone else's welfare but their own. The soul discovery is to first accept pleasure and bring joy into their own lives. Only then will they have the energy to serve others.

- **Hips**—In helping the body move in several directions, hip joints are capable of many kinds of movement. The soul discovery of people with arthritic hips is to be flexible from every standpoint.

- **Spine**—The spine supports the whole body. A problem with the spine may indicate a lack of support in one's life. Arthritis of the spine may be a red flag that signals anger. After all, self-criticism shows a lack of self-support. The soul discovery of people with spines that are inflamed with arthritis is to stand up for their beliefs and support "who they are".

The basic message of a joint inflamed with arthritis is this: *I want to be free to move in all directions, to develop my full potential, and to validate, trust, and love myself at my core.*

Rheumatoid arthritis is a progressive disease that's usually systemic and thus can affect many parts of the body. If an individual learns the soul discovery from the area first affected by arthritis, the disease may not progress to another part of the body. And if the individual learns not to be critical of self and others while bending in reaction to life's events, then the arthritis may not become systemic. The soul discovery has been learned.

Osteoarthritis, the most common form of arthritis, occurs when the cartilage that cushions the joints breaks down and becomes rough and thin. With no cushion, joints swell, become irritated, and overproduce synovial (joint) fluid. As osteoarthritis progresses, the cartilage disappears, forcing the bones that meet at the joint to rub against each other and develop bone spurs. These can be extremely painful, and, of course, inhibit movement of the joint.

When an individual has unbending beliefs and attitudes, these thought processes may cause the elastic cartilage material to become rigid. As a result, the body overproduces synovial fluid in its effort to lubricate the joint and promote movement. Instead, this action combines with the inflammation caused by suppressed anger or rage and results in swollen and painful joints. Too much synovial fluid can cause synovitis, which is an inflammation of the membrane of the joint. This can make the joint puffy or swollen and cause pain and is usually treated with an anti-inflammatory drug. However, it's possible that one's thoughts may actually result in producing the inflammation by sending out the synovial fluid to protect the joint and, in the process, they generate too much.

Nearly 40 million Americans suffer with arthritis, and by the year 2020, experts expect this rate to double.[1] According to traditional medicine, arthritis results from changes in the immune system, but it's unclear why this happens. The answer may be that when individuals are self-critical and essentially attack their own bodies, their immune systems "get the message" and join in the attack.

Think about how you may criticize yourself and others as a pattern in your life. Humans are all simply made of energy that attracts like energy. If people constantly find fault with themselves, they may continually attract others who disapprove of them. Wouldn't it make you angry to receive tremendous criticism? Wouldn't resentment build up?

On top of that, people tend to become angry when they feel powerless. The instinct is to attack, yet civilized people suppress this instinct. Suppression doesn't dissipate the inflamed thinking, however, so the body obliges and attacks itself, creating physical inflammation to mirror that of the emotions. To prevent and cure arthritis, a person is wise to learn the soul discovery of the affected area then release the emotional sufferings of arthritis using the MO Technique.

Can you imagine how joyful your life would be if you never criticized yourself again? What if you didn't attract critics in your life? Wouldn't it be wonderful to accept and approve of yourself, thus attracting people who praise you and allow you to be who you are? If you let yourself peacefully connect with your own being and others, it might also allow different parts of your body to connect harmoniously and do their job well. This, of course, doesn't mean you have to simply accept everything you or others do. You can always give loving, instructive feedback.

The Emotional Sufferings of Arthritis

The main themes in the emotional lives of those suffering from arthritis include:

- Signature emotional suffering: Difficulty connecting with self and others
- Criticizing oneself and others
- Feeling unworthy
- Feeling not good enough
- Feeling abandoned
- Feeling unsupported
- Unique emotional suffering
- The Common Thread—lack of self-love, resentment, anger/rage, powerlessness

Case History 1

Bea, a 68-year-old avid golfer and gardener, was becoming progressively less mobile due to her arthritis. She couldn't swim or hook her own bra. With such pain, she had trouble sleeping. She finally retired and told me she wanted to swim, golf, and work in her yard without the searing pain that made it difficult to enjoy physical activity.

As Bea grew up, she had believed that no one in her family was "there" for her, that she had no one to trust or lean on. She was always told to be a good girl and behave, so she believed her parents thought she was bad. No one in the family showed her affection. Her stepfather's alcoholism prevented them from planning family gatherings, so Bea didn't form any sense of family connection. In her mother's eyes, she could do nothing right. Playing the role of parent most of the time, Bea became overly responsible. Strong-willed, she stated her mantra as, "I'll show ya!"

When Bea was young, she preferred playing with boys and never had any close girlfriends. Living with anger, this showed up in her worldview, which was starkly black or white. As an example, she was very angry with President Bush and the war in Iraq. Her face became flushed when she'd talk about it. So we examined her responsibility in this and questioned what she could do about it. She realized she could only vote for those she thought would do a good job in the presidency and leave it at that. Realistically, she said she really couldn't do anything about the war. Anytime her anger about Bush and the war came up, she'd feel the anger and then find the anger in her body and release it, then fill her body with the energy of joy. Doing this didn't mean she was okay with world issues, but she found she could help her situation by putting her energy into creating a positive environment for her family. When she first released this out of her body, she saw bombs and chaos and felt disruption in her rib cage. She now blesses Bush and lets her anger go. She cleansed her ribcage with streams of water and put a beautiful loving energy back into her rib cage. At the soul consciousness level, she said, "I bless him and let him go."

Sometimes we project our insecurities into the world (like Bea did on Bush) so it seems like the problem is "out there" instead of "in here". I helped her to let go of things she couldn't control. As she becomes peaceful and harmonious on the inside, she will project that energy out into the world and to her immediate family.

This approach does not dismiss that the world is chaotic and crazy. However, our job is to find our own spiritual peace inside. Then we can cope with the world by healing ourselves first. I believe that has to happen before we can heal the world.

As an adult, Bea had been married four times. None of her marriages worked out. She said her relationship philosophy could be summed up with, "It's my way or the highway." She believed she had finally found a wonderful man in her fifth husband, but she resented his children and had problem after problem with them. The arthritis that began in her left foot and shoulders was getting worse and progressing to other parts of her body, leaving her in unbearable pain.

During her first session, Bea released self-criticism (lack of self-love), her tendency to be overly responsible, feeling unsupported (powerlessness), and her deep anger. I was delighted when she called me after 40 days of programming her conscious mind, which is part of the MO Technique. She told me she'd been out working in her yard and exclaimed, "I can't believe this! The pain is gone!"

Bea later wrote me saying that when anger comes up for her today, she is able to view the situations differently and just let it go. She now has a refreshing new relationship with her husband's children. As she was able to connect and accept herself, she was able to be more approving of them. Bea has been free of arthritis and pain since February, 2005.

Case History 2

A 60-year-old woman from Ireland, Jane had spent half of her life living unhappily in the United States. Her husband had landed a good job in the U.S., so she felt obligated to move with him— although she longed to be back in Ireland. For 30 years, she had been angry over this decision. Her anger had turned to rage and left her feeling powerless.

The daughter of a school principal, Jane said she never felt she could do anything well enough in her father's eyes. She didn't feel supported by her father, and because of the energy she put out, she married the same type of man. Like her father, who had been strict and unavailable, Jane's husband rarely spoke to her.

Jane's mother was also critical of her. Consequently, she learned to be critical of herself. Jane suffered from arthritis in her hands, shoulders, knees, and hips. When she imaged self-criticism doing the MO Technique, she saw a picture of her mother. She released that image out of her heart. As she imaged what she would feel and look like if she didn't criticize herself at the soul level, she saw herself as patient, tolerant, relaxed, fun, and free from the fear of her mother. She instilled this positive energy at the soul level.

As she imaged her anger or rage, Jane saw a picture of herself alone, without support, and lacking the knowledge to care for her first child. She sensed the same image was weighing on her heart, so she released it from her heart area.

Jane tried to image lack of self-love and explained, "I never received love as a child. I was never hugged or told 'I love you'." She then imaged her childhood experience as a big sign reading "NOT WANTED" lifting out of her heart area. At her soul level, the "NOT WANTED" sign turned into a beautiful, loving light that surrounded her. Jane then instilled the energy of that beautiful loving light and truly knew and felt that she was deeply loved.

In other sessions, Jane released unworthiness, powerlessness, and feelings of not being good enough. Lo and behold, her arthritis began to improve. Next, she wanted to release perfectionism. When she imaged perfectionism, she saw herself never being satisfied with anything. She mentally placed that image on her right knee, which had been hurting that week, and she released it. At her soul level, when she imaged perfectionism, she felt forgiveness for herself. She also saw herself talking with her husband and asking for help when she needed it. In these ways, she instilled love and forgiveness at the core of her being.

By her fourth session, Jane felt so much better, both physically and emotionally, that she and her husband had decided to go on a trip to Ireland. Not only was she excited about the trip, but about the rest of her life. She wanted to discover her life purpose.

Specifically, I helped Jane tap into the wise, loving, caring part of herself when she was in a relaxed state and then guided her to bring in her inner wisdom. In this state, she saw several things:

- She had used her arthritis as an excuse to retire from her job because it did not feel fulfilling.
- She saw her weight gain as the result of self-pity for having to leave her beloved Ireland.
- She saw how she'd come to help the sick—a neighbor with cancer—and that she could, and would, start helping others in this way.
- She realized her surgeries were the cause of her resentments and that she'd been blaming everyone around her, instead of making choices that empowered her.

Jane later told me she and her husband were communicating again, and things were going well for them. Why? Because she'd learned that the qualities she desired in her husband—love, support, and compassion—had to first be a part of her own core. Once that happened, the relationship improved dramatically—and it wasn't because he *changed. Having done the work, Jane understood she had to change her thought process every time the old tapes of criticism began. And for her arthritis to heal completely, her new way of thinking had to be continuous and real.*

Jane had come a long way from thinking that her arthritis was punishment for not supporting her husband's decision to come to the

United States. She understood the irony of wanting support from him, but not offering the same in a heartfelt way. At her soul level, she asked for forgiveness and a chance to start a new life with her husband. And she did!

Arthritis, one of the most pervasive diseases ever, is the leading cause of disability and the number one crippler in the U.S. It can create deformities and damage to the body's vital structure and organs.

The first step in releasing the emotional component of arthritis is ridding oneself of negative self-talk. The second step is to nurture and connect with ourselves. Arthritis is usually treated with anti-inflammatory drugs, and some of these medications have serious side effects. Some have to be taken for life. The best prescription is a loving, kind, accepting relationship with oneself and others.

Chapter 14: Cancer

"For every minute you are angry, you lose sixty seconds of happiness."
– Ralph Waldo Emerson

The Disease

Cancer is the term for abnormal cell growth. Over one million people in the United States are diagnosed each year with some form of cancer. It is the second leading cause of death.

The MO of Cancer Sufferers

After heart disease, the second leading cause of death is cancer. We all have cancer cells in our bodies, so what triggers these cells to grow abnormally? What is the commonality of the programming and MO of an individual with cancer?

Internal beliefs that we deem "right" causes judging and blaming → energy of anger or longstanding resentment builds up → adverse event happens → *we are wronged* → we feel powerless → body lacks foundation of self-love = the perfect setup for cancer cells to erupt.

Why does someone die of cancer every minute? Have we as a society been programmed to be the judge and jury on the value of everything that we encounter? Do many of us believe that our values are right and others' values are wrong?

We as a society have been programmed to blame outside sources for disease. Have we been misguided? Should we be programmed to bless others and have compassion for those that have different opinions than ours? To not only look at the bigger picture but look at all sides of the picture without judgment?

How does the body respond to judgment? The body festers from the anger of being wronged and eventually deteriorates because the body thrives on love and compassion. When the adverse event happens and we feel we have been *wronged*, the body responds to the judgment by allowing the anger to erupt a symptom, condition or disease. What would the world look like without judgment? The belief that there is only one "right" way would disappear.

Greg Braden, in *Walking Between the Worlds*, stated, "The seeds of compassion and blessing are rooted within your nature, laying dormant until the time that their value may be recognized; their memory awakened. Perhaps that time is now."[1]

With one person dying of cancer every minute, perhaps it's time to replace judgment with love and compassion.

Cancer may be triggered in the body when an adverse event has a devastating effect on an individual's life, leading to feeling powerless. The foundation of the body—self-love—is absent. Anger, rage, and resentment can build in the body. Resistance, blaming, and judgment build up energy blocks of anger. If we don't work through these blocks, they get suppressed and start affecting the body. In other words, what we resist, persists.

The soul discovery of the individual may determine which area of the body will be affected with the cancer. Although cancer individuals share a commonality of programming and MO, each area of the body where the cancer erupts reflects a different soul discovery. For instance, the unique soul discovery of breast cancer is to nurture the caretaker or ourselves first; then we have the energy to nurture others joyfully.

We are raised with certain beliefs that become embedded in our consciousness throughout life—that is, unless we consciously change them. If we didn't have some type of internal beliefs that we deem "right", then we wouldn't react with anger (as we sometimes do). In the realm of regaining health, the soul discovery presented by cancer requires replacing cell-altering judgment with acceptance—which starts with accepting ourselves. Someone who develops cancer may have had years of inner conflict and suppressed anger before the trigger shows up. But it's the adverse event that ignites the festering coals of cancer. Remember the actions of others are never to blame; rather, something inside our bodies causes the anger, even though the actions of others can trigger it.

For example, when anger comes up for me now, I feel it, image it, find it in my body, and release the energy being held there. I then look at why my "anger button" got pushed. Usually I've uncovered a feeling of powerlessness that I've allowed. I know that a deep fear inside me needs to be reconciled. So I ask, "Maureen, what do you need?" I discover the fear, fulfill the need, and move on in life. I no longer suppress the anger or hang onto it for days. I direct the energy into fulfilling what I need in the moment. This process releases feelings of blame and judgment, and lets me accept others for who and where they are.

Using the MO Technique, we can release judgment of self and others, and replace it with love and compassion. It may be helpful to look at every situation in life as an opportunity to learn and grow. How do we stop cancer? We release The Common Thread of Disease and make our "new house", or our body, the house of our dreams. For me, every time I start to judge, thinking that my way is the "right" way, or that I've been wronged, I recognize it and delete it from my hard drive and instill love and compassion. Reconciling judgment can only be done with love and compassion. We will then look at the world in a new way. All aspects of our life will just *be*—without judgment. Euphoria!

Once this way of life became a habit for me, I learned to quickly transform anger into a positive emotion that helped me understand myself. I could then confront the issues that needed to be healed and go forward. While I was going through my divorce, I started releasing anger every time it came up, before it had the chance to build. Today, when I experience a loss of any sort, I nurture and take care of myself. I feel my negative emotions but always release them out of my body. Coping with life for me means knowing every problem has a solution. I have a deep trust in the Divine and I know I'm protected. If situations don't work out exactly how I want them to, I have faith that a much better plan is in store.

Think about Western medicine, and the model it sets for coping. Usually a medication is prescribed to deal with symptoms, not to address the soul discovery behind the disease. Another approach is to view cancer as a message about what needs to be healed—the cause of the anger that erupted inside. Healing means feeling more worthwhile, having a sense of purpose, and beginning the journey of self-love.

As we learn from disease, our perspectives can expand, and life may hold more meaning and make more sense.

The Universal Soul Discovery of Cancer
To heal judgment of self and others in the world.

The universal soul discovery of cancer is to heal judgment of ourselves and the outside world—but how do we do that? When a person dies of cancer every minute, this disease has really been trying to get our attention! With the MO Technique, we can learn to recognize a judgment or blame and release it and replace it with love and compassion. Once we have the awareness, we can make it a habit. Once it's a habit, we'll make great strides toward creating a compassionate and loving world. Write down how many times a day you judge or blame. Listen to television and others around you and write down how many times you witness judgment and blame. I bet it will surprise you!

The Emotional Sufferings of Cancer
The emotional sufferings of cancer all tie in with The Common Thread of Disease.

- Signature emotional suffering—Judging and blaming; feeling wronged
- Feeling helpless and hopeless
- Unique emotional suffering
- The Common Thread—lack of self-love, resentment, anger/rage, powerlessness

Case History

At age 55, Georgia was diagnosed with stage IV lymphoma. The lymph system defends the body from invasion by viruses, bacteria and fungi. The soul discovery of lymphoma is for the afflicted individuals to learn they have the ability to defend themselves against attack from outside forces or their own self-rejection.

I first asked Georgia whether a major event in her life might have triggered the disease. She explained that her husband had died suddenly of a heart attack six months before her diagnosis. Having lost her partner, Georgia was also abruptly faced with financial obligations and had no experience dealing with them. Because her husband had paid the bills and taken care of all business matters, she had separated herself from these tasks. After he died, she was angry and blamed herself for not knowing the details of their finances; she felt powerless and helpless. Although she'd been an intelligent, self-reliant registered nurse all her working life, she became self-rejecting, hopeless, and full of rage over her dilemma. These feelings may have been programmed in childhood. Almost inevitably, the loss of one's caretaker activates feelings of helplessness, causing anger and may trigger the abnormal growth of cancer cells.

Georgia and I had three sessions during which she released everything she believed could have been emotionally connected to her cancer. She was also undergoing conventional cancer treatment, including radiation and chemotherapy.

I always begin my sessions by establishing if the person truly wants to heal and has the belief system to support this desire. Georgia both wanted to heal and believed her healing was possible.

First, she released the powerlessness out of her cellular memory. She began by recalling an image of her grandmother telling her to select a strong branch she could use to whip Georgia. At that point, she determined she had no personal power. So Georgia found the image of that branch in her stomach and released it. When she imaged going to her soul level, she saw the branch in a glass box, which reminded her to take her power back. Then she instilled the belief and feeling that she was safe, protected, and powerful at a deep level. Next, she worked on rage. She saw an image of an aunt who told her she was ugly and had no right to exist. She found the energy of a snapshot of her aunt's image in her heart and released it. At a deeper level, she saw loving arms around her and felt the energy of love, protection, and support, and she instilled that energy.

Georgia now knows what emotionally triggered the cancer for her. If she experiences another loss, she'll know how to nurture herself and release her anger and grief. She knows she has choices, so she won't feel powerless again because she now has the tools to defend herself. When Georgia arrived for a fourth session, she came only to tell me she was completely cancer free!

When we have a sense of personal power, love ourselves at our core, have tools to cope, and know how to release resentment and anger every time they come up, we don't provide the cancer cells with the weakness they need to take over.

The concept that disease teaches us soul discoveries is new to most people, but once understood, it can empower us. With the MO Technique, we learn how to take care of ourselves so the match that lights the festering coals of anger and resentment is extinguished or not even lit. Cancer cells lie dormant when we know what triggers them and how to regulate our emotions especially anger.

Chapter 15: Breast Cancer

"When we are in rhythm with ourselves, we can join in harmony with others."
– Dr. Lauren Artress

The Disease
Breast cancer is abnormal cell growth with an uncontrolled spread of malignant cells in the breast.

The Soul Discovery of Breast Cancer
Breast cancer soul discovery is to nurture ourselves. Neglecting our own needs may produce feelings of resentment, anger/rage, and powerlessness. Resentment understandably builds for women who nurture everyone else but don't get their own needs met often enough. These women may develop a feeling of powerlessness that builds into suppressed anger. As time goes by, this inner rage may become toxic and explode if triggered by a devastating event.

As with other cancers, these feelings of powerlessness and rage usually stem from childhood events. Cancer appears where the body is out of balance and the particular soul discovery is to be addressed. Since the breasts symbolize nurturance, breast cancer may erupt in women who are over-nurturing to others but deny nurturance to themselves, thus arousing subconscious resentment. This may suppress the immune system and block nurturing life energy to the heart chakra, allowing the cancer to manifest in the breast.

The Universal Soul Discovery of Breast Cancer
To embrace the feminine and bring the feminine back into
balance in the world.

The universal soul discovery of breast cancer is to change and heal the role of women in the world. In the late Middle Ages, masculine energy came to dominate feminine energy, and everyone has paid the price. If we learn the soul discoveries of breast cancer, will the feminine return? Is that what this cancer is trying to tell us? Breast cancer's soul discoveries may bring back the receptive, feminine aspect of ourselves that nurtures our spiritual nature and feeds our souls. As women, we will learn to nurture ourselves first so anger and resentment do not build in the body.

In the United States, more than 178,480 women were diagnosed with invasive breast cancer in 2007. Women living in North America have the highest rate of breast cancer in the world.[1] The chance of a woman developing breast cancer over her lifetime is one in eight. One in one million men develop breast cancer, while children rarely get this disease.

Although a great deal of research has focused on environmental, lifestyle, and genetic risk factors, many questions remain. For example, why do some women with no family history of cancer and no other known risk factors get breast cancer, while others who have this family history remain disease free? Why does this particular cancer strike predominantly women and only the breasts?

We feed and nurture our babies at the breast, which is a universal symbol of maternal caretaking. Breast cancer may be thought of as the breasts screaming, "You are out of balance! *This* body needs nurturing." The social role of women revolves around being the mother figure who takes care of other people, often at the expense of her own health. This may explain the statistics of why one in eight women develops breast cancer while one in a million men contracts this disease.

Women are taught to nurture others first and themselves last, if at all. In fact, many believe their very acceptance in life depends on this. But such a belief is entirely wrong. Every breast cancer patient I've worked with feels fed up with being last!

Resentment and anger/rage follow that "fed up" feeling. Anger is vital for survival, so it shouldn't be denied or suppressed. The anger serves to shout the message that "something is very wrong with this picture!"

A powerful way to prevent breast cancer is to release anger and resentment out of cellular memory every time it comes up so it doesn't build into rage and then fulfill your deep need inside every time. A primary lesson of breast cancer is for women to nurture themselves first—and only then will they have enough energy to nurture others joyfully.

This disease offers an opportunity for life-enhancing personal growth, so women can fulfill their divine life plans. When we, as women, nurture ourselves and use our DNA healing power, everyone can benefit because we have taken care of the caretaker first.

Think of a well where everyone comes to draw water. If the well is not replenished, it will go dry. The idea of women nurturing themselves may be in opposition to everything we think we know about women, mothers, and history. However, it's an idea long overdue, as breast cancer threatens millions of lives every year. We must question this social role and the effect it has on our health. It's time to change it—but how?

It's a woman's nature to want to nurture others, and we'd like to continue to do so.

We can—but let's do it joyfully, with a desire to share that can only happen naturally when our own needs are being met. I suggest that we—Rejoice!

- Rejoice—not feel guilty if we fulfill our personal needs
- Rejoice—stop feeling selfish for taking time out for ourselves
- Rejoice—accept the idea that we deserve nurturing as much as anyone else
- Rejoice—validate and love ourselves so we can be there for others with strength that's not tainted by resentment.

Julie Motz, author of *Hands of Life*, harnesses the body's energy to help patients survive operations such as those often required in breast cancer. She wrote, "Eventually I came to see the disease (breast cancer) itself as a ghastly expression of the crisis around nurturing that the whole society is experiencing, a tortured longing to be loved."[2] To that, I would add that the first step toward a solution is learning to love ourselves. Most people look to the outer world for validation of their worth, but we can't count on it. We must validate ourselves at the soul level first, and then we will receive it from the outside world.

This is the mirror principle in action—and for most people, mirroring happens on a subconscious level. For example, women may not consciously realize that resentment and anger are building when they give, give, give, and don't fulfill their own needs. This buildup might eventually lead to a painful event. In turn, this event may produce more powerlessness and rage, further inciting cancer cells to multiply out of control. It's crucial for all people, not just women, to become *conscious* of how their feelings can create disease and to learn to love themselves—a completely drug-free antidote.

Many of my female clients have lamented, "But, Maureen, if I change my role, it will upset the apple cart at home!" I reply, "You now have the knowledge of the soul discoveries of breast cancer, and you have choices. You can keep your pattern of nurturing everyone else first, not getting your needs met, and building up resentment and anger, which may lead to breast cancer. Or, you can nurture yourself first, retrieve your DNA healing power, and learn to release anger out of your cellular memory every time it comes up and fulfill your need. With the second choice, you have a much greater chance of remaining cancer free. After all, if you upset the apple cart, the only apples lost are the ones you don't need anymore."

The soul discovery is about empowerment—the power to make healthier choices. Knowing this not only may help eradicate breast cancer, but also strengthen the feminine role globally.

Besides feeling a lack of nurturance and validation, people diagnosed with cancer often feel a loss of control. This feeds the feeling of powerlessness, which provides even more impetus for *uncontrolled* growth of cancer cells. Then, to make matters worse, in our society we usually give up what's left of our power to our physicians. But we need our DNA (Dynamic Natural Authentic) healing power to heal ourselves as we take responsibility for our health and working *with* physicians.

We claim an incredible power when we accept responsibility for our own experiences. As this DNA healing power strengthens the immune system, it gives us the power to overcome the disease by tapping into the innate healing wisdom of the body— our natural, biological right.

Taking time for physical exercise is part of taking responsibility for ourselves and doing so can help more than people realize. Understandably, those diagnosed with cancer can feel overwhelmed as they face many new problems. They may cut back on exercise or just not have energy to do it. However, research shows that just a few hours of physical exercise each week can reduce a breast cancer patient's risk of death by 50 percent, or *half*. A 2005 article in the *Washington Post*, "Exercise Can Cut the Risk of Dying from Breast Cancer," echoed this fact.

Being physically active boosts the odds that breast cancer patients will survive the disease, according to the first study to produce evidence that exercise improves the prospects of beating any malignancy. The findings, from a large, well-respected study of U.S. nurses, found that breast cancer patients who walk or do things of moderate exercise for three to five hours a week are 50 percent less likely to die from the disease than sedentary women. [3]

Why does exercise help? Because you're nurturing yourself. You show that you deserve and value yourself enough to take time out for yourself, thus creating a feeling of being in control and rejuvenating your personal power.

It also helps release negative energy. According to Julie Motz, anger is stored in the muscles and blood. As you exercise, your blood starts pumping and gets your muscles moving, which releases the energy of the anger. Exercise may help nurturing life energy flow to the heart chakra because by taking care of *you*, you're loving yourself. This kind of self-care may thus reduce the risk of breast cancer and help those who've been diagnosed to beat the odds.

The Emotional Sufferings of Breast Cancer

Listed below are the emotional sufferings that need to be released out of cellular memory to help empower women.

- Signature emotional suffering—Not nurturing oneself
- Feeling abandoned
- Feeling a lack of validation
- Feeling over-responsible
- Feeling out of control
- Feeling guilty
- Grieving
- Unique emotional suffering

- The Common Thread—lack of self-love, resentment, anger/rage, powerlessness

These case histories demonstrate how the MO Technique erases emotional sufferings and old beliefs from the subconscious memory and instills a new belief in the superconscious, at the soul level. It also reprograms the body and mind on the conscious level. Thus the Technique takes into consideration all aspects of a person: the emotional body, the soul, the conscious mind, and the physical body.

Case History 1

At 54, Trudy had just finished her last round of chemotherapy for breast cancer. Frequently nauseated, she'd lost all her hair and was suffering with severe joint pain. Understandably, she felt like hell. When Trudy came to my office, she was elated to learn the MO Technique has no negative side effects.

As previously explained, the trigger for cancer usually happens about six months to a year before the illness appears. In Trudy's case, she and her husband had owned a business that her husband had decided to sell just six months before Trudy's diagnosis. For several reasons, Trudy didn't want to sell, but she believed her opinion didn't matter to her husband. This disregard for her opinions had been a pattern. Not surprisingly, Judy's resentment and feelings of powerlessness had built over the years. The event with the business had been the last straw that may have been the trigger.

Trudy had silently aimed her rage at her husband, not realizing it would have a worse effect on her own body. When she was diagnosed with breast cancer, she underwent a mastectomy. Trudy persuaded her doctor to remove her other breast as a preventive measure. At that point in her life, sacrificing her healthy breast was the only way she knew of to take care of herself and prevent a recurrence of the cancer.

As we talked, Trudy immediately recognized herself as the queen of nurturing everyone else, but never herself. She had four children, six grandchildren, and a husband—and all their needs came before her own, in her book. In fact, she felt guilty if she put her needs first. Trudy also admitted that she believed if she healed completely, she would miss the care and nurturing she'd received since becoming ill. Being well meant she had to return to her old life and resume her role of taking care of everyone. I assured her I could teach her how to recreate her role so she could receive what she needed to stay healthy.

As Trudy began the emotional healing, she first imaged the enormous rage she was carrying and the disappointment in herself for never setting boundaries or standing up for herself. She felt the image in her right shoulder and released it. When Trudy imaged going to her soul level—her truth—she looked at the rage from a new perspective and saw a butterfly. She suddenly realized we come into the world with everything we need, and she felt the joy in that. Trudy then understood it was okay to feel anger—but it was also critical to release it.

She imaged her powerlessness as a limp rag in her heart, which she released. As she went to the soul level, she heard the words, "listen to your heart and your body." Trudy immediately understood she had choices. She'd allowed her life to fall into what it had become. Now she knew she needed to choose.

She also began to feel compassion for others on their own journeys, as one human being acknowledges others' pain without rushing in to save them. At the soul level, she let this in as deeply as she could. She saw the possibilities of living a new way, and she instilled her personal power.

When Trudy looked at the lack of her own self-care, she imaged herself under a massive pile of paperwork and saw the papers flying away. Then when she went in her mind to her soul level, she heard, "Love yourself at your core." At this level, she instilled nurturance.

In the sessions that followed, Trudy released self-rejection, guilt, over-responsibility, lack of self-love, and not feeling validated. A unique emotional suffering of Trudy's was the fear that her family would abandon her if she changed, so she also released her fear of abandonment. She talked to everyone in her family about this fear, and they assured her they just wanted her to be well. She courageously made changes and it has paid off. Her relationships with her husband and her children have greatly improved, as she explained the importance of taking care of herself first. She claims she has more love and more energy to give. She feels immense joy when she's honest about her own feelings and able to release anger in a healthy way. She now recognizes she has the tools to survive.

Case History 2

Margaret called to make an appointment and wanted tools for long-term healing so her breast cancer wouldn't return. She'd recently dealt with cancer in her right breast, enduring a course of chemotherapy.

An attractive, petite woman of 30 with angelic blue eyes, Margaret sat down and began telling me her story. In her family, Margaret's sister was considered the "cute one". Her sister told Margaret she was fat and stupid. Her mother teased her about having a bulbous nose. None of these were true, but Margaret bought these untruths at a deep level. The first-born in the family, she'd been labeled the "responsible one". She always strived to get good grades. She felt her acceptance was based on being responsible and caring for everyone else, and that she couldn't let others down — ever.

Margaret married a man who degraded her. He had a daughter from a previous marriage who treated Margaret like dirt. No matter how hard she tried, she could do nothing right in their eyes. In the school where she taught, the school administrator also degraded her and often verbally attacked her.

Together, we looked at what Margaret had always been attracting in her life, and everything pointed to people who degraded her, just as her mother did. Margaret didn't feel appreciated or valued, no matter how hard she tried. To stop attracting this in her life, she needed to stop degrading herself and believing these untruths. She had to deal with the resulting resentment and anger built up in her body.

Two events may have triggered her breast cancer. First, the stepdaughter who had always degraded her didn't invite Margaret to her wedding. Tears streamed down her face as she spoke about this insult. It had been intensely painful, especially as Margaret had tried so hard to get along with her. Not only did Margaret's husband fail to validate her feelings on this matter, but he actually took his daughter's side. Secondly, her father—who was her main support and whom she greatly loved—discovered he had throat cancer. Because her mother was ill, Margaret took care of her father and was devastated when he died. At this point, she felt exhausted, depressed, and lost without him. Within six months of these two incidents, she was diagnosed with cancer in her right breast.

Margaret felt anger/rage and powerlessness, and she didn't nurture herself in any way. Dr. Lincoln writes that cancer of the right breast signifies these individuals are fed up with the way they're being used and being required to respond. They feel ashamed and don't like themselves. This struck a cord with Margaret. She said, "This describes me to a T."

Margaret lamented that, before she would take any time out for herself, everything had to be done perfectly—which just never happened. If she didn't do everything, it wouldn't get done, or at least not done right. She felt unappreciated and unvalued, yet at the same time kept trying to be responsible for others in hopes that, someday, they'd recognize her worth.

Ironically, what Margaret gave to everyone else is what she desperately needed to give herself, which was just to be appreciated and valued. Yet she kept this cycle going until the disease took hold and told her, "This cycle needs to change! You're out of balance."

Through the MO Technique, Margaret first released powerlessness out of her cellular memory. She imaged a black color in her forehead, then erased it and filled the area with a loving energy. At the soul level, her truth, she saw herself strong, confident, and happy, laughing and with good posture. She instilled her power into cellular memory.

She then imaged her rage as a fire in her stomach. She released it and instilled at the soul level that she would release anger every time it came up. Her lack of nurturance was actually physical as well as emotional. She didn't eat enough. This energy she felt in her calves. She let it go by tying balloons to a picture of her not eating and releasing them. At the soul level, she felt a love for herself and saw herself being happy and healthy with lots of energy. She realized at this core level that she must nurture herself first. Only then would she have energy to nurture others. She released grief and lack of self-love using the same imagery.

After the session, I explained she had released the emotions that may have been related to the cancer out of the body and subconscious mind, where our beliefs and feelings of value and self-worth are stored. We don't even know they're there, but they remain—even though they hold no truth—until we reprogram the subconscious with what we now know is true.

At the soul, or superconscious, level Margaret instilled her truth. The soul perspective is one of real worth and love. The soul is always perfect, whole, and complete. Margaret would reprogram the conscious mind at home by reading her affirmations over for 40 days in a row, making this new way of being a conscious habit and part of her.

As a result of the session, Margaret felt uplifted and positive. She wanted to give up her teaching job and do something she'd always wanted to do—become a personal organizer. She decided to take classes and work on her passion. She understood she needed to change to make her life the way she envisioned it to be. Nurturing herself was going to be such a treat. She even planned a room just for herself—a retreat where she could read and nurture herself every day.

I showed Margaret her energy field, or aura, as generated by a computer program and the Win Aura System. This machine shows the electromagnetic field surrounding the body, assigning colors depending on the level, or speed, of the color's vibration. It prints the energy, color, and description of each chakra.

Specifically, it describes the color of each of the chakras and what that color means. It includes a hand plate where clients place their hands so it can pick up their energy. It allows us to see any energy shifts and transformations, signifying a change in their consciousness or a healing. This provides an emotional blueprint of the person. After a healing session, clients feel changes in their energy, but it's confirming to also see these changes. After Margaret's session, her root chakra, which is where family beliefs that support our identity are stored, emanated completely white light. This white light is divine healing energy. I see this energy enter people's energy fields, or auras, when they heal the soul discoveries they came to learn.

Now that Margaret has reprogrammed herself at the conscious, subconscious, and superconscious levels, she can see her life from a new perspective. She let go of her old limiting beliefs, or consciousness, and created a world that met her deepest needs.

These are only two examples and we all have a different story, so please understand that different MOs and soul discoveries are associated with each disease. I'm providing some food for thought with these two examples. I've been asked, "Isn't it worth considering that the feelings of these women in the examples such as weariness, self-abandonment, and shame may also be a *result* of the disease?" Yes, the feelings can be a result of the disease, but the crux of this book is for us to relate the body part to the disease and what it may be messaging to us. To prevent breast cancer we have to know how it is set up, and these two case studies provide examples of programming that may explain why the cancer erupts in the breast. The soul discovery of breast cancer is nurturance of self, whether it's a man or a woman who develops the disease, because the breasts are the symbol of nurturance.

In conclusion, since breast cancer affects mostly women, breast cancer then teaches that when women change their role in the world and become empowered and self-nurturing, then feelings of powerlessness, resentment, and anger/rage won't build in the body. Think of what the world would look like if every breast cancer patient learned breast cancer's soul discoveries. And then what would happen if all of those women who wanted to prevent breast cancer (all of us, right?) learned these soul discoveries? We lost the feminine in the Middle Ages; let's find what we lost. When we feel in harmony with ourselves, we can then be in harmony with others. The feminine principle of nurturing, intuition, connection to the sacred whole (feminine and masculine), and reverence for Mother Nature would replace the fears, domination, violence, and human darkness that has polluted our world.

When our bodies are in harmony and balance, we also have the power to create healthier, more conscious lives. We then have the energy to nurture others joyfully—and everyone benefits.

Chapter 16: Prostate Cancer

"You da man!"
– Street talk

The Disease
Prostate cancer—abnormal cell growth in the prostate gland

The Soul Discovery of Prostate Cancer
"You da man!" was once a popular expression that fits prostate cancer like a glove. In terms of many social norms—at least in Western cultures—the patriarchal culture has changed, and the role of the man is quite different than it was even a generation ago. For example, many more women have entered the workforce and are competing with men for higher positions, creating much different roles for men at work and at home. Roles for men and women are becoming mixed, and a greater equity exists between the genders. Now it's even more acceptable for men to express emotions. But in spite of these large-scale changes, the patriarchal role that's been embedded in the male psyche for thousands of years may still be lurking in the cellular memories of men. The soul discovery for individuals with prostate cancer is to understand the role of a man in their own consciousness.

This confusion about the "correct" social role for a man has wreaked havoc with the prostate gland. Prostate problems other than cancer have increased dramatically over the last 20 years, (although PSA tests and exams have helped decrease the cancer risks) and prostate cancer is now the most common type of cancer contracted by men in North America. It is second only to lung cancer in mortality rates.

What functions does the prostate gland perform? Its first role is to produce a milky fluid that forms part of the semen and protects the sperm. The second role is to squeeze this fluid with its sperm into and through the urethra during sexual climax.

What would make this gland malfunction? A feeling of weakened masculinity, or disempowerment or insufficiency as a man. When do these feelings begin to take root? Men with such issues are usually raised by a possessive mother and a patriarchal father or no male role model at all. If the individual had a father involved in his upbringing, the father was usually a patriarchal figure who instilled certain values about what it means to be a male. Masculinity in a patriarchal culture is represented by a strong, powerful, macho man. In this time-honored view, men "rule the roost and bring home the bacon". This role has become so enmeshed in a male's subconscious memory that, if he doesn't meet these standards, he may feel inadequate, powerless, and ashamed. If the male in a young man's life is weak or alcoholic and unreliable, or there is no male role model, this too can create confusion of the male role.

The mother may have wanted her son to take care of her emotional needs and be her "safe" male. Usually these women would like to "kick anything with three legs," as Dr. Lincoln puts it. They have an unconscious dislike of men. Many of their husbands are alcoholics and abusive or controlling; their son represents a form of male energy that can be controlled and safe. In striving to please both parents, this conflict may create much confusion and shame. The boys may feel they just can't measure up to what *either* parent wants.

Likewise, if boys had no male role model, they may be confused about what a male should be and how he should act. The soul discovery they came to learn is to figure out their role as a man and accept the role they choose.

The prostate gland first grows early in puberty, which is when the male is capable of reproducing sexually. If he feels he's not the man he should be, he may reject himself, an attitude that can negatively affect the prostate gland. He denigrates his

148

masculinity, which the prostate gland represents. Thus, the body may produce a reduced amount of testosterone and a higher amount of estrogen, which is known to promote cell growth or enlargement of the prostate in large amounts. This risk increases as men age and their testosterone decreases, creating a relatively high level of estrogen.

Uncontrolled growth of cancerous cells in a man's prostate may follow an adverse event that foments his familiar but painful feeling of male inadequacy. Resentment and anger/rage has built up over his lifetime, and a disempowered feeling sparked by this event puts him over the edge, inciting cancer.

Their soul discovery requires men with prostate cancer to examine their beliefs about manhood and decide what kind of man they truly want to be—a lesson in self-acceptance. To eradicate prostrate problems, men may need to bring their masculine and feminine energies into balance. This integration may be the key to changing and healing the masculine role in the world. It means balancing masculine power and feminine vulnerability in their careers, their financial lives, and their relationships with others as well as themselves.

The Universal Soul Discovery of Prostate Cancer
Understand the role of the 21st century man.

The Emotional Sufferings of Prostate Cancer

- Signature emotional suffering—A feeling of not measuring up to society's role of the man
- Feeling male shame
- Feeling not good enough
- Feeling guilty
- Rejecting oneself
- Having to feel too responsible as the "man of the house" at an early age

- Unique emotional suffering
- The Common Thread—lack of self-love, resentment, anger/rage, powerlessness

Impotence may be a precursor to prostate cancer. If men release the emotional suffering of lesser diseases or conditions such as impotence, they are likely to prevent more severe diseases.

The prostate gland is in the sexual chakra, which sends energy and support to the sexual organs. The energy of this chakra directly reflects how comfortable we are with our sexuality and how we relate to others sexually. The feeling that one doesn't measure up as a man may block the free flow of energy in this chakra and cause dysfunction of the sexual organs. As we've seen in many instances, health relates to beliefs. That is, if we don't believe we're good enough, our health declines.

When working with men with prostate cancer, I first ask them to examine their beliefs about what it means to be a man in the world today. I explain that our beliefs control our thoughts and actions. Which beliefs are creating desired outcomes? Which are not? Beliefs that aren't serving the individual's health and happiness can be released from cellular memory using the MO Technique.

Not all men develop prostate problems, but by age 80, most men experience problems of urinary obstruction due to an enlarged prostate. As men grow older, they may start losing some of their power and control over their lives. The loss of a spouse may also affect the sexual chakra. Testosterone may decrease as a man's power diminishes, which can also cause prostate enlargement. The key to empowerment is for a man to examine his belief system regarding the masculine role and to make it work for him so it doesn't affect his health.

Case History

Jason was 59 when he came to me for help. Jason's biological father was a weak man. His mother had been married four times, and three of her husbands were abusive alcoholics. When his mother was depressed, she would ask Jason to hold her. Often, as a teenager, when Jason went out with his friends, his mother would cry and tell him she needed him. He would feel enormous guilt and frequently changed his plans to meet his mother's stated needs.

Instead of having a normal, healthy adolescence, Jason ended up taking care of his mother's needs. The men in his life—mainly his stepfathers—were intimate with alcohol so his mom would look to Jason as a source of emotional support. His biological dad was not an alcoholic but still a weak man.

Before Jason retired, he realized he hadn't found his life purpose and his life lacked passion. This awareness may have triggered feelings of anger and it was translated into mild depression. Relating with his wife in a second marriage, he would get very angry at things she did where he didn't feel valued. Having problems with impotence made the matter worse. This really troubled him because he craved more purpose and passion in his life. He believed his passion involved writing and helping people.

In one of his imagery sessions, Jason said, "There are so many tears that need to be released." He never understood what all of his ailments were trying to tell him. He wondered why he'd ever signed up for the mother he had and abusive alcoholic stepfathers or an absent weak father figure for role models for men. I referred to my theory that they were giving him the experiences that his soul signed up for—his soul discoveries.

Before this diagnosis, Jason suffered with back problems, pain in his Achilles tendon, and arthritis. He had also undergone heart bypass surgery. Emotionally, back problems relate to not feeling supported in life. Achilles tendon problems indicate the individual was made to feel wrong for who he is. And the emotional suffering of arthritis is about being critical of oneself. Heart bypass surgery represents not allowing the flow of love. At a deep level they may believe everything is their fault, they're never good enough, and they deserve to be sick. Jason's body had been trying to get his attention for a long time.

Jason believed his previous ailments had logical explanations. He was active and athletic, hence the back and tendon problems. His arthritis he attributed to genetics. The athletics and genetics may have played a part, but they weren't the underlying emotional cause. The emotional suffering underlying all of Jason's physical problems was The Common Thread of Disease—resentment, anger/rage, powerlessness, and lack of self-love. The manifestation of these experiences did not occur in his professional life where he excelled but they were themes in the emotional and spiritual aspects of his life.

In Vibrational Medicine, *Dr. Gerber stated that "total avoidance of a particular lesson can result in blockage of the chakra and inadequate vital energy flow to the associated organ."*[1]

In Jason's case, dysfunction of the prostate gland was urging him to learn the soul discovery that he is good enough and that, in fact, he does measure up as a man. For Jason the message that he received from his mom was that he needed to meet her needs and that was not possible so the "measure up" part was more about being a caretaker verses a traditional male.

When Jason released powerlessness out of his cellular memory, he imaged a little boy crying alone in the corner. He felt this image in his prostate area and released it. The area was cold, so he imaged bringing in warmth. At his soul level, he saw a powerful adult who was there to help people in a variety of ways. It was Jason's first glimpse of his life purpose. He saw that it was helping people through his writing, and he got excited about it.

When he released guilt, he saw a little boy all by himself crying. When he released isolation, he saw a little boy sitting in a corner all by himself, crumpled over. When he released self-rejection, he saw a

little boy in a corner looking up at a woman. When he imaged depri-
vation, he saw the two outer corners of his sacral chakra that had
deep scars and felt frustrated that he couldn't get warmth to those
areas. I think it helped him take care of his inner child, realizing that
he needed to work on helping himself feel loved and accepted.

Jason came to me for only two sessions, while also using traditional
therapies for prostate cancer in which he healed his cancer. He found
the MO Technique beneficial. He discovered how his body had been
trying to reach him through his ailments, and he learned the impor-
tance of acknowledging his emotional history. He also learned how
to prevent another episode by knowing and releasing the emotions
that might trigger a relapse.

World-renowned therapist Alice Miller states:

The truth about our childhood is stored up in the body, and
although we can repress it, we can never alter it. Our intellect
can be deceived, our feelings manipulated, our perceptions
confused, and our body tricked with medication. But,
someday the body will present its bill, for it is as incorruptible
as a child who, still whole in spirit, will accept no compro-
mises or excuses, and it will not stop tormenting us until we
stop evading the truth.[2]

Once men see their truth, they can be whole again. The popular
phrase "You da man!" can now represent something entirely
different. How about "You da *new* man!" —a man of the 21st
century with a role that's more fitting for today's realities. This
acceptance of a new role creates balance and harmony in the
body. Men, your prostate gland will thank you.

Chapter 17: Cholesterol Problems

*"The message we give our bodies—one of irritation or acceptance—
is the message to which our bodies will answer."*
– Debbie Shapiro

The Disease

Cholesterol, which is produced by the liver, helps carry fat and
lipids (fat-soluble molecules) to parts of the body that need it for
energy and repair. Too much cholesterol can build up in the body.
The excess can clog arteries and prevent the blood from flowing
freely to the heart and brain, thus increasing the risk of heart
disease and stroke.

The Soul Discovery of Cholesterol Problems

The soul discovery of cholesterol problems is to feel protected
and supported. The individuals I have seen with high cholesterol
were raised in a rigid, strict, sometimes almost militaristic
environment. People who experience this type of environment
may not feel protected or supported, even if the strictness is
meant to be a protective measure.

The psychological meaning of cholesterol problems is a "grin
and bear it" orientation to life. These sufferers may believe life is
one long problem to be solved. They have the distinct impression
that they are not supposed to be happy or contented. They may
also compensate with superficial, self-indulgent, comfort-
concerned, luxury-loving lifestyles that follow a "live now–pay
later" (if ever) pattern. They had to maintain sanity and deflect
disaster at the expense of any form of enjoyment.[1]

The body uses cholesterol to repair and protect the cells or
make them waterproof so they don't become porous and fragile.
Fat cells are an essential fuel for body metabolism and regulate
the production of cholesterol and transport it through the body.

They also insulate us from the cold, protect us from injury by providing padding for the vital organs, and help us digest our food. The cell walls, or membranes, need cholesterol to produce hormones and make vitamin D. Serotonin, the "feel good" hormone that creates our feelings of natural joy, can't work without the proper amount of cholesterol. Louise Hay, author of *Heal Your Body* states that high cholesterol is "clogging the channels of joy. Fear of accepting joy."[2] So if we have a lack of joy, our serotonin will likely be decreased.

Glucocorticoids are major hormones that regulate our blood sugar levels or our "sweetness in life". Individuals who had a strict and contentious upbringing may not have been allowed to feel joy, and when they did, they may have had a terrifying sense they'd be attacked. They may also have been taught they don't deserve joy. An upbringing with rigid discipline can result in a regimented life that's just one never-ending chore.

Serotonin, which produces our natural joy, may decrease when individuals believe they don't deserve joy and don't allow themselves to feel it. The strict, rigid discipline of these individuals may also create chronic stress. The corticoids produced by the adrenal glands are cholesterol-based, and these hormones normally relieve stress of all kinds. But the adrenal glands can become exhausted with too much stress. When this happens, the adrenals may fail to produce adequate levels of the stress hormone DHEA (dehydroepiandrosterone) and too much cortisol. This is dangerous, because DHEA buffers us from stress. When the adrenals malfunction, all associated systems do as well, which can cause cell damage. The body may interpret cell damage as a signal for the liver to send out more cholesterol to protect and repair the cell membranes. Too much cholesterol may then build up because of an individual's sustained stress level.

In its normal state, cholesterol is a waxy, fat-like substance, but in individuals with high cholesterol, it becomes a hard, thick plaque. Chances are the lack of joy and the rigidity of these individuals cause them to have an inflexible belief system that gets mirrored in the body by the hard, inflexible plaque. This "bad" cholesterol, or LDL, sticks to and narrows the walls of the arteries, restricting blood flow. Over time, this buildup can cause hardening of the coronary arteries, which can lead to heart disease.

These individuals may develop a live-now pay-later attitude to compensate for their regimented life and lack of joy they've experienced. Imagine a rubber band stretched as far as it can go for a length of time. What eventually happens? It wears thin and finally breaks. These individuals feel stretched into a tight line and, after some years of living that way, may snap. They let go, live for today, and deal with consequences later. Perhaps they believe that if they "let go", it will surely bring them the joy they so desperately need. Unfortunately, letting go often means they don't take care of themselves. They may eat or drink excessively and skip exercise, or they do it in a hit-or-miss fashion. They may not be financially responsible and may not prepare for the future. All these situations can cause more stress.

Not being able to love themselves or feel joy, these individuals begin to weave The Common Thread of powerlessness, resentment, and anger/rage into the fabric of their lives. These constant negative emotions can strain the adrenals, and the circulatory system may malfunction as a result.

The "good" cholesterol, or HDL, helps the body get rid of the bad cholesterol. HDL takes excess cholesterol from the body's cells and carries it back to the liver to be converted to bile. HDL thus reduces LDL cholesterol in the circulating blood, but it can't do its job when the adrenal and circulatory systems are depleted.

The liver and adrenals are located in the area of the third chakra. This chakra is related to our personal power and how we project this power into the world. This chakra also supplies energy to most of the major organs for purification. Domination or control over others and anger/rage can cause malfunction of this chakra. In Brad's case (the case history in this chapter), he had to dominate his grandchildren and thought his strictness was the only way to raise good children because it had (apparently) worked with his own children. Perhaps it made him feel in control. People with such a strict approach believe it helps deflect disaster in any situation because of their rigid control (although it rarely works, which frustrates them).

Frustration is one of *the key emotions* that many individuals with high cholesterol say they feel. Frustration results when these people feel they can't change their situation. This can cause anger and disappointment, and because this happens all the time with these individuals, it brings up powerlessness. This blockage of motivational energy and rigid controlling can make the cholesterol become rigid or plaque-like over time. Frustration is hard on the nervous system and the heart because this emotion produces too much cortisol. I help my clients use the words "it's a challenge" instead of "I'm so frustrated".

People who try to rule with an iron fist can feel as if they're hitting their heads against a wall most of their lives, trying to control others but never in a satisfying or effective way. This frustration may create additional anger and rage, thus intensifying The Common Thread that leads to disease.

The Universal Soul Discovery of High Cholesterol
To protect and support each other in the world.

The universal soul discovery of high cholesterol is to believe in the Universe and allow oneself to be protected and supported as well as to protect and support each other. As the protective cholesterol, HDL cleans out the excess cholesterol that can cause problems. When the individual doesn't feel protected or supported, this emotional attitude may be reflected in low HDL and/or difficulties with the HDL ridding the body of the bad LDL cholesterol.

How can individuals increase their HDL levels and decrease their LDL levels? Not surprisingly, it requires the following supportive self-care practices:

- Aerobic exercise, losing weight, not smoking and maintaining a healthy diet increase HDL levels because the individual is choosing good self-care, which may release the live now/pay later attitude. Exercise may decrease the LDL cholesterol because it produces serotonin, which creates a natural high. This increase in joyful feelings may improve blood flow and decrease hard plaque buildup. Such an overall "loosening up" may help release mental and emotional rigidity, enabling the person to flow with life more easily.
- Because they are pure and not artificial, good fats from vegetables, nuts, and fish work with the body to reduce the LDL and increase the HDL. The body interprets trans fats in processed foods as foreign because they are artificial, thus the body may have to send out more cholesterol to protect and repair.

Even though the Eskimos in Greenland, referred to as Inuit, eat a diet rich in fat (even blubber), few cases of cardiovascular disease or high cholesterol are reported in that culture. It's because the fat is primarily fish oil, which is high in EPA, a beneficial fat. Could this good health record also be due to the traditional life of this society? The Inuit believe their children are treasures and rarely punish them. Men and women are treated as equals. They believe in helping each other and living peacefully. They are strong in spirit and soul, and their beliefs are built on kinship and family. They have revered traditions that have been handed down for generations, rooting them in the DNA of the people.

This society, mainly composed of hunters, believe they need to appease the soul of the animal killed in the hunt. A loving society,

Inuit don't have an attitude of live now/pay later nor were they raised with a strict regimen. Could this possibly be why the high amount of fat they consume does not turn into high cholesterol and hard plaque that causes heart disease?

The Emotional Sufferings of High Cholesterol

A pattern emerges for those who end up with high cholesterol, including the following subset of emotions: Each client determines which of the following emotional suffering resonates with them.

- Signature emotional suffering—Not feeling protected and supported
- Frustration
- Having an strict attitude, rigidity
- Lacking joy
- Having a live now/pay later attitude
- Believing that life is just one long problem to solve
- Unique emotional suffering
- The Common Thread—lack of self-love, resentment, anger/rage, powerlessness

Case History

When Brad read Dr. Lincoln's psychological meaning behind high cholesterol, he was more than a little hesitant to see himself in this way. Brad's wife, however, thought it described him perfectly. It's funny how others never see us as we see ourselves.

Brad's wife confirmed he had raised their children with an iron fist and was now equally as strict with their grandchildren. Brad failed to see anything wrong with his approach, as his children turned out well—as a result of his being so strict, of course. Now, however, his two grown children, who are thin and exercise regularly, also have high cholesterol. Brad's wife also said Brad embraced a live now/pay later attitude. Although he did exercise, he failed to curtail his diet in any way. At age 54, Brad had just begun to put away money for his retirement. To his wife, it seemed as if Brad believed life was one long problem to solve, and he failed to plan ahead. His father had been an alcoholic, leaving the responsibility of being the "sane one" to Brad. Due to his own strict upbringing and his father's alcoholism, Brad admitted it was difficult for him to feel joy.

Brad was open to try the MO Technique of healing, although he was skeptical. He didn't want to take the cholesterol medication his doctor had prescribed, as he'd heard the medication affected one's sex drive. As it turned out, Brad was smart. Right after my sessions with him, this medication was taken off the market.

Much to Brad's amazement, the MO Technique not only had no negative side effects, it worked.

When Brad imaged his own "iron fist" attitude, he saw Adolph Hitler. This stunned him, as he didn't perceive himself in this way. He felt this image in his chest and, to the best of his ability, released it. As he journeyed to a deeper level, he felt a loving energy around him as the image of Hitler gradually disappeared.

Brad also told me he had severe rigidity in his back and was unable to touch his toes. The rigidity of his upbringing was not only manifesting in high cholesterol but also rigidity of the back which may have been from the lack of support and not feeling protected. Our soul discoveries can show up in many ways.

He then addressed his feelings of powerlessness, imaging a puppet, as he said he'd always felt like his father's puppet. As he released that image from his heart, he saw that he had choices about his own power.

As Brad imaged anger/rage and his belief that life is one long problem to solve, he saw a mushroom cloud over his head. He watched it disappear and witnessed blue sky and sunshine taking its place. His image of lacking self-love was a white flag in his head, which he released and replaced with loving energy.

After two sessions, Brad's cholesterol readings without medication or change of diet showed significant improvement, as evidenced by the following chart.

	Before	**After**	**Normal**
Total Cholesterol	285	273	135-200
Triglycerides	226	185	<150
HDL	45	63	>30
LDL	195	173	<130

Here's an easy way to remember which is the "good" cholesterol: H is for Happy cholesterol and L is for Lousy cholesterol.

Brad released his lack of joy and the feeling of doom from his body. We determined his internal conflict with his father had triggered his cholesterol level to rise. To keep improving and prevent future problems, Brad will need to continue working on what his condition is teaching him and bring joy into his life every day.

Without joy in our hearts, the body is sure to rebel and may create disease. Brad understands this today, and he's lightened up on his grandchildren and himself. He's also found compassion for his father, which is the beginning of a loving attitude.

After a few months, Brad's cholesterol readings showed even more improvement. His total cholesterol went down to 249, triglycerides to 140, HDL to 49, and LDL to 172. Even though his lousy cholesterol dropped only one point, the rest of his cholesterol chart was improving and coming into balance. No longer a skeptic, he'll continue to release the emotional sufferings of high cholesterol. Still working on letting go of his rigid beliefs, I'd say he's 50 percent more flexible than he was—his big soul discovery this time around. Brad has been working hard at his soul discoveries. He replaced the word frustration, *which he said constantly, to "it's a challenge." He still was not ready to watch his diet, so he chose to use a natural formula (red rice yeast) to help his cholesterol as he keeps working on feeling joy and letting go of his strict rigid way of life. His*

cholesterol just keeps improving. His LDL—the lousy cholesterol—
went from 201 on 5-17-05 to 149 three years later—46 points! He
promised me that he would incorporate the right diet as he is
working on the "live now/pay later" part of his soul discoveries.
Brad's lousy cholesterol (LDL) keeps improving.

	Before	*After*	*Normal*
Cholesterol	*249*	*231*	*135-200*
Triglycerides	*140*	*128*	*<150*
HDL	*49*	*56*	*>30*
LDL	*172*	*149*	*<130*

High triglycerides result when the body has difficulty processing fats and sugars. The psychological meaning of high triglyceride according to Dr. Lincoln is they believe they don't deserve love and joy in their life at a deep level. Growing up, they likely had a simultaneous conflicting love-hate relationship with family members. Or they may harbor resentment because they had to sacrifice their joy and be the "responsible" one, the rescuer. Their underlying attitude may be outrage that the world does not come through for them.[3]

For a person with a mindset about not deserving positive experiences (including joy or love) who carries built-up resentment and anger, triglycerides may not get broken down properly and may remain at high levels in the bloodstream. Fat and liver cells synthesize and store triglycerides. Fat represents protection and the liver is the seat of anger, so when a person gets angry and doesn't feel protected, this mechanism may also malfunction. In Brad's example, his triglycerides came into a normal range as he released his anger and resentment, and allowed joy and love into his life.

None of us likes to admit we have deep-seated issues to resolve, but this resistance is self-defeating in the long run. Most of us have some kind of soul discovery to learn, and we might as well get on with it. It seems men *and* women don't "see" parts of themselves, and other parts they just don't want to look at. Often, these parts are in the subconscious and have to be nudged into the conscious mind.

Statins may lower cholesterol, but the soul discovery of high cholesterol will keep knocking at the door. The body malfunctions for a reason, and it's best to discover the underlying cause and release it rather than cover it up and hope it will go away. When something goes wrong in the body, the problem can only be fixed permanently (without side effects) by learning what it came to teach you.

Chapter 18: The Common Cold

"Listen to your body. If you respond to its whispers, you won't have to endure its cries."
– Author unknown

The Disease
The common cold is a bodily disorder associated with chills, a runny or stuffy nose, sneezing or coughing, swelling of the sinuses, and sometimes a sore throat, headache, and a fever.

The Soul Discovery of the Common Cold
I've been able to evaluate and observe exactly what emotions trigger a cold. I've concluded that the main trigger, or cue, is suppressed grief. Our soul discovery for the common cold is to feel our grief when we experience a loss but release it out of the body every time it comes up, as with anger. We then get in touch with our feelings. We can take time out to handle the issues that are bothering us instead of taking medication and shoving our grief down deep in our lungs. We can look at our life and see what is not working in some area and find solutions. If everyone did this who caught a cold, we would have a world of happy people because everyone would look at their grief and take time out to handle their mental and emotional issues. Who could imagine that the common cold is a signal to be compassionate with ourselves?

Because almost everyone has had a cold at least once, we share a common bond with this disease. All of us experience grief, but we've not been taught how to release it out of the body each time it comes up.

We usually "catch a cold" when we have a lot going on, we feel stressed out, and our immune systems are run down. The prevailing thought is that colds are caused by over 200 different viruses, such as rhinoviruses or coronaviruses. However, I believe the virus is the *trigger*, not the cause, because viruses are around us all the time. Grief is stored in the lungs and respiratory system. When an adverse event strikes, it may cause great sadness, heartache, and suffering. Resentment and anger/rage may build up because we can't accept what has happened. We may feel helpless or hopeless about the situation. This vulnerability brings suppressed grief to the surface, which then triggers the cold. Our feeling of helplessness creates congestion and anger induces inflammation.

The event that triggers the cold usually relates to a recurring deprivation, or loss and suppressed grief from childhood. It brings up from the subconscious the old familiar feeling of despair so that each time we get a cold, we're reminded that it's time to confront and release the issue being presented.

When we have a cold, mucus builds up and we experience difficulty breathing through the nose. We may cough, sneeze, and experience a sore throat, sinus swelling, chills, and sometimes a headache and fever.

Mucus is a slippery secretion of the lining of many membranes in the body. It protects us by catching foreign matter in an effort to prevent it from entering the body. An increase of mucus is always a symptom of the common cold. The membranes lining the respiratory track become inflamed and produce excess mucus, and we cough to help get rid of it. We may have difficulty breathing. Often an underlying emotional theme is questioning our self-worth or wondering if we're "good enough". Many people may feel non-deserving and that perhaps the triggering event was their fault.

A sore throat may be a sign that we're unable to say what we'd like to say for fear it will cause "World War III" among those around us. Feeling or even anticipating a loss may bring on sneezing. Sinus problems may represent an "inner crying". The chill may be a fear of the world, with a desire to retreat and pull away. A headache may result from a feeling of abandonment, while fever may relate to burning up with anger. This is quite a witch's brew of symptoms!

To sum up: the cascade of emotions and resulting bodily reactions from an adverse event triggers anger/rage that, in turn, triggers suppressed grief stored in the lungs and the respiratory system. The body puts up a protective shield (the excess mucus), and this creates a blockage. Fear or anticipation of loss initiates inner crying, which plugs up the sinuses. Finally, the "not good enough" feeling of being at fault brings up powerlessness and the immune system collapses, allowing the cold virus to attack.

The loss may be abandonment by a loved one or another emotional issue. The individual often "burns up" over this problem yet is not usually aware of it. Even the trauma felt after a collective, severe loss like the tragedies that happened on September 11th, 2001, can cause people to feel as if they just can't breathe in life.

The Universal Soul Discovery of the Common Cold
To heal the grief and suffering in the world.

The Emotional Sufferings of the Common Cold
It's sad in itself that the common cold is so common! It means that many, many people are walking around with these emotional sufferings:

- Signature emotional suffering—Grief
- Feeling not good enough
- Feeling undeserving
- Feeling abandoned
- Feeling deprived
- Feeling helpless and hopeless
- Unique emotional suffering
- The Common Thread—lack of self-love, resentment, anger/rage, powerlessness

Grief may be the most dreaded human emotion because it's associated with a form of loss that can cause great pain. I, myself, have mourned my childhood, my divorce, and the deaths of many loved ones and beloved pets. The pain felt excruciating; the grief from this pain was stored in my cellular memory. Specifically, after my divorce, I had to confront my "never-ending" grief. I hope to help others do the same and prevent the emotional component of diseases that stored grief can trigger.

After I started healing my own grief, I worked as a hospice bereavement counselor for teenagers. My experiences with this enormous volume and intensity of grief helped me support, comfort, and assist others to find meaning and growth through the grieving process. When we work through this powerful emotion, we grow and expand ourselves.

I've concluded that our *attachments* to relationships, non-permanent material items, cherished pets, and the idea of having things go "our way" can cause this great pain. With each loss or failed expectation we encounter, we feel grief. It's stored in the lungs and respiratory system. There, it gets suppressed because we haven't been taught to release it out of cellular memory whenever we have a loss or deprivation in our lives. Thus, it builds, grief upon grief, until it finally erupts and causes a respiratory problem—most commonly, a cold. When a cold erupts, the body is telling us to look for a loss or deprivation that may be at the bottom of it.

Then we can use the MO Technique and get to the root of it, feel it, and learn how to release the grief so it doesn't build in the body. If we learn to release grief and The Common Thread at the cold stage, perhaps we can prevent more severe problems, such as pneumonia, emphysema, chronic obstructive pulmonary disease, and lung cancer. Because at the cold stage, we can turn grief into recognizing and fulfilling what we need.

Case History 1

Jerry, now my husband, and I both came down with colds at the most inopportune time of the year—just before the holidays. I was busy seeing clients and working on this book, with a looming deadline. AND, we were getting married January 15th. Did I have enough on my plate? This was the second marriage for both of us. Jerry had been single for twelve years and I for seven, so we knew marriage was a big step for us. We were both stressed to the max, and as a result, we both caught terrible colds. I went into my office and released the emotional sufferings that were coming up for me, and the symptoms disappeared the next day. In spite of the fact that Jerry took medications that temporarily helped his symptoms, his cold hung on for another week and a half. Today, he knows how the MO Technique works and he releases grief any time he experiences or anticipates a loss, releasing his symptoms quickly.

My sister also had a cold. She was actually in bed with her box of Kleenex as I read the emotional sufferings of a cold to her. She had just gone through a traumatic episode with her teenage son. It brought up old feelings of helplessness we'd both felt as children when our dad would go on his alcoholic rampages. We talked about the current event that had triggered the suppressed grief and released it with the MO Technique. She called the next day to tell me her cold had disappeared. Now she's able to release the emotional grief each time she feels a cold coming on.

Suppressed Grief

How does grief store up in the body and become suppressed grief? We may grieve and release grief in many ways, such as writing about our sadness or loss. We may work it out with physical exercise, by playing the piano, or with free-style dancing. I would like to add to these wonderful ways to release grief and work through the grieving process.

As noted throughout this book, my theory states that grief

builds up in the body. It needs to be felt and then released out of the body every time it comes up, which can be accomplished with the MO Technique. Then, with compassion, we can look at the trigger and find solutions.

Clients have told me they thought they'd worked through their grief, but releasing it with the MO Technique created a much more powerful effect than ways they had tried earlier. I do a computer energy reading before and after each session. The color of the energy that comes in when people release grief is gold, which signifies forgiveness. Forgiveness of ourselves and others is a potent healer.

Case History 2

One of my clients, Anita, had just been through radiation after a mastectomy of her right breast when she came to me. Her body had become toxic from the radiation and had developed several serious complications, including shingles. Her childhood had been marred by loneliness. She'd felt abandoned by her parents as a child, saying, "They just didn't pay a lot of attention to me. I'm 60 years old now and I still can't be around my mother very long." While she was releasing the emotional suffering of abandonment, a great deal of grief surfaced. She felt deep sorrow like she'd never felt before, even though it had surfaced on the conscious level many times during counseling. After releasing with the MO Technique, she said, "My eyes are involuntarily watering, but I'm not crying." I explained that the grief was also releasing out of the body through her watery eyes. She said, "When I was releasing the abandonment I felt as a child, I could sense it strongly in my body. It felt so good to release it. I didn't realize it was such a big deal, but my body sure knew it was. Then when I filled my body with the positive energy at the soul level—declaring that I would not abandon myself but would instead always be there for myself—I could discern who could be there for me and allow that. It was like my body was saying yes, this is my truth. What a joyous sensation."

Grief can result from many events, depending on the strength of a person's emotional attachments around the situations involved. The event could be any major change in one's life, such as experiencing a miscarriage, a divorce, the death of a loved one or pet, or a child moving away to college. Moving to a new house, losing a job, going through menopause, surgery, or a terminal illness can also cause grief. The bottom line is that any *loss or deprivation* can trigger this emotion, affecting one's body if it's not released.

In my work with clients, I've found that major and minor traumatic childhood memories come up most when releasing emotional sufferings. A similar situation occurring in adulthood resonates with the old memory of grief in childhood; the suppressed emotions can manifest in a cold.

I, myself, suffered from severe colds and bronchitis as a child. The grief in my lungs and anger in my body would manifest an infection of the bronchial system every time it was triggered. I remember being desperately ill with pneumonia while in high school. I played guard on the basketball team and I was asked to give up my uniform to a freshman because of my illness. I felt devastated. I would lie on the couch and hold my coughs so my dad would let me go and play basketball. I took massive antibiotics and eventually became well enough to suit up for the basketball team, but the emotional damage had been done. Today, I can see how suppressing my emotions just made the pneumonia worse.

If I had known as a child how to release the emotional sufferings and the grief out of my cellular memory every time they came up, I wouldn't have spent most of my childhood in one illness after another. The medications we take may clear up symptoms, but rarely do people address the underlying causes of illness. That may be why one billion people in the world suffer from colds each year.

Children may get 6 to 10 colds a year. A prevailing theory is they get so many colds because they're in close contact with other infected children in daycare or school. One other reason may be that certain children are vulnerable because they hold suppressed grief from some sort of loss or deprivation at home or school. In addition, they may be under more stress, which increases their vulnerability.

Fourth Chakra

The fourth chakra, or emotional center, houses the lungs, heart, and circulatory system, shoulders and arms, ribs, breasts, diaphragm, and thymus gland.

The emotional sufferings that especially affect the fourth chakra include stored grief, lack of joy and nurturing, abandonment, self-rejection, fear of failure, co-dependency plus feeling undeserving of love, unconnected, overly responsible, and not good enough. These emotional sufferings can cause circulatory, respiratory, breast, and shoulder problems. The opposite of grief is joy, and joy is so powerful it will not only help keep the heart healthy and help with diabetes, but also may keep the lungs clear.

Joy and Love

I instill joy and love into my cellular memory in my daily meditation with the MO Technique. It gives my body the powerful emotional energy it needs, thus keeping my body joyful. Those with heart, respiratory, or immune problems (or any other disease, for that matter) will benefit from instilling love and joy into cellular memory every day.

Love sometimes comes in the form of chicken soup (thus the popular *Chicken Soup for the Soul* series). When my young children got colds, I concocted homemade chicken soup. My mother told me chicken soup could cure a cold, and she said her mother swore by it. Then, in nursing school, I found out chicken soup contains a mucus-thinning amino acid called cysteine, which helps congestion by replacing white cells called neutophils. When my grown children get sick, they still want homemade chicken soup, and I make it for them when I can. I think it's mainly the love they feel when I nurture them they crave. This soothing warm soup reminds them of how much I love and care for them.

In fact, when they were growing up, I had a spice can labeled "love" and I shook the "love" into everything I cooked. My son use to tease his sister that his soup had more love in it than hers. There's no real proof that chicken soup will cure a cold, but I know *love* helps. Indeed, love helps heal all disease across the board.

We've been programmed to pop cold tablets and guzzle cold medicine, drink lots of liquids, rest as much as we can, and hope that a cold goes away soon. But even the common cold—an unfortunately common bond among people—carries a message that something is out of balance. The underlying emotional sufferings need to be released and replaced with their antidotes—joy and love. In this way, it may not develop into something more serious.

It's important to learn our soul discoveries with a relatively benign cold. When you catch a cold, make it a habit to release grief and find out why it's there every time you experience a loss. Remember, it's never "just a cold".

Chapter 19: The Flu

"Some see a hopeless end, while others see an endless hope."
– Author unknown

The Disease
Influenza, commonly known as the flu, is a virus infection that attacks the respiratory system causing fever, coughing, and severe muscle aches and fatigue.

The Soul Discovery of the Flu
Individuals with internal conflicts who feel trapped and believe they have no viable way out may be susceptible to flu viruses. Internal conflicts may have originated from a family situation in which the individual was expected to uplift the family and felt depended upon, but was given no support or validation in return. He or she may feel responsible for working out solutions for everyone else, but feel alone and alienated within, resulting in a hopeless or helpless feeling.

I've seen these situations so often in my practice that I've termed this overly burdened individual the "family hoist". However, it's a good sign that I see this, because those who seek me out want to take responsibility for their condition or disease—and that's the first step in healing.

Hopeless, helpless feelings may come from the lack of support and validation in childhood—leading to a belief that there's no solution. This may collapse the immune system and allow a virus to take hold. Yet the message of any virus—any strain—is that a viable solution exists for every problem.

Lung problems involve difficulty in receiving the life energy needed to "breathe with life". The lack of feeling accepted in childhood may deplete this life energy and lead to feeling unworthy of taking in life fully. This creates the lack of joy and

173

love needed for the fourth, or heart, chakra to function properly.

As noted earlier, the heart chakra directly affects the energy flowing to the heart and lungs. Grief stores in the lungs and blocks the life-giving energy to the lungs and heart. Grief and the hopeless, helpless, alone feeling result in the lack of joy and love. The person may be deeply afraid or may not know how to obtain love and joy. This can lead to heart and lung dysfunction, allowing a virus to attack.

The individual's childhood programming induces the futile feeling, which impairs the immune system and allows the flu to take hold. Hence the soul discovery is to support and validate oneself, and to bring responsibility for self and others into balance.

The Universal Soul Discovery of the Flu
To heal hopeless, helpless feelings about the world.

The Emotional Sufferings of the Flu Virus
Although the flu shares several emotional sufferings with other diseases, it has its own emphasis.

- Signature emotional suffering—Feeling hopeless and helpless
- Not feeling validated
- Feeling unsafe
- Feeling alone
- Feeling unsupported
- Difficulty coping with life's demands
- Feeling overly responsible for others
- Unique emotional suffering
- The Common Thread—lack of self-love, resentment, anger/rage, powerlessness

Buddha asserted, "All that we are is a result of what we have thought." Our thoughts often reflect our childhood

174

programming, our way of looking at life, our *modus operandi*. Consequently, if we had been taught there *is* a solution to every problem, we would feel hopeful about coping with life's demands. Yet because it's not commonly taught, many people turn to antidepressants or succumb to addictions to get through their days.

Negative thoughts or emotions influence the physical body to develop disease, including the flu. Positive emotions such as joy, happiness, and peace tend to create health. Throughout time, various cultures have included teachings about the influence of negative thoughts and emotions. Here's a great story from a Native American elder:

One day the elder was teaching his grandchildren about life. "There is a fight going on inside me," he told them. "It's a terrible fight, and it's between two wolves. One wolf represents fear and anger, hopelessness, helplessness, powerlessness, and resentment. The other wolf stands for love, faith, personal power, kindness, joy, compassion, and peace. This fight is going on inside you and every other person, too." The children thought about this for a minute, and then one child asked his grandfather, "Which wolf will win?"
The elder simply replied, "The one that's fed."

Like the elder instructing his grandchildren, the flu tells us exactly what emotions we are feeding. Everyone has been programmed with distinct emotions—our MO—since the womb. Looking at the symptoms of the flu can tell us exactly what thoughts and emotions allow the virus to attack; it indicates which emotions we're feeding.

Symptoms of the flu are nausea, vomiting, diarrhea, headaches, body aches, fatigue, sore throat, and sometimes fever. Nausea may be a sense of queasiness about something in one's life, and vomiting may be trying to get rid of it. Aching may be a desire to be held and loved that seems futile. Headaches may result from a feeling of abandonment. Diarrhea may be a sign the physical body is unable to assimilate or absorb the experience. Fever may indicate a burning up with anger and resentment. A sore throat may signify not being able to verbally express one's thoughts. Fatigue may represent weariness from trying to cope and from life just not working. Feelings of futility and power-lessness allow the virus to take hold. After all, the signature soul discovery of the flu is to rid the mind and physical body of this hopeless, helpless feeling.

In the old days, patients were swaddled and taken care of while the virus worked its way out of the body. So at least patients had love from their caregivers and were tended to, so they felt supported and connected. How do we treat the flu as a society now? Aspirin, maybe some flu medication, and rest. Not much sympathy for the flu—is there? "Boy, I feel as if I just got run over by a Mac truck," I tell my doctor. The reply? "Sorry, Maureen, there's nothing I can give you. It's just the flu, and you'll have to let it run its course." The only good part of that scenario is that by letting the flu run its course, I'm building up immunity to help fight off future viruses. But when I have the flu, I just want someone to take care of me and help me and give me hope that I will be over it soon.

If you look back at what was going on in your life before you caught the flu, you can usually link it to something that was disturbing you. We're all under stress, but one thing usually puts us over the top and causes our immune systems to fail. I think most of us can relate to situations that didn't seem to have a solution or when we've felt trapped or had a loss that made us feel powerless. The hopeless, helpless feeling could come from a difficult circumstance at work or at home, a troublesome situation with children or losing a loved one through death, divorce, or a breakup. That feeling might also come from seemingly hopeless financial difficulties.

An example may be situations as common as people feeling they aren't getting paid enough for the job they do. They work at a job they dislike because it pays the bills, but feel stuck in it. This alone may trigger hopeless, helpless feelings. They may build up anger and resentment until one adverse event puts them over the top. That feeling of powerlessness allows the virus to attack.

Here's an example. A client told me her adult daughter has a severe drug problem. She's been in rehab several times but just can't stay clean. Because of this, her daughter couldn't take care of her child, so my client has picked up the pieces to take care of her grandchild. This was not her idea of retirement! But she believed she had no choice except to adopt her grandchild. Today, her adopted granddaughter is the light of her life! She has been able to turn around the feeling of hopelessness and helplessness by concentrating on thoughts that her grand-daughter is a gift at this time in her life.

These kinds of situations happen every day. Learning to keep our power, release the anger, and love ourselves by seeing these situations in a positive light, we can prevent the hopeless, helpless feelings—and prevent getting the flu. We may need professional help to see it in a different light, though.

Severe family environments that include abuse and molestation also set people up with powerless, hopeless, and helpless feelings. When we understand what triggers disease in the body, we can see why people in our world get sick.

Case History

The influenza pandemic of 1918, known as the Spanish flu, was the most devastating epidemic in recorded world history and the most deadly for those between 20 and 40 years of age. We normally think of newborns, children, and the elderly as being most vulnerable to the flu. Why were people in their prime more vulnerable in this situation?

Let's look at what was happening in the world. In the fall of 1918, World War I was winding down in Europe. As these young people were fighting in the war, they endured some of the most brutal conditions. These conditions can cause a futile feeling, but equally as important is the fact that war generates hate and intolerance. It weakens our common bond as fellow human beings, a bond that provides the foundation of life on this planet. Yet war results in the loss of fathers, mothers, children, family members, and friends, and the smashing of that bond. This enormity of the loss in WWI set the framework for a huge hopeless, helpless feeling among the populace and especially among those young people involved. Devastated, people couldn't find a solution to massive losses and horrors they experienced. This conflicted mightily with what humans have been born to learn—living a life of unconditional love.

What's Really Wrong?

Hate, intolerance, and loss from this era may have spread exponentially throughout generations, allowing feelings of injustice or victimhood to become embedded in our collective cells. On a physical level, hate and intolerance weaken the heart chakra and lungs. So when we live through wars and devastating events such as 9/11, an individual body's cell memory can react to the "victimhood" set up and elicit hopeless, helpless feelings. In turn, these feelings may cause respiratory weaknesses that collapse the immune system and allow a virus to attack.

In part, an uncontrollable flu might attack people in their prime because of the situation currently embracing our world. We're still at war, the economy is a mess, and millions have lost half or more of their savings and retirement funds. Are these negative events breeding hate, intolerance, feelings of loss, and powerlessness?

As a society, we have chosen to rely on medication instead of learning to cope with health issues in self-contained ways. We've become a population that hasn't been taught to cope with life's problems, a situation handed down from generation to generation with no fault or blame attached.

A standard way for helping people who feel hopeless and helpless has been to put them on antidepressants—the second largest class of prescription drugs, exceeded only by heart medication. Out of a population of 300 million . . . "overall use of antidepressants continues to grow, with nearly 190 million prescriptions dispersed in the United States last year, according to IMS Health, a health care information company."[1] (Reported by Melissa McNamara in CBS Evening News on December 13, 2006. Her piece "A Look at Antidepressants" is available at http://cbsnews.com/stories/2006/12/13/fyi/main2255769.shtml)

How do antidepressants work? They increase the serotonin level in the brain, creating a false sense of joy.

Similarly, learning to cope creates a support that can release natural serotonin so we feel naturally happy and joyful. Then the hopeless, helpless feeling disappears. Fine-tuning our coping skills helps us to take control and feel happy so that we can manage our lives well. We gain a sense of strength and confidence when we know we have choices and don't feel trapped. This creates a strong immune system that can more easily ward off viruses. The energy of feeling happy is more powerful than food or drugs.

If there is another pandemic flu virus, it may be because, as a society, we have not addressed the underlying cause of conditions and disease. Masking diseases and conditions with medications has been a dangerous solution. The only way to prevent a future superbug is to look at flu in a new way and address the underlying cause—futility and hopeless, helpless feelings.

How Does This Apply to Disease of All Kinds?

At the base of every disease, not only flu, is a situation that weakens a person's immune system. If we examine what went on before the onset of disease, it can usually be linked to something that disturbed or stressed us. When the stress gets too great, one thing tends to put us "over the top". That's when the immune system can collapse..

As an example, Bill decides he has to stay stuck in a hated job so he can pay family bills. His "stuckness" triggers feelings of hopelessness and helplessness. Over time, this situation builds resentment and anger. Then an adverse event happens—he loses his parents—and the grief he feels puts him "over the top". His immune system gets compromised.

What could Bill do to avoid contracting a disease? Having an awareness that a situation like this could compromise his health, Bill could proactively identify and seek several options. Doing this shows he believes that a solution exists for every situation. Because of that belief, he doesn't allow himself to sink into a hopeless, helpless state.

One solution could be seeking professional help such as life coaching or therapeutic counseling to assist him in moving forward in life. The process could help him find a greater purpose or passion in his work. In that way, he could draw a fresh roadmap to help him manifest exactly what he desires.

Another option is using the MO Technique that, in effect, reprograms the subconscious, super conscious, and conscious minds. This technique first gets him to release any "stuckness" out of his subconscious mind so he can move forward. How does he do that? By imaging his feelings of stuckness, locating negative energy in his body related to feeling stuck, and releasing that energy out of the area where it hangs out. Then he would reprogram his super conscious mind by looking at and accepting options that come from his higher self. He replaces all the negative energy he's identified with positive energy and "instills" it into his body. How can he reprogram his conscious mind to accomplish this? By repeating an appropriate affirmation for 40 days. His affirmation might be something like this: "From this day moment, I make all decisions based on knowing that I'm moving forward in life with ease. All doors are now open for manifesting the future I desire."

Reprogramming all three minds makes lasting change possible. And by increasing his awareness, Bill might see doors open for a new job that he hadn't noticed before. Even if he needs to stay in his job, he can now regard it with a new perspective — one that could give him greater satisfaction than ever before.

Let's say your seven-year-old daughter Mollie comes down with the flu. As a parent, you have the knowledge that the flu is caused by a situation that has led to a hopeless, helpless feeling. Your first question to Mollie is, "Honey, is there something going on at school or at home that's bothering you?" She replies, "The kids make fun of me all the time." This may be really taking place, or happening only in her mind, but both are genuine in Mollie's experience.

You've just found out what's causing these feelings for Mollie and discuss choices with her. She could talk to the teacher, make friends individually, or other possibilities. You then assure Mollie the situation can be resolved. From this experience, she learns how she can feel hopeful by finding a viable, healthy solution to her problem.

Let's follow the same pattern assuming you have the flu (or any disease). What do you do? You examine the situation and determine what's going on that may have been causing feelings of resentment or powerlessness or anger/rage or hopelessness/helplessness. If you've faced emotional setbacks before, you may already know of ways to release the powerlessness, anger/rage out of the body. That's what you want.

Is a Pandemic Flu a Wakeup Call for Humanity?

Traumatic situations can set up powerlessness, hopeless, helpless feelings, even rage and anger. Those who understand that a viable solution exists for every problem and have life skills to cope aren't as likely to get caught up in this problem as those who don't. In contrast, when people feel trapped with no solution in sight, many turn to antidepressants or other unhealthy solutions to cope.

Suppose another super bug invades the United States, fear sets in that lives will be lost, creating a massive feeling of hopelessness and helplessness. Look around. Many have reason to feel hopeless and helpless in numerous ways—the type of situation ripe for a superbug to invade.

Are we being set up for a perceived pending pandemic? To learn from the Spanish flu epidemic of 1918, we'd have to ask why it reached pandemic proportions. Remember, World War I engendered hate, intolerance, and loss on a gargantuan scale. Anything to do with intolerance and hate violates our collective purpose and may be lethal to our bodies. If we don't learn to replace these deadly feelings with unconditional love, we may be faced with something as devastating as a flu that's uncontrollable.

On 9/11/2001, terrorists struck New York's Twin Towers— buildings that represented power, money, and possibly even greed. Can we trace today's "bust" economy back to greed? The swine flu represents the pig, which could be interpreted as being piggy or greedy. This may sound far out, but the Universe keeps sending us messages, begging us to pick up on them and change our ways.

This grave lesson from greed, hate, and intolerance that sets up the hopeless, helpless feeling doesn't have to become an uncontrollable flu for us to get the lesson. People can learn to cope and gain control over their lives, choosing unconditional love instead of hate and intolerance. It will be the only way to create peace and harmony in the world.

How Do We Prevent A Pandemic?
Right now, we can take positive action. We can each determine our own modus operandi and learn to cope with life's demands, possibly seeking professional help. Our MO includes our programmed emotional beliefs and our emotional roots. We can release any hopeless, helpless feeling out of cellular memory

using the powerful MO (Modus Operandi) Technique. Those who deal with depression can get the help they need to feel powerful again. Those who already know the Technique can help others learn to cope.

Building a system of support that addresses the underlying causes of disease will teach us not only to cope but to feel genuinely happy. This is the freedom from all viruses. Then we'd be able to create a much more powerful—and certainly healthier—nation and world.

Chapter 20: Fibromyalgia

"A crippled spirit makes us forget who we are."
– Maureen Minnehan Jones

The Disease
Fibromyalgia is a musculoskeletal disorder with symptoms of pain and fatigue.

The Soul Discovery and MO of Fibromyalgia
Fibromyalgia individuals may have been undermined as children. This undermining may have been subtle or obvious, but regardless of its form, these behaviors instill in children a belief that it's not okay to be who they are. Individuals with this kind of upbringing may consistently feel they aren't good enough and may fail to value themselves, crippling their spirit and causing deep pain. This pain expresses itself in the muscles because that's how we move in life.

The word *fibromyalgia* means pain in the muscles, ligaments, and tendons—the soft, fibrous tissues of the body. Fatigue sets in because the individual feels drained of energy. Muscle turns energy into motion. The brain sends a signal to the nerve cells to instruct the muscles to contract and flex and propel the body to move. The soul discovery for those who acquire this disease may be to become flexible, flow with life, and love who they truly are. The programmed inflexibility of their mind may then cause the same in their body, which is why the pain goes straight to the muscle. Fatigue may result from trying hard to be "good enough", a state they believe could never be attained in the eyes of their parents. This conflict may eventually cause extreme exhaustion.

Individuals suffering from fibromyalgia may be programmed by family members to believe they must be super-successful, but *only for the family.* Every time they get close to succeeding in the world or in relationships outside the family, pain in the muscles may surface and immobilize them, or they may sabotage themselves in some way. The amount and severity of pain depends on the degree to which they've been undermined.

These beliefs have been subtly programmed into the subconscious. At their core, individuals with fibromyalgia may believe they're never good enough, thus setting up The Common Thread cycle of disease: lack of self-love, resentment, anger/rage, and powerlessness. When an event demands feeling competent, confident, and moving forward, their "keep them around the old homestead" programming may sabotage these individuals. Their undermining may instill a lack of trust, so they may not trust themselves. Executing plans and accomplishing things may become extremely difficult, thus creating a cycle that can become frustrating and cause them deep pain.

The Universal Soul Discovery of Fibromyalgia
To heal the deep pain and "crippled spirit" in the world.

.

The Emotional Sufferings of Fibromyalgia
Family of origin programming may create the following emotional sufferings in individuals with fibromyalgia.

- Signature emotional suffering—A "crippled spirit," caused by being undermined as a child
- Feeling restricted as a result of "keep them around the old homestead" programming
- Feeling not okay to be "who you are"
- Lacking trust
- Not feeling good enough
- Feeling unconfident and incompetent
- Feeling unsupported
- Punishing oneself

- Feeling undeserving
- Feeling guilty
- Unique emotional suffering
- The Common Thread—lack of self-love, resentment, anger/rage, powerlessness

The deep muscular pain and aching of fibromyalgia is a signal from the body that a deep need inside is aching to be filled, that these individuals need to be loved for who they are. Muscular pain indicates being immobilized and afraid to move in life. Pain in general is a form of self-punishment generated by feeling they deserve this lot in life. When they were undermined by their parent(s) as a child, they took it as "God's word".

Seventh Chakra

The seventh, or crown, chakra involves the muscular system. It's our spiritual connector. When we understand this, it's easy to see why a "crippled spirit" would adversely affect the muscles. When we are unable to trust our parents, we may be set up to distrust our own divine connection. By mastering the lesson of the seventh chakra, we learn to connect with the divine energy, to trust life, and to find our personal meaning. When a child is undermined, the natural flow of energy through the seventh chakra—the connection to our spirit—may get blocked. Repeated programming that cripples the spirit may cause heaviness or fatigue and block this chakra from pure divine healing energy.

The crown chakra spirals down and touches the pineal gland, said to be the seat of the soul. It's the line of communication to our spiritual quest, our true meaning. Activation of the pineal gland can be accomplished by meditation or relaxation. The MO Technique helps individuals relax and settle into a meditative state. Seventh chakra dysfunction affects the whole body, so the pain of fibromyalgia can be felt throughout the entire body. The painful aching of fibromyalgia may be the soul aching for us to find our truth and our purpose. Once we find our truth and soul connection and reprogram the body with the MO Technique, this disease may no longer be needed.

Case History 1

Janet, 54, was a highly intelligent woman in a prestigious position within her company. Despite this, Janet lacked confidence and often felt like a fraud. During our interview, Janet mentioned that her mother always undermined her; even today, her mother ridiculed the way she dressed. Despite her mother's behavior toward her, Janet was devoted to her and assumed responsibility for her care.

At the time of Janet's father's death, Janet was going through a divorce, so it seemed logical to move her mother in with her. At first, Janet welcomed the company; however, the "keep them around the old homestead" issue arose. She turned down a position in another city because she felt she couldn't leave her mother. Shortly after this, fibromyalgia began to immobilize her.

Dr. Lincoln explained that the "keep them around the old homestead programming" involves parents seeking to "guarantee their off-spring will never want or be able to leave them." This programming is based on the parents' abandonment anxiety and dependency. They want to keep their children "home where they belong."[1]

It's been my experience with clients who hold this type of parental programming that the inner knowledge of their dilemma is often so suppressed that it's difficult for them to see where the problem began—or to see it at all. People aren't eager to explore their "shadow" side. In addition, it may be difficult for these clients to see how little feeling of competence or confidence they have, as they are often high achievers. This drive to succeed may be the result of parental undermining and the child's overreaction to it. They are always striving to be "good enough" but never feel they are. On the outside, they look like winners rather than "children" who are constantly trying to prove they're okay. They never receive approval from the one(s) who programmed them to be successful for the family only and to otherwise fail.

Fibromyalgia can be triggered by old tapes (of being undermined) by the subconscious. This "crippling of the spirit" weakens a person's support system to a point of immobilizing them. The immobilization can cause pain in the muscles of our bodies; our muscles help us move forward in life. As an example, a friend had been told by her mother over and over that she was an ugly duckling. She'd taken in the message as if it were God's word. This beautiful woman, a registered nurse, said, "I just want to be told I am a beautiful swan, but if someone did tell me that I wouldn't believe them." When she went through a divorce, she became immobilized and was in severe pain. The diagnosis—fibromyalgia. Her soul discovery was to heal her "crippled spirit" and love herself at her core.

Again, the body may present a soul discovery in the disguise of a condition that prevents us from moving further without pain.

Janet was an exception, as she clearly saw just how her mother's programming had affected her life and ultimately her health. She was able to release the emotional sufferings at the soul level and see it was okay to be who she was.

Janet's Win Aura Printout

The energy of Janet's before and after treatment was dramatic. The energy of her heart chakra filled in. All four quadrants of her brain lit up. She came into balance, and all of her organs demonstrated significantly more energy.

Energy Of All Organs Of Patients

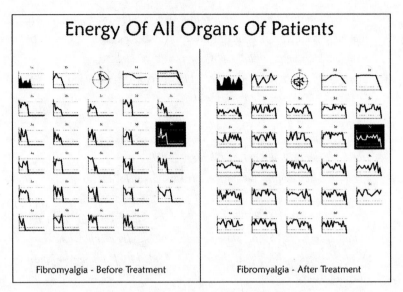

| Fibromyalgia - Before Treatment | Fibromyalgia - After Treatment |

Diagram 3: Janet's Win Aura Printout

Case History 2

Diane was a 65-year-old nurse practitioner and was about to retire. She had fibromyalgia and wanted to get to the root cause so she could enjoy her retirement. Diane told me her parents never allowed her to show anger so she always turned it inward. If she spoke up, she was put down and constantly criticized. Her stance became, "I'm not going to let any of you get to me! I don't care about you — you can't hurt me." She said she wouldn't allow herself to laugh or cry — "not on your life" — and made a decision to hate her parents. Diane left an eastern women's college at 19 to marry a hometown boy. They had attended school together in Texas, but the following March she discovered that she was pregnant, and would be unable to complete her senior year. She left her husband when their child, Joe, was two years old, and raised Joe as a single mother. Joe was severely hyperactive, and at age six was diagnosed with ADHD. His tantrums and learning/behavior problems were so serious, his doctor recommended a special school. At considerable sacrifice,

Diane managed to arrange for this. Even after two years of highly specialized education, Joe's behavior remained a significant problem. At age seventeen he had a schizophrenic break.

"This broke me emotionally," Diane confessed. After the short difficult marriage, and so many years of trying to help her son function better, his mental illness was devastating. As a hardworking single mom, she never allowed herself to be creative or to find a job that she really enjoyed. During the years of Joe's mental illness, she began to suffer from chronic fatigue, and then fibromyalgia.

As Diane planned to retire, she was able to find a separate supportive place for Joe, now 43 years old, to live. She was excited to start her new life, and hoped to find relief from the pain of fibromyalgia.

During our first session, she released the feeling that it wasn't okay to be who she was. She felt it in her left side, the back of her legs, and up around and behind her left arm. She let it evaporate. At the soul level, she described what she would look and feel like if it was really okay to be who she was. She described it as being like a free and innocent child, respected and smiling, and instilled that energy at the soul level.

Diane also released the anger/rage and grief. She tapped into herself as a child and talked to this inner child, saying it was okay to care and not be so hard-hearted. She let that child know her importance. As we talked after the session, Diane felt it was okay to speak, be heard, and feel respected.

My computer program has been a great tool to show what energy needs to come into the body for it to help itself heal. Before and after each healing session, I showed Diane her energy field. After her first session, the color turquoise (representing compassion) came into her energy field, the color white (divine healing energy) and the color blue (communication) came into her solar plexus. Once Diane saw her truth at the soul level and instilled it, her energy changed to match her truth.

During the second session, Diane released lack of trust, power-lessness, and lack of self-love. After this session, white light and blue light came into her heart. She said she felt free and believed she could lighten up.

In the third session, she was ready to release the unique emotional suffering that pertained only to Diane. This was her stance that adamantly affirmed, "I'm not going to let any one of you get to me! I don't care about you—you can't hurt me." Because she'd been so berated by her mother throughout her life, Diane had erected an impenetrable psychological wall around herself for protection. Knowing this would be huge for her to release, she was nervous but excited. As she imaged the stance, she saw a barrier at arm's length encircling her and keeping people at a distance. The barrier was belly high, gritty with tar, and rough like roof shingles. She removed the grittiness and kept imaging the barrier close to the ground so she could step over it. She couldn't step over it, so she asked what it needed from her. It said to be forgiven. As she acknowledged the forgiveness, she sobbed and repeated to herself, "I forgive you."

The barrier then disappeared. At the soul level, she saw her truth— that the past had no power over her and anger was no longer needed. The pain and sadness in her heart dissolved when she forgave herself. She was able to recognize what others were feeling and send them love, saying, "I am not hurt by them."

She also released the feeling of not being safe. She said, "I used to think, 'Dammit, I won't be happy and that's the way it is.'" But after this session, she felt more in touch with her truth. In her new stance, she was now flexible, movable, and able to flow gracefully with life. She gave herself permission to feel good and allow happiness. More colors came into her energy field: yellow (happiness), green/yellow (healing), turquoise (compassion), green (growth), and gold (forgiveness).

Diane wrote to me and said that all of our sessions helped her very much and she is still working on these issues. A great deal of her anger that was unconscious has since come to light and she continues to work on healing. She stated that she experienced some relief from pain with energy healing but specifically it helped Diane be less afraid of her emotions.

Once people suffering from fibromyalgia master their soul discovery and know it's okay to be who they are and know they can trust and have success in the world and their relationships they can flow with life. Once they have these positive convictions within, the outside world sends them more of the same—people who are supportive, trustworthy, and successful, affirming that they are, too. That's called the Law of Attraction in which like attracts like. This means negative energy attracts more negative energy and positive energy attracts more positive energy.

Individuals who cripple the spirit of others may feel powerless themselves. They may somehow see the individual as a threat, with the undermining being an inappropriate way of trying to establish their own sense of power. Usually, these individuals were programmed to operate like this and just don't know any other way. Empowerment is the antidote.

Teaching our children to be empowered and showing them they're loved and secure can provide the trust they need to flow with life. Educating both children and adults about their soul connection and divine love can help prevent the "crippled spirit" and deep pain of fibromyalgia.

Chapter 21: Heart Disease

"We are all born for love. It is the principle of existence and its only end."
– Benjamin Disraeli

The Disease
Heart disease is an umbrella term for a number of conditions that affect the heart, usually involving the vessels that supply blood to the heart or the heart muscle. It's the leading cause of death in the United States.

The Soul Discovery and MO of Heart Disease — the #1 Killer
The soul discovery of heart disease is self-love—complete acceptance of ourselves. Heart disease will continue on its path as number one killer until every single body has self-love.

Heart disease may result from a failure to love oneself. Given the grave consequences of this failure, it's amazing to realize how many of us must have had poor, or no, role models for loving ourselves. How many have actually been *taught* to love themselves? Self-love, including all our faults and human failings, may be the most difficult kind of love to achieve. Ironically, it's this kind of love that keeps our hearts healthy. When the body doesn't have self-love, the heart can weaken. And without self-love, we cannot fully love others. All love begins "in the heart".

One of my clients with heart disease programming plus MO had all the following elements:

Self-rejection → work feverishly to be good enough → try to prove self-worth → Type A personality → emotional stress → lack of self-love and joy

---

Regardless of doing well, this person never felt good enough. What happens? This sets up The Common Thread of Disease, made up of feelings of resentment, anger/rage, powerlessness, and lack of self-love.

When self-love is not the foundation of the body, the body lacks its foundation and becomes weak. Anger and resentment build if not released. When the body feels powerless, the immune system breaks down and it allows disease to set up house. This starts the crumbling effect well ahead of having an adverse event. Heart problems are often triggered by losing a loved one, either through divorce or death or another adverse event. Grief, sadness, loneliness, and depression may all factor into shutting down the energy of the heart chakra.

The "not good enough" belief leads to not deserving love. The cycle continues and in this emotional setting, it's difficult to feel joy. The undeserving feeling and lack of joy may create an energy shield around the heart. This shield is meant to protect the person from being hurt but also blocks love to and from the heart chakra. Serotonin, dopamine and endorphins—the biochemicals of love—are neurotransmitters that may alleviate the hurt we endure in our lives. These chemicals communicate and dispatch love in the body. Deprivation of joy and love lower dopamine and endorphin levels, and a powerless feeling lowers our serotonin level. The amount of energy that flows through the heart is controlled by self-love and relates to getting love needs met. Those who have heart disease may have never known self-love due to deprivation in childhood or perhaps withdrew love energy due to emotional stress in their lives. Being hurt emotionally breaks down the immune system, blocks the heart chakra or energy to the heart, and weakens this essential organ.

Fatty deposits in the coronary arteries are often deemed the culprits in heart disease. These fatty deposits block the flow of blood and narrow the coronary arteries of the heart. This narrowing can cause abnormal clotting or sudden rupture of the plaque. The rupture of this plaque caused by stress blocks the blood vessel and starves the heart muscle of blood, causing a heart attack.

Fatty deposits develop when a person does not feel safe. *As a protector, fat is sent out to areas of the body that need protection.* In effect, it clogs the arteries and blocks love to and from the heart. (When individuals are hurt, abandoned, betrayed, or do not feel good enough, they may feel that anyone can hurt them emotionally—a very unsafe feeling.) Once sent out to the arteries, fat transforms into hard plaque due to hardened thoughts like "love is a poison apple", or "I'm not lovable".

Think how your life would be if you healed the soul discoveries of heart disease? Your MO could be one of loving yourself at your core, treating yourself as a treasure, as one of the most precious gems in the world. You would feel good enough, be there for yourself, feel safe, and have your DNA Power. You would know how to feel and release anger or resentment every time and fulfill your need right on the spot. Your heart would be filled with joy and your body response would be euphoria! I imagine the *wisdom of heart disease* transforming our planet.

Universal Soul Discovery of Heart Disease
To love ourselves unconditionally.

What we learn in childhood about fairy-tale endings is often what we strive for in our lives. In reality, living can be difficult and our experiences around love painful. Once we've been hurt in some way, it's easy to shut down the energy to the heart chakra. This shutting down can start in the womb, be programmed throughout childhood, and continue up to the diagnosis of heart disease. The earliest memories of emotional deprivation of love leave the deepest imprint.

Dr. Arthur Janov, author of *The Biology of Love*, wrote:

Love is not just recommended; it is the sine qua non of child development. Love makes the brain develop in positive ways. When love is not made available early in life, the system "shrinks" and figuratively does not develop the proper 'love receptors'. The capacity to receive and give love will be diminished for a lifetime. In this sense, love is not an abstraction but a literal neurochemical event.[1]

When a child receives love, the natural chemicals serotonin and dopamine increase. Serotonin, dopamine, and endorphins—the biochemicals of love—are natural neurotransmitters that may alleviate the hurt we endure in our lives. These chemicals communicate and dispatch love in the body. A lack of love may block these natural chemicals that help us cope. All lack of love—as simple as not comforting a crying infant to extreme cases of mental or physical abuse—can set up a person for heart disease.

Heart problems are often triggered by losing a loved one, either through divorce or death. Grief, sadness, loneliness, and depression may all factor into shutting down the heart chakra. Still, the crux of all diseases may be the failure to love oneself. Many people are able to emanate love but can't receive it. A healthy heart chakra requires a balance of receiving and giving love.

Once you've reached the soul level and have acquired unconditional love for yourself using the MO Technique, no one can take it away. I insist that all my clients release lack of self-love first, as this emotional suffering is thought to be the core of every disease and the crux of heart disease. When you make decisions based on self-love, you don't give resentment, anger/rage, or powerlessness any strength to rupture arterial plaques or develop factors that weaken the heart. In fact, if you begin to love yourself soon enough, you may not have any arterial plaques to rupture!

The lessons of love—the message of heart disease—are the

most critical ones to learn on this planet. Given that it's the number one killer, why aren't we getting the message that self-love is crucial to a healthy heart?

Primary Risk Factors for Heart Disease

Here are the primary risk factors in the development of heart disease. Can you see how these factors might relate to the lack of self-love?

- Smoking
- Obesity
- Physical inactivity
- High cholesterol
- Diabetes mellitus
- High blood pressure

Smoking. Dr. Lincoln, in *Addictions and Cravings,* explained the reason people smoke this way: "They are feeling-suppressing, pain-blocking and joy-destroying, grief-deflecting, self-numbing. It is a self-disgust and self-destruction via attacking their own heart. It's a form of helplessness and rage, oral gratification, and self-medication for nurturance-starvation in reaction to intrauterine and subsequent maternal rejection."[2] People can actually come into the world with self-rejection stored in cellular memory from the womb. This self-rejection may create situations from infancy in which these individuals feel rejected in some way. So they are given the opportunity to conquer the soul discovery of self-love. Now that this information is available, we can see how smoking may be a trigger for heart disease. It's also a form of self-rejection and lack of self-love that can lead to heart disease.

Being overweight is one of the primary risk factors for heart disease. How does obesity relate to heart disease? Deprivation of love and not feeling safe and protected form the core emotional sufferings of those who are overweight or obese. The Common Thread cycle begins when deprivation causes resentment, powerlessness, and anger/rage, and self-rejection sets in. These individuals may numb out as a way to survive.

In the end, they may abandon themselves and eat too many things that may be psychologically nurturing to them but poor choices in terms of calories, fat and sugar content, and portion size. Overweight people may be craving love; food may be the substitute they use to try to fill the emptiness. It's likely that the absence of love deteriorates the heart. Obesity is therefore a factor in heart disease. It may be a failure to love oneself that creates the unhealthy eating pattern.

Physical inactivity is another primary risk factor for heart disease. Following simple logic, if you love yourself, exercise will be a priority for you. When you exercise, you take time out for yourself and nurture your body. Keeping physically fit pumps the blood and oxygenates the body, which is crucial for health. Exercising can also release resentment, anger/rage, and powerlessness from the body because you are releasing energy and taking charge of yourself. Exercise also tells your body that you are important—a way of saying, "I love you."

High cholesterol is a serious risk factor for heart disease. This book also has an in-depth chapter on cholesterol, but here's a brief synopsis of how cholesterol relates to heart disease. Individuals with high cholesterol have usually been raised in a rigid environment. They believe that life is one big problem to solve, so they just grin and bear it. This "grin and bear it" attitude may set up feelings of powerlessness that they can't solve life's one big problem. They may set up resentment and anger/rage. A strict attitude may have been programmed into cellular memory in childhood, which may have set the stage for lack of self-love and lack of joy. It's difficult to bring joy into one's life when every day one's thoughts revolve around the belief that life is just one long problem to solve. Arteriosclerosis often results when individuals have a profound fear of accepting and expressing joy. This fear blocks the life flow, providing an excellent foundation for the buildup of plaque, which then clogs the arteries and may trigger a heart attack.

Diabetes mellitus. The core emotional suffering of diabetes is lacking sweetness in life, which causes a lack of joy. This may stem from the programming of having to fend for oneself and having difficulty asking for help. The body responds to this programming by the cells not accepting the insulin that *helps* the glucose get into the cell to be used as fuel. Insulin doesn't heal diabetes. Rather, insulin receptors in the cells refuse to work, leading to diabetes because the soul discovery of diabetes is: bring joy into one's life and allow people to help. Glucose that can't get into cells becomes useless as a fuel source. When insulin won't help the glucose enter the cells, then the cells turn to other means of fuel—fats and protein. The resulting excess fat turns into ketones and makes the blood acidic. Use of excess proteins causes muscle wasting and weakness. This reacts with one's eyes, nervous system, kidney, and blood vessels—gradually setting up the environment for a weakened heart. When people experience self-love and learn the soul discoveries of diabetes, they can bring in the joy needed to not only help heal diabetes but also have a happy heart.

High blood pressure. The core emotional suffering of high blood pressure is suppressing one's anger/rage because of feeling a lack of control over one's life because there is never "enough time". Anger may build like a seething volcano and turn into rage, which can tighten the arteries of the whole system, causing blood pressure to rise. Of course, suppressing anger also blocks joy in life, which can cause artery problems that may turn into heart disease. The Common Thread for all the risk factors in heart disease is not loving oneself.

The Emotional Sufferings of Heart Disease

- Signature emotional suffering—Lack of self-love
- Lacking joy
- Feeling not good enough
- Feeling abandoned
- Feeling betrayed
- Unique emotional suffering
- The Common Thread—lack of self-love, resentment, anger/rage, powerlessness

As I've mentioned, I use the Win Aura System before and after each healing session to show the energy of the heart chakra. Nearly every client I've seen in the last 12 years has had a marked diminished energy to the heart chakra before the session. This means that almost every client could have had a potential for heart disease. These individuals may have been shutting down energy to the heart because of the emotional pain and hurt they'd been through—because they lacked self-love at their core.

To keep the heart chakra healthy, we first acknowledge that this chakra exists. Second, we can prevent attacks by knowing what causes the heart chakra to shut down. Third, we can protect the heart chakra by deflecting negative energy that comes toward us. To do that, we can image harsh words or feelings directed at us bouncing out into the universe. That way, we don't take on other people's negative energy. If a surprise attack catches us off guard and we've taken another person's negative energy, we can find it in our bodies and release it with the MO Technique.

Few of us are taught how to protect our heart chakras. I often see women taking on energy that's not theirs, primarily in their marriages and at work. More women are dying from heart attacks than all forms of cancer combined. Women are now in the workforce and simultaneously taking care of the responsibilities of family and home, which may overload their circuits. The Common Thread cycle sets in and weakens the heart.

As Dr. Gerber states, "Love is truly the great healer, for when it is absent, the heart chakra and eventually the physical heart tend to suffer dysfunction and dis-ease."[3]

Case History

Matt, 52, had gone to the emergency room several times with "heart spells". He had both high blood pressure and high cholesterol, and also suffered from sleep apnea (a cessation of breathing during sleep), which correlates with heart problems. Matt felt sure one day he would have the "big one". After all, his mother had recently died of a heart attack and both his parents had undergone two heart bypass surgeries. His father also developed diabetes and ended up with gangrene in one foot. He eventually died of a heart attack.

When Matt arrived for his first session, he announced that he was "doomed by his genes." I explained that our thoughts can precip-itate disease, and if he continued to think he was going to have a heart attack, his thoughts might make it happen. As for genetics, I also explained that emotional sufferings, or thought patterns, are passed down from generation to generation. These ideas greatly affect our DNA. Indeed, once the emotional suffering is released out of cellular memory, our DNA may change.

The one person in the family who avoids a genetic disease may be the one who doesn't take on the passed-down emotional suffering. Unfortunately, Matt had not been that person in his family, so the first thing to do was reprogram his way of thinking or MO. Then he'd stop putting energy into "being doomed".

Matt explained that his parents had had a turbulent relationship. His father had been an alcoholic, and Matt remembered having to stop him from beating his mother several times. His parents had eight children including Matt, and paid little attention to each child. Even when he'd ask for his mother's time, she would say, "later." Of course, later never came. Matt never felt loved by his parents.

He eventually married a woman with a similar background—an alcoholic father and an overwhelmed mother. Matt and his wife both felt unlovable, so their commonality was being "wounded partners". Even in his marriage, Matt didn't feel loved. He tried to fill this void by working hard—and succeeded in making millions of dollars. He purchased a magnificent home and many expensive toys. When this failed to make him happy, he bought more. He couldn't figure out how he could be so unhappy when he had so much.

When people grow up feeling unloved, how can they possibly love themselves at their core? Many don't know how. They don't even know they're supposed to. As a society, many of us have not been taught to love ourselves, and this has been true generation after generation. Perhaps this sad legacy makes heart disease the number one killer. It's time to learn how to love ourselves so heart disease can be eradicated.

In Matt's session, he released lack of self-love, lack of joy, self-rejection, powerlessness, anger/rage, and feeling not good enough out of his cellular memory. He also released the belief that he was undeserving and that love was a "poison apple". Finally, Matt released the belief that he was doomed. All of his images were located in his heart. At the soul level, he instilled unconditional love for himself.

Matt later told me he had felt lightness in his heart area when he released these emotional sufferings. He knew at a deep level the material things in his life would never bring him the joy he needed. Matt saw at his soul level that helping others would help bring him joy. He was excited to recreate his life to match his inside joy to the outside world. Using the Win Aura System before the session, I could see that Matt's energy to the heart was barely visible. After his healing sessions, the energy of the heart chakra filled in completely.

As mentioned, Matt also suffered from sleep apnea. Each symptom and disease strives to give a message. If we don't get it, the symptom won't merely give up and go away; rather it finds another way to get our attention.

According to Dr. Lincoln, sleep apnea is a consequence of maternal deprivation. In his view, deprived individuals are:

...intensely fearful and longing for mother love or love from someone close. They are overworked and very angry and bitter about that. But at the same time, they dare not express or even acknowledge these feelings out of the total rejection and abandonment they experienced. There is a great deal of deep-seated guilt, shame, and grief arising out of this, and they are joy-avoidant, happiness-squashing, and love-deflecting all in the misguided hope of finally earning some love. In effect, they are self-suppressing and suffocating themselves.[4]

Can you see how these feelings could lead to heart disease?

Matt felt bitter and angry that he had to work so hard. Although he had many material rewards, love is what he really wanted. In fact, if Matt had healed the emotional sufferings of his first problem of high cholesterol instead of just taking a medication for it, it may have saved him from developing high blood pressure, sleep apnea, or heart problems.

Rampant heart disease broadcasts the soul discovery of needing self-love in our society loud and clear. We have lots of work to do, yes, but the rewards are infinite. If, as a society, we could learn our collective soul discovery and achieve self-love, perhaps we could eradicate disease and peace would become possible.

Dr. Lincoln wrote, "Individuals with heart problems constantly put out reams of heart energy and service in the heart of their heart and they dream someone will be there for them someday. They are unable to manifest agape and universal love and to process love."[5] But these qualities have to start with the inner heart or self-love. When you learn self-love, you'll always be there for yourself, which attracts people to be there for you also. You can then manifest agape—the purest kind of love.

Adult children of alcoholics can also be afraid of intimacy, causing feelings to be suppressed, and have difficulty forming close intimate relationships. This can manifest as heart disease. Children of alcoholic may take the following paths, according to literature from Adult Children of Alcoholics:

- Become people-pleasers to protect themselves and lose their identity in the process.
- Find a way (such as being a workaholic) to relieve their feelings of abandonment.
- Develop dependent personalities terrified of abandonment.
- Choose insecure relationships because they matched their childhood relationships.
- Stuff feelings as children and keep them buried as adults. They confuse love with pity, tending to love those they can rescue.
- Become self-defeating and addicted to excitement in all of their affairs, preferring constant upset.

Suppressed grief. Grief stored and not released often resides in the chest and eventually causes dysfunction in the heart chakra.

Dr. Gerber wrote, "Depending upon the specific impediment, disease will manifest in the organ that most closely resonates with the chakra ruling the particular difficult lesson. When the difficult lesson being learned by the personality involves being able to love others and feel love for oneself, blockages of energy flow through the heart chakra can manifest as physical afflictions of the heart, thymus gland, bronchial tubes, and lungs."[6]

We are only here to learn and grow. Soul discoveries will be continually presented or mirrored until they're learned. A healthy heart houses self-love and joy. Why not know of our soul discoveries and go through the lessons joyfully and keep our hearts healthy?

Give yourself the greatest gift—the gift of self-love!

Chapter 22: Hepatitis C

"We cannot rise higher than our thought of ourselves."
– Orison Swett Marden

The Disease

Hepatitis C virus (HCV) invades the liver and is transmitted primarily by blood and blood products. Hepatitis is a Latin word meaning inflamed liver.

The Soul Discovery and MO of Hepatitis C

The soul discovery of hepatitis C is to believe in oneself. People who suffer with this disease, experience a deep-seated self-doubt that arose from a family who expected too much of them at a young age. The self-doubt may be instilled from a non-supportive family and cause competence-anxiety and feelings of powerlessness. The self-doubt and non-support can create resentment and anger/rage that gets stored in the liver.

Inflamed thinking or self-attack may cause the inflammation of the liver. Once inflamed, toxins and wastes build up in the liver due to the lack of life force (our innate energy to cope) or lack of energy needed to remove them. Emotional blocks such as self-doubt can cause energetic, psychological, and physical metabolic changes in the body tissues and circulatory system.

Any kind of self-attack may affect the heart. Depression or loneliness may also create blockage to this chakra, which can cause a loss of glandular function. The immune system may weaken and allow the virus to attack. The liver involves the third chakra or our personal power, which includes self-esteem and self-confidence. This chakra also entails the emotional issues of fear and trust, and how we feel supported in the world. Self-doubt, competence anxiety, not feeling supported, lack of trust, and difficulty coping can block the life-force energy of this chakra. The filtering system of the liver then gets blocked and hepatocytes (liver cells) fail to tell the cells what to do. These cells become scarred or die altogether. Then blood, our life force, can't flow freely through the liver and becomes blocked, causing the liver to malfunction. In this state, the liver is unable to filter and may release the virus into the blood.

Our liver is essential to life itself. Without the survival tools of self-confidence, competence, and ability to cope and support ourselves, it may not be able to function properly. A traumatic event or loss may trigger the anger/rage and powerlessness feeling. This sets up The Common Thread involving the heart and third chakra, allowing the virus to attack those individuals whose soul discovery is to master competence-anxiety, release self-doubt, support themselves, and competently manifest and cope with their intended destiny.

The Universal Soul Lesson of Hepatitis C Virus
To believe in oneself.

Approximately 170 million people worldwide and 4 million in the United States are infected with the hepatitis C virus (HCV). It has been called the silent epidemic and silent killer, for it can reside in the body for 40 years or more before symptoms occur and the disease can be diagnosed.

Our early childhood programming may set up the emotions that cause hepatitis C and eventually cause the thymus gland to malfunction. Eventually, an adverse event later in life may trigger the virus to erupt, which may be why the virus can lie dormant in the body for years. According to the National Institutes for Health, chronic HCV is now the most common reason for liver transplantation and leading cause in the United States for developing liver cancer.[1] This disease differs dramatically in every individual who contracts it. Some will have minimal liver damage and never develop complications. Others will have cirrhosis of the liver and develop end-stage liver disease. But what are the variables that predict who will experience life-threatening liver disease as a result of hepatitis C?

Many writers and researchers have attempted to address this question. The liver, wrote Louise Hay in *Heal Your Body*, is the seat of anger and primitive emotions.[2] Energy healer Julie Motz stated that on an emotional level the liver is thought to hold unexpressed anger.[3] Dr. Gerber wrote:

> According to the Chinese five element theory, the organs of the body are connected with a certain emotion or emotional state. . . . For instance, the liver is associated with the emotion of anger, while the emotion of excessive fear is thought to be connected with the kidneys. As such, in Chinese Medicine, someone with a great deal of repressed anger due to a sense of overwhelming responsibility might be expected to develop liver problems due to a solar plexus blockage.[4]

The solar plexus is where our DNA (Dynamic Natural Authentic) Power is stored. When it's programmed with self-doubt, people may feel inferior and live with low self-esteem, displaying a lack of confidence that creates the competence-anxiety. The loss of personal power can stem from constant criticism about who they are. These individuals may be overwhelmed by too much responsibility placed on them at a young age, continuing as a habitual pattern throughout their lives.

Julie Motz wrote that bone marrow, at the very core of the skeleton, regenerating our blood, carries love.[5] Our blood is our life force that carries the emotion love and sustains us. Hepatitis C affects the liver with its message to heal stored resentment and anger/rage due to the self-defeating patterns, then it may attack the blood. The body allows the immune system to weaken, leaving room for the virus to attack. According to Dr. Lincoln, any viral infection sets in when people harbor "a feeling like everything is one long series of responsibilities and that there is no joy in their life. They are in effect utterly unable to experience the beauty, good, and joy of the universe."[6] Physician Mona Lisa Schultz wrote, "How well your life's blood flows through your heart, arteries, and veins is linked to the degree to which joy flows through your life."[7] Therefore, lack of joy sets up The Common Thread (powerlessness, resentment, anger/rage, and lack of self-love), which in turn can damage the liver and restrict the blood flow.

Three factors that contribute to hepatitis C are:

- Blood transfusions before 1990 (after 1990, the blood gets routinely tested for this virus). Screening of blood donations was implemented in the U.S. in May 1990 when a reliable blood test became available to check for hepatitis C.
- Sharing objects or needles that could carry the infected blood and pass it on. Objects include razors, earrings, toothbrushes, gum, etc. Sharing needles for body piercing, tattoos, acupuncture, shots, or even sharing straws for cocaine. Alcohol abuse can also contribute.
- Transmissions through sexual intercourse or mother-to-baby during pregnancy.

Blood transfusions. For a person to have to receive a blood transfusion, it's reasonable to assume a traumatic event has happened. That traumatic event can set off the powerlessness and anger/rage that breaks down the immune system and allows a virus to attack. This virus will attack those whose souls need to learn the soul discoveries of hepatitis C—including being able to cope with life's demands when traumatic life events occur. In fact, that may be why some who received blood transfusions before 1990 did not get hepatitis C. Testing for this virus in blood transfusion since 1990 has not stopped the disease. More than 35,000 people in the United States develop this disease each year.

Sharing objects or needles. For those who contract hepatitis C through illegal drug use, this may signify they have low self-esteem and reject themselves. The self-rejection or self-attack may be exactly why the virus attacks. This also applies to those who abuse alcohol.

Sexual contact. This poses a potential risk for spreading the disease, especially for those with many partners, while those in long-term relationships with one partner have low risk. Dr. Lincoln wrote, "Those having sex with many partners are engaged in worth - and validation-seeking."[8] This can be another indication of low self-esteem, which can trigger this disease.

Hepatitis C rarely passes from mother to baby. But there's a greater risk to the baby if the mother has HCV and is HIV positive. Chapter 10 on HIV explains that those who have HIV may strongly believe they're not good enough, leading to self-rejection.

Do you recognize a double conviction of self-rejection with both diseases, which may be passed on to the baby as a soul discovery? Emotions can be handed down in the womb; the soul decides which ones will be picked up.

The Emotional Sufferings of Hepatitis C

- Signature emotional suffering—Low self-esteem
- Experiencing competence anxiety
- Difficulty coping with life's demands
- Feeling abandoned
- Feeling unsupported
- Feeling betrayed
- Feeling overly responsible
- Feeling guilty
- Hopeless, helpless feeling
- Lack of trust

- Unique emotional suffering
- The Common Thread — powerlessness, resentment, anger/rage, and lack of self-love

In 1990, country music star Naomi Judd was struck with hepatitis C and given just three years to live. Today, she is in remission, which may be partly due to learning the soul discoveries that hepatitis C presented to her.

Naomi survived poverty and domestic violence, and has endured harsh lessons involving the soul discoveries of hepatitis C. In an article titled "Naomi Judd's Voyage of Self Discovery", Lydia P. Boyle wrote, "By now in her 20s, married and divorced, she was living in Hollywood with her daughters, Wynona and Ashley, on welfare. They were so poor; they didn't even have a car, that is a necessity in Southern California. Judd says at this point she felt responsible for her parents' divorce and her brother's death. 'On a scale of 1 to 10, my self-esteem was around 2, she remembers now."[9] Naomi's low self-esteem, feeling responsible, and a hopeless, helpless feeling may have been the emotional component of hepatitis C for her.

If a soul discovery for certain individuals is to gain competence and cope with life's demands, situations will be mirrored to them many times over in their life so they can learn it.

If the flu gets healed at the minor stage and the soul discovery of a virus learned, people may never develop hepatitis C because at that point The Common Thread of Disease would be released and self-love would be their foundation.

As a society, many people take prescribed antidepressants without ever fixing the underlying problem of feeling hopeless and helpless. We mask the soul discovery by taking a drug instead of removing symptoms. Yet symptoms act as a compass to direct us to the real problem being manifested in the disease.

Today, Naomi is in remission. In her journey of healing, she has written a book called *Naomi's Breakthrough Guide*. In fact, she has used some of the esteemed healers of our time as well as members of the scientific community to help her heal. She meditates and believes in guided imagery. She is teaching others what the hepatitis C body symptoms were sent to tell her. She is a self-esteem coach not only for herself but in sharing that information with others. "Judd says self-esteem begins with trust, and we begin to trust as infants."[10]

In this book, she wrote, "Self-esteem is about how well you appreciate and value yourself. Self-love is truly the magic wand that can keep you on the right path, prevent illness from taking hold, and make current problems solvable."[11] She wrote that real security comes from within and advises readers to honor their intuition or inner wisdom, to take risks and believe that God has a higher purpose and bigger dream for us than we have. "I'm living proof that all of our difficulties can be the stepping stones to self-actualization and fulfillment,"[12] she declared. These beliefs and practices may have helped Naomi's hepatitis C go into remission.

Naomi Judd wrote the song *Love Can Build a Bridge* inspired by Paul Overstreet, a Christian singer, who said, "Sometimes the only way we can cross life's great divide is to let love build a bridge."

Chapter 23: ALS Disease

"Abilities wither under faultfinding, blossom with encouragement."
– Donald A. Laird

The Disease
ALS (amyotrophic lateral sclerosis), or Lou Gehrig's Disease, attacks the nerve cells in the brain and spinal cord, usually resulting in a complete shutdown or paralysis of the body.

The Soul Discovery and MO of ALS
Individuals with this disease have difficulty feeling successful inside, no matter how successful they are on the outside. Their soul discovery is to acknowledge their self-worth and be accepted. Look at the end stages of Lou Gehrig's: Usually a complete shutdown or paralysis of the body results, signifying how these individuals may feel on the inside.

No cure has been discovered for this disease. Those who develop Lou Gehrig's appear to be highly successful. *They become successful because they work tirelessly to gain acceptance.* However, if they've been programmed to feel unworthy and have no real self-acceptance, it's easy to understand why the muscles and backbone that move us forward—the support system of the body—might deteriorate.

This disease attacks the nerve cells in the brain and spinal cord, possibly from these people suppressing the "unacceptable" aspects of themselves and not connecting with their true feelings. Clients I have seen were taught not to show their feelings and were punished if they did. The thought process of the non-acceptance programming causes the nerves, our vehicles for feeling, to become numb.

In everyone else's eyes, ALS sufferers may seem to have it all. But, inwardly their MO may be feeling like a failure. *The outward life may not match the inward one—which is why this disease has been so difficult to get a grip on.* Following is how an ALS sufferer may feel inside.

The Emotional Sufferings of Lou Gehrig's Disease

- Signature emotional suffering—Deep need for acceptance
- Not feeling worthy
- Not feeling good enough
- Difficulty feeling success
- Needing hands-on control
- Unique emotional suffering
- The Common Thread—lack of self-love, powerlessness, resentment, anger/rage

Now what would you feel like if you knew at a very deep level that you are a success no matter what happens in your life? It's been written that failure is nothing but the first step to something better or a step closer to success. For those with Lou Gehrig's disease, success comes from first accepting themselves. Once they accept themselves unconditionally, success soon follows. How would their body respond? By contacting their true feelings and accepting themselves, the cells of the brain and spinal column would radiate, not deteriorate.

Universal Soul Discovery of Lou Gehrig's Disease
To learn that success is the total acceptance of oneself.

In this disease, the conditional love of the parent or caregiver may set up feelings of non-acceptance, causing sufferers to feel "not worthy" or "not good enough". No matter how hard they try, they feel unsuccessful because they weren't accepted by a parent or authority figure they adore. This programming may cause The Common Thread to be set up in the body. As the resentment builds, an event triggers the powerlessness and anger/rage, which eventually erupts as a disease in the body.

On June 19, 1939, his 36th birthday, Lou Gehrig was told he had amyotrophic lateral sclerosis or ALS. This is a fatal neuromuscular disease that later—because of his renown—came to bear his name. Characterized by progressive muscle weakness, it results in paralysis and, ultimately, in death. When Lou Gehrig was told he had ALS, he was basically handed a slow and agonizing death sentence. In his famous farewell speech to his baseball career, he said, "Today, I am the luckiest man on the face of the earth." Understanding the the emotional component of Lou Gehrig's disease explains why this man who suffered from this disease would *say* he was lucky.

Lou Gehrig died on June 2, 1941, just 17 days short of his 38th birthday.

Lou Gehrig's disease can result from an individual's failure to acknowledge self-worth and an extremely deep need for acceptance. According to Dr. Lincoln the psychological meaning of ALS is as follows:

They deny their success and they are totally unwilling to accept their self-worth. Very clearly, especially the mother conveyed that any form of self-manifestation or success in the world and commitment elsewhere would be committing the ultimate betrayal, would destroy the family and this immobilizes them. This got started at a time when there was no difference between their mother and the universe, so if they recognized their self-worth or sought success they would be destroying God and all its creation. So to avoid the 'ultimate calamity' they sacrificed themselves.[1]

As I interviewed clients with Lou Gehrig's and discovered their *modus operandi*, I found this definition applies. How does it relate to Lou Gehrig himself? How was he programmed? Why did he end up with this devastating disease?

I have used Lou Gehrig's life history to illustrate one way this disease may be programmed into the body. This theory may provide a new perspective on ALS. Perhaps we can now ask the right questions to help those with this disease: Do you accept yourself completely? Do you feel successful? Do you feel good enough and worthy?

Lou's mother, Christina, a German immigrant, had four children and lost three of them as babies. Only Lou survived infancy. With the family deeply hurt by these losses, Lou became the center of the universe. His mother wanted to keep him all to herself and even ruined all of his girlfriend relationships. It was said that no one thought he would marry because he was so in love with his mother. Lou didn't marry until he turned 30.

Christina worked tirelessly cleaning houses, cooking for the wealthy, and taking in laundry to make ends meet. Lou's dad, in poor health, had a hard time finding work. Jonathan Eig, author of *Luckiest Man, The Life and Death of Lou Gehrig*, wrote that, "If there were a Hall of Fame for mamma's boys, Gehrig would have been a shoo-in."[2] To Lou, the "muscular, unemotional" Christina was a heroine. "He would write her when the team went on the road, and when he returned, he would greet her on the train platform with long hugs and tender kisses."[3]

Lou worked alongside his mother at a young age, so he didn't have a lot of playtime. But when he did, Lou played baseball, soccer, and football. Although he loved and lived for sports, Lou was programmed with comments from his mother, who thought sports were a waste of time.[4]

Lou was known to be ambitious, but shy and insecure. Being born of German immigrants, he was frequently ridiculed and felt unworthy because of his lack of social polish. In *Lou Gehrig, the Luckiest Man*, David Adler wrote, "Christina Gehrig had great hopes for her son Lou. She dreamed that he would attend college and become an accountant or an engineer."[5] When Lou quit college and signed up with the Yankees (pro baseball team), "Lou's mother was furious. She was convinced that he was ruining his life."[6]

In *Lou Gehrig Baseball Legends*, Norman L. Macht wrote:

In 1927, the Yankees won 110 games, a league record that stood for 27 years. Then they swept the Pittsburgh Pirates in a World Series that Gehrig almost missed. His mother was still his best girl, and he did not hesitate to let the world know it. Gravely ill, she needed an operation at the time of the Series, and Gehrig felt it most important to be at her side, rather than with the team. Christina Gehrig and Michael Huggins persuaded him to play in the Series.[7]

Lou was always trying his hardest to be accepted, specifically by his beloved mother who couldn't understand that baseball was his life. To someone who has a deep need for acceptance, negative comments about one's passion can be understandably devastating. *Any* success for Lou would be the ultimate betrayal, a belief that represents a significant emotional suffering of Lou Gehrig's disease.

Macht gave many insights into Gehrig's character. He wrote, "Lou was shy and lacked confidence to be a leader."[8] In spite of this shyness, "Gehrig's .373 batting average and league-leading 175 RBIs earned him the American League's Most Valuable Player Award."[9] But he "never got used to his popularity and did not handle it well."[10]

Yet Gehrig was one of the most talented and greatest baseball players of all time. Being successful presents the ultimate paradox. Individuals with Lou Gehrig's disease are most often highly successful people *but one reason they're highly successful may be because they work tirelessly to gain acceptance.*

As previously mentioned, in everyone else's eyes, ALS sufferers may seem to have it all. But regardless of what they've accomplished, inwardly they may feel like failures. This makes aspects of Lou Gehrig's disease confusing because the *outward* life doesn't match the *inward* one.

An adverse event frequently triggers the disease to erupt in the body, usually happening six months to a year before diagnosis. Lou's programming of non-acceptance leading to resentment may have been set up in his body throughout his life. What may have caused the powerlessness and the anger/rage that may have triggered the disease in his body?

Eig wrote that, "In 1938, things were different. Over the next eight games, Gehrig continued to play miserably, striking out six times and accumulating only four hits."[11] "Fans in Philadelphia and Washington took to mocking Gehrig when he came to bat, something they would never have dared before. Lou couldn't let things roll easily off his shoulders." "He dropped from fourth to sixth spot in the lineup. It was reported in *The New York Times* his batting average was .133—the worst hitter in the American League."[12] Gehrig went from all-star player and movie star to the biggest slump of his career in 1938, approximately one year before his diagnosis of ALS. Did this event make Lou Gehrig feel like such a failure that it erupted the disease in his body? Those who attract this disease use hands-on control extensively as a major survival tool. So when an individual loses control (such as when Lou's performance slumped), the body starts to do the same thing—that is, lose control. This can be only a theory; the one to know would be Lou himself.

Lou called himself "lucky" through humility and grace, but most likely because of his deep need to be accepted. He wanted to please people so much; that may be why he said he was lucky even though he had a fatal disease.

I believe that our soul discoveries are a pre-determined soul contract that we sign up for in the school of life—sometimes arriving in the form of disease. I also believe we can learn the soul discoveries and prevent it from taking hold if we know what it's trying to tell us. With ALS sufferers, the disease becomes part of their soul work, their contract to feel worthy of their success. Most important, it's imperative for them to accept themselves at the deepest level, the soul level.

The disease usually starts with stiffness and muscle weakness. The psychological meaning of stiffness is they are displaying rigid and stiff thinking. They are of the conviction that "one strike and I'm out!" According to Dr. Lincoln, muscle problems indicate:

- Confronting unsettling memories
- Dealing with issues and feelings associated with success
- Feeling immobilized

Such issues arise from an intense self-distrust that encourages these people to stay around the family who programmed them to be simultaneously super-successful (for the family *only*) and to otherwise fail. With the MO Technique, this first symptom can be treated and the issues and feelings associated with success would be addressed at this stage.

Often one of the first symptoms is tripping frequently. Our feet help us step forward. Dr. Lincoln wrote:

A problem with the right foot indicates they have a hard time stepping forward in life. Relationship concerns–They have deep conflicts over how to get life and love support. The left foot indicates–"Sealed Unit"–they are handicapped with vulnerability issues, unwillingness to receive support and refusal to allow themselves to be taken care of by the Universe or other people.[13] The right leg indicates an individual is experiencing issues in the realm of love, not enough love or they are commitment and relationship avoidant, as a result of being forever fettered to their mother. They have a hard time standing up for themselves. Left leg is they are manifesting support issues in the form that they aren't supported.[14]

It would be interesting to see if this rang true for Lou.

Lou's symptoms started with leg stiffness. When people have stiffness in the legs, they may feel ungrounded and may feel they have difficulty impacting the world. They may fear the future and not take risks to climb the ladder of success and make a "stand" for themselves. Can you see that if individuals learned the soul discoveries of leg stiffness and released The Common Thread of Disease, the disease might not progress?

The right side of the body is the masculine side, which generates power and authority in the world. When a problem lies with the right side, the person may have difficulty manifesting his or her power. During Gehrig's hitting slump in 1938, was he feeling this way?

Problems with the left side of the body in males "represents the negative impact of the mother and the maternal and all aspects of the receptive mode. Finally it also reflects the distortions of their manifestation of masculine nobility, power, creativity, and initiative by the negative impact of their dysfunctional family."[15] Was this true for Lou?

It was noted that Lou had hurt feelings toward his father and resented that his father didn't work as hard as his mother. This may be partially why Gehrig had difficulty with male authority figures and became so emotionally connected to his mother.

Mostly, ALS attacks the spinal cord, which supports the whole body. When individuals have a problem with the spine, they may have been systematically undermined in their confidence. Lou wasn't supported for his passion with sports by either parent. This may have affected his brain. Why? Because of serious conflicts between what he signed up to do (his soul contract) and what he was accomplishing. Problems with one's brain may indicate that it's time to work on divine purpose or soul intentions.

In ALS, paralysis eventually ensues. This may result from the sufferer's programming of being unacceptable. In addition to eventually immobilizing the individual, ALS can also attack the hands, speech, swallowing, breathing, and all the voluntary muscles—all related to the lesson of accepting who one is at the soul level.

Let me make it clear that Lou didn't get his disease because of his mother or father. Rather, he (and any individual who acquires this disease) may have signed up to be programmed with conditional acceptance as one of his soul discoveries. With this knowledge and information, we can start learning our soul discoveries at the symptom stage instead of masking symptoms while the underlying disease continues unabated.

Case History 1

One of my clients, Bart, was diagnosed with Lou Gehrig's disease, which was affecting his right side and moved to his left. He also participated in physical and occupational therapy. Bart related unequivocally to the message of Lou Gehrig's disease—that is, when he released his "not feeling successful", he imaged a picture of his mother. Like Lou Gehrig, Bart loved his mother dearly. He'd been programmed with conditional love and felt both overly responsible and under-appreciated.

Bart's constant need for approval kept him from deepening the relationship with his wife and others. He said he always suppressed feelings of closeness to people when, in fact, closeness is what he craved most. Everything he did focused on getting approval from others. At a soul level, he saw that he had a great fear of trusting that it was okay to be who he was. As he did the work of releasing his emotional sufferings with the MO Technique he began to listen to himself and trust himself more. He felt that it was okay to be who he was. This was a start for him to feel successful.

Case History 2

George, 58, had been having problems with restless leg syndrome and balance problems. At work, he'd fall down suddenly, creating embarrassment and shame. His physician prescribed a medication but couldn't find what caused George's symptoms. Experience has taught me that not releasing these symptoms out of cellular memory can eventually lead to a more serious illness such as Lou Gehrig's disease.

According to Dr. Lincoln, restless leg syndrome happens to those who'd say, "I'm all I've got. One strike and I'm out." So their survival tool becomes hands-on control. The individual may be sick and tired of the demands of too much responsibility and account-ability. They were meant to be the 'sane' ones in their families, but sanity wasn't attainable, thus setting them up for non-acceptance and for contracting a disease in which they lose control over their bodies (like ALS sufferers). The body is giving a strong message to bring the desire for control into balance.

To the outside world, George had it all: a successful career, promi-nence, a winning personality. He was well liked and much admired. Yet his internal life was another matter. His dream and passion was to be a writer, but it never manifested because his mother told him his "dream" would never pay the bills. So George didn't pursue his passion, but he thought about it all the time. He resented the work he did, but needing acceptance, he didn't delegate, taking on all the responsibility of the job. Resentful that no one volunteered to help him, still, he was incapable of asking for help. As a result, George felt unworthy and unsuccessful, despite all of his achievements.

The trigger for the balance problems appeared when George was asked to take early retirement. He'd sacrificed a great deal and given his "all" to a company that no longer wanted him. For George, who thrived on acceptance, this was devastating. Most ALS patients have difficulty accepting themselves at their core and when, on top of that, the outside world doesn't accept them, their bodies may begin failing.

George and I discussed the idea that perhaps the Universe allowed him to retire with good pay so he could pursue his real passion. We applied all the steps of the MO Technique, and in one session, he released feelings of unworthiness, not feeling successful, and not being good enough. At the soul level, he instilled self-love and acceptance. When George came back for his second session, he was shocked that his balance problems had disappeared. I explained that the MO Technique not only brings about psychological changes in the body but physiological ones as well.

Lou also told his beloved wife that he wondered if he could ever feel worthy of her. He kept the "unworthy" programming up all the way to his farewell speech. In fact, he said he'd give a month's pay to get out of the ceremony honoring him.

Love and Life Purpose

As we raise our children to become "successful," it's imperative we not put conditions on their progress. We cannot withhold approval, believing that children will do better because they'll strive for more. This may set them up for approval-seeking behavior and ultimately disease. Instead, fully loving and supporting our children—accepting them for exactly who they are—teaches them how to love and accept themselves.

Using Dr. Lincoln's work in my practice has taught me that what people show to the outside world may differ greatly from how they really feel inside. That's why it's been so hard to heal the diseases discussed in this book. *The outward life does not match the inward one.* This may help us to see disease in a whole new light. We now may be able to halt these incurable diseases, and learn our soul discoveries in the process. As we learn our soul discoveries, we create a more loving world because we learn to love and accept ourselves first.

If conditional love and acceptance can affect the body so drastically, imagine what unconditional love and acceptance can do. Lou Gehrig's life purpose was not only to be a baseball legend and hero; *it was to present this disease to the world so we could learn from it.*

I consider one of my life purposes to be educating others not only about Lou Gehrig's disease but about the the psychological meaning and soul discoveries of all diseases in the hope of showing how they can be prevented and healed. In my lifetime, I know at my soul level that we'll see the prevention and healing of ALS as a truth, rather than a hope.

Chapter 24: Menopause

"The emotional, sexual and psychological stereotyping of females begins when the doctor says, 'It's a girl.'"
– Shirley Chisholm

The Condition
Although menstruation stops naturally, the resulting state of menopause is a condition that can include adverse symptoms.

The Soul Discovery and MO of Menopause
Menopause is a natural process of the aging female body; however, problems associated with this process may be caused by feeling that one must "earn" one's acceptance and by preventing the creative power of the feminine to be birthed. The soul discoveries of the adverse symptoms of menopause are to accept oneself and embrace one's feminine power.

Menopause—the "change of life" that usually occurs in a woman's 50s—is natural and expected, yet women have varying experiences with menopause. Interestingly, some women glide right through without difficulties. Others have irritability, mood swings, hot flashes, sleep problems, and bodily changes. Women who bear these symptoms may have been programmed to be the "mother of the house" at a young age, and the father may have filled his void of female energy through his daughter. Some of the women I've seen in my practice appear feminine in their looks, but they see themselves as more masculine (believing they can "do it all"). Therefore, the creative power they put out to the world has masculine tendencies. This confusion of the feminine/masculine balance can contribute to menopause symptoms.

The women with menopausal problems I've seen as clients were all raised in families in which they experienced love as being highly conditional. As children, they learned the only way to gain acceptance was by continually "overdoing". But no matter how hard they tried, the acceptance they craved never came, so they typically recreated the same scenario in their marriage or relationships because of its familiarity. This kept the cycle of trying to gain acceptance going.

For some women, menopause also signifies the loss of being able to procreate, ending "girlhood", which can be particularly significant in cultures that celebrate youth. One hundred years ago, when life expectancy was around age 47, menopause meant that a woman's life neared its end. But with women living 30 to 40 years longer than their great-grandmothers ever did, we can look at menopause as a new surge of energy at mid-life. It can be a time of freedom, offering opportunities to tap into our feminine creative power and make it especially fulfilling. We simply have to learn the soul discoveries of menopause.

Menopause sometimes brings on a fear of aging and, for some women, feelings that they are no longer lovable or desirable. They may have feelings of abandonment, seeing themselves displaced by women much younger than they are. Because of childhood programming, they may feel not good enough and reject themselves, thus adverse menopausal symptoms could stem from the rejection or non-acceptance of self.

The Universal Soul Discovery of Menopause
To embrace the acceptance of the feminine and the power of the feminine.

The Emotional Sufferings of Menopause

- Signature emotional suffering—Feeling they have to earn their acceptance
- Having difficulty with their feminine power
- Being the "mother of the house" at an early age

- Being afraid of aging
- Feeling not good enough
- Feeling abandoned
- Not pursuing creative work
- Unique emotional suffering
- The Common Thread—resentment, anger/rage, power-lessness, lack of self-love

I remember welcoming this phase of my life. That's when I started creating this book and began feeling more fulfilled than ever.

As with everything, if we understand the soul discoveries of hot flashes and other symptoms, we can prevent them. Although taking medication may cause symptoms to subside, their real cause is rarely addressed. What are these causes?

For some women, hot flashes are as enjoyable as sticking a finger in a pan of hot grease! A hot flash happens when the body heats up dramatically and quickly. The face and neck may become flushed, red blotches may appear on the skin, and heavy sweating can occur followed by cold shivering.

I believe a hot flash is the body's response to anger/rage that explodes when a woman thinks about a situation she deems unfair. When one of my friends was having hot flashes, I asked her what she was thinking about every time she felt one. Each time she had one, she was thinking about a wedding she was orchestrating. Her hot flash reflected her anger about being the "woman who has to do it all". On a conscious level, she was pretending everything was fine, but that day, she saw how her hot flashes related to her emotions.

Another friend described her hot flash as sweating profusely one minute and freezing the next. "Hot" means burning up about something and "cold" signifies being afraid of the anger. Women who suffer this adverse symptom of menopause may have learned in their family that it was bad to feel anger. Because acting it out only made things worse, they retreated into their core, causing the hot/cold sensations.

Anger can build up in the body when we're raised in a patriarchal society and have been discriminated against or exploited. The woman may feel overly responsible, convinced that everything is left up to her to do or it won't get done. I know many women who feel this way. These feelings build up if we've been rejected, shamed, treated unfairly, or abused. If we retain anger about how our lives have gone (like a victim), then anger and resentment builds.

Hot flashes reflect the body's response to the anger/rage combined with femininity issues. Releasing the resentment and anger/rage using the MO Technique every time it comes up will help prevent a build up of hot flashes. You can also stop a hot flash as quickly as it comes on by acknowledging the anger/rage and powerlessness you are feeling in the moment and releasing it and fulfilling your need.

Why do some women end up having a hysterectomy and some do not? Those who have hysterectomies may be experiencing a rejection of the feminine. The uterus is the seat of our feminine power. Having to remove it may mean rejecting one's creative feminine part. According to Dr. Lincoln, excessive bleeding from the uterus is "seething leakage" or a lot of undirected anger that is draining out the joy of life. A problem with the uterus is a feeling that says, "I don't dare manifest my creativity due to fear of rejection and abandonment." The feminine was greatly feared and devalued by those in the family.[1] These women believed they had no recourse. The intense anger they were subjected to could have been passive-aggressive so that the child didn't even understand what was happening. Perhaps she believed it was unsafe to use her feminine power for fear of rejection or abandonment.

One client told me she was diagnosed with cancer in the lining of her uterus after her husband told her she just wasn't fun anymore. Likely the problem was really his, but my client felt deep pain. She questioned her feminine nature and role as an intimate partner, becoming self-rejecting and intensely angry. Her anger may have triggered the cancer when she allowed herself to feel powerless. Questioning her feminine nature may be why it ended up in the uterus. Once she released her anger/rage and feelings of powerlessness plus understood what may have erupted the cancer cells, she felt much better about the situation and her surgery was successful.

Hormone Therapy

There is much controversy about using hormones to relieve adverse symptoms of menopause. Menopausal hormone therapy (MHT) or hormone replacement therapy (HRT) comes with unknown risks. Let's look at the psychological meaning of hormone problems.

Low estrogen levels. This may result from a woman suppressing feminine qualities as a result of viewing her feminine role model as weak or having no mother role model at all. Low estrogen could also be from taking on the qualities of a man due to a father who was a strong role model. It may come from a family where women were put down and children were ruled in a patri-archal way. For instance, my father told me I had the ugliest knees he had ever seen. Repeatedly, he beat and verbally abused my mother in front of us children. These kinds of patriarchal, power-abusing authoritarian actions can set women up for having estrogen problems.

As we come into the heart chakra era in the next few years, the feminine and masculine will become more balanced. Currently, we're dominated by masculine power, yet as we heal feminine power, the world will become more balanced, with less violence and aggression.

Estrogen levels can come into balance when the soul discovery of estrogen is accomplished and released. Although this hormone is primarily produced by the ovaries, smaller amounts are produced in the breasts, liver, and adrenal glands. When adrenal problems show up, it may indicate resentment and anger/rage—that is, women who experience adrenal problems may believe they must constantly work at generating success, recognition, influence, or a station in life, according to Dr. Lincoln.[2] Producing the right amount of estrogen during menopause may result from releasing the corresponding emotional sufferings.

Osteoporosis. This also applies to osteoporosis, another serious symptom of menopause, because estrogen helps control bone loss. Dr. Lincoln stated that those with osteoporosis as children were left to their own devices. They may not feel the support they need because they never had it growing up. The bone supports our bodies and produces our cells, so developing osteoporosis signifies a support and trust issue. Once the soul discoveries of osteoporosis and estrogen are learned and their emotional sufferings released, old bone tissue can be replaced with new bone.

Heart disease. After menopause, women are more likely to develop heart disease. If related emotional sufferings are going on, then it's easy to see that self-rejection or non-acceptance of oneself would be related to heart problems. Do you see how so many diseases are interrelated? They have the same emotional sufferings and can be addressed by understanding that they present soul discoveries and by using the MO Technique.

The Second Chakra

The energy of the second chakra, or sexual chakra, involves the sexual organs and energizes the sexual organs. In *Anatomy of the Spirit*, Carolyn Myss stated, "The illnesses that originate in this center are activated by the fear of losing control. Problems at menopause such as hot flashes and depression are second chakra dysfunctions."[3] If we have to earn our acceptance as children, it makes sense that, as adults, we may believe we have to continue in the same way or sell ourselves out, thus creating problems with our feelings of control. Blockages in this chakra can stem from adultery, abusing ourselves or others, and being dishonorable and untruthful in our relationships. Control, power, or sexual problems as well as lack of financial support, greed, or ruthless dealings with money may affect the energy of this chakra. Abortions, rape, and sexual molestation also severely affect it.

When working over the sexual chakra, I can usually sense if there's been a loss of some sort. When I tell clients I'm feeling some sort of loss over the sexual chakra, they often say something like, "I didn't mention it to you but I did have a miscarriage." Some will tell me they had an abortion or were raped or molested. When this happens, I feel a deep sadness; imagine how that deep sorrow and negative energy must be affecting the person herself!

I then help clear the energy and my clients make peace with their sufferings. They tell me the clearing experience is powerful, cleansing, and relieving. Often, they have no idea they'd been carrying around that painful energy. Yet it affects menopause and any dysfunction of the sexual chakra. Having clear energy of our aura and chakras both prevents and heals disease, not only in the sexual chakra but in all the chakras.

Western medicine doesn't acknowledge this energy or the chakras, although great healers from our era and from ancient times have been putting out this information for all to see. Unfortunately, researching the next new miracle drug doesn't bring us closer to learning our soul discoveries. Rather, it puts these discoveries on the back burner, waiting to show up in another way.

Case History

Karen, who experienced severe hot flashes, was very attractive, which had been a definite advantage in her life. However, she believed people were drawn to her for how she looked on the outside, rather than for herself on the inside. For this reason, she never felt loved.

Karen's mother felt jealousy toward Karen. When she was not belittling her daughter, she was ignoring her. Growing up, she adored her father and viewed him as the strong one in the family.

Understandably, Karen felt royally ticked off about her life and how it had played out. Although she had everything money could buy, all she really wanted was love. And because she lacked self-love, she attracted people who continually rejected her in some way.

In an effort to build her self-esteem, Karen had several plastic surgeries, including breast implants, a tummy tuck, a face-lift, and liposuction. As I talked with her about what needed to be released out of her body, she became very defensive. She didn't want to look at her truth; she just wanted to take a drug and have the hot flashes go away. She decided to seek treatment that would give her the medication rather than work on herself through the MO Technique.

I have a few clients like Karen who aren't ready to look at the emotional underlying causes of their symptoms or their soul discoveries. I regard them as I would a wrapped mummy—if you start to unravel the binding just a little, you have to put it right back in place. And that's okay, as we can't force people to awaken if they're unwilling or not ready. Each person clings to an idea of control until the pain gets unbearable. Sadly, Karen ended up being diagnosed with an immune disorder and cancer.

One of my big lessons as a healer was to realize that pain is different for everyone. All I can do is share information; what people decide to do with it becomes their choice alone. Although difficult, I've had to let go and allow people to continue on their paths.

Body Wisdom

As we pause to heal and release our emotional sufferings, we build our strength. As we learn the messages of the body, obstacles and blockages disappear. Fulfillment comes from doing the creative work we've come on earth to do. Learning our soul discoveries brings peace, love, joy, and well-being. All this is called "Body Wisdom".

Respect for feminine power is desperately lacking today. Accepting and bringing it to the world will result in much needed respect and awaken our intuitive perceptions of the whole. Once that happens, the intuitive mind will balance the rational mind and creativity will fulfill the soul's hunger for connecting to its intuitive nature. Looking at menopause can provide a great awakening!

Using the MO Technique can help us connect to the divine within—the naturally creative beings that we are. Balancing the masculine and feminine in each of us (men and women) will balance the lopsided scale of aggression (the masculine) and receptivity (the feminine), putting us on the same path to unity and peace. Learning to work together can be hard, but we can do it. Imagine celebrating our differences and viewing them as guides to growth and fulfillment.

The universal soul discovery of menopause is about rallying all females to *accept* the feminine power by first accepting ourselves. If we perceive menopause as the way to rediscover this incredible feminine power, this energy will positively affect life as we view it now. Maybe that's why menopause is called the "change of life"—we really are meant to change the way of life for ourselves in the world today.

Menopausal women, we have a big job to do! Are you up for it?

Chapter 25: Migraine Headaches

"The maxim 'Nothing but perfection' may be spelled 'Paralysis'."
– Winston Churchill

The Condition
A condition marked by reoccurring, severe headaches, often accompanied by nausea and/or vomiting; sensitivity to light, sounds, and smells; sleep disturbances; and depression.

The Soul Discovery and MO of Migraine Headaches
The soul discovery of migraine headaches is to be there for ourselves at all times and to flow with life. Individuals suffering from migraines aim to overachieve to gain love from their mothers or mother stand-ins, and may come from a family where the mother is often caught up in serving the patriarch or doing other things instead showing their children they are loved for who they are.

Their headaches may be set off when they figure out that whatever project they're doing or whatever relationship they're in may never bring them what they want—*maternal love*. This ongoing feeling of inadequacy may lead to self-rejection, with resentment and anger/rage building up in the body. When the project or relationship fails to be perfect enough, they may feel powerless. This Common Thread can ignite severe pain in the head.

Subconscious programming of not giving maternal love may be handed down through generations—a programming most don't even know exists. And because they were raised that way, they may raise their own children with that programming. Of course, most mothers did the best they could with the knowledge they had. But today, we can offer a new understanding—that is, many conditions and diseases can be prevented by knowing how our programming sets us up.

When children can't get the love they desire, some become perfectionists. As perfectionists, they tell themselves if they keep trying to get it right, they will have success, love, and acceptance. But usually the opposite happens. Their method of no mistakes and high standards may cause them to *abandon themselves*, thus setting them up for frustration and disappointment. In addition, the individual's value may come from the approval of others. In contrast, those who understand healthy striving see mistakes as opportunities to grow and learn.

Perfectionists tend to be raised with many "shoulds" from their parents. When they live by strict, rigid rules, a "because it should be done" belief may spawn a lifestyle in which they don't consider their own wants and desires. This is a form of abandonment.

As humans, we are imperfect. I believe we were set up that way so we could learn our soul discoveries. Learning that perfection is an illusion and unattainable—that it's okay to be a human with flaws—is part of the soul's discovery here.

Yes, perfectionism comes with inherent values such as striving for a goal and following through with the commitment to achieve it, as top athletes do. This kind of perfectionism is encouraged in our society. We see that as *healthy striving*, which involves feeling good about ourselves as we attain our goals. However, when a person's body message is to strive for approval from others, not for the satisfaction of achieving something they truly desire for themselves, migraines can result. Eliminating migraine headaches can happen when you love and accept yourself enough to let go of unrealistic expectations.

The Universal Soul Discovery of Migraine Headaches
To be there for ourselves and others in the world.

The Emotional Sufferings of Migraine Headaches

- Signature emotional suffering—Abandoning ourselves
- Seeking approval from others
- Needing to earn the right to love
- Over-achiever
- Striving for perfection
- Not trusting
- Not feeling good enough
- Fearing failure
- Lacking commitment
- Unique emotional suffering
- The Common Thread—resentment, anger/rage, power-lessness, lack of self-love

When my children used to come home from school and tell me their accomplishments, I would say, "Pat yourself on the back—good job!" They would do that to feel proud of themselves, not because they sought my approval. They got that, too, of course, but to this day when they tell me about something they feel proud of, I see their hands on their backs giving themselves a pat. It's an automatic response for them, creating a healthy self-pride that may prevent disease in their bodies.

Other symptoms of migraine headaches include nausea, vomiting, sensitivity to light, sound, and smells, sleep disturbances, and depression. Headaches may stem from blocking the flow of life. Nausea may be a sense of something in our space that makes us feel sick. Vomiting is the attempt to get rid of that something. Dry heaves may be the unsuccessful attempt to get rid of something. Sensitivity to light, sound, and smells may be trying to tune everything out. Sleep disturbances may come from an out-of-sync feeling. Depression comes about when we aren't able to live the way we want; we have to live within other people's limits yet we sense a soul longing to live our life purpose.

The message from these symptoms is to not abandon ourselves but to flow with life, accept ourselves unconditionally, and achieve our destinies through healthy striving. We aim to feel good about ourselves as we attain every goal in our lives.

Sixth Chakra

The sixth chakra, or brow chakra, is our mind's eye, located in the middle of the forehead. This chakra can become blocked by perfectionism and lack of self-love. Dr. Gerber wrote, "A key issue of the sixth chakra is our ability to look truthfully at our lives, to evaluate our flaws and failures, and to acknowledge our strengths and accomplishments. One of the key relationships of the sixth chakra is the relationship between the mind and emotions."[1] Perfectionism may deprive these sufferers of the very love and acceptance they want so badly. How does it do this? Demanding standards that are beyond reason and setting themselves up for failure may severely deplete the pituitary gland. The emotional dysfunction of the pituitary gland involves being unhappy and believing they're at fault.

Perfectionism may also set them up for not mastering what they set out to do—not only in projects and work but in relationships. The pituitary or master gland produces ACTH, a hormone that stimulates the adrenals to produce cortisol to help cope with stress. When the mind and emotions block this critical area, the pituitary may not function properly. This could deplete the body of important adrenal hormones.

Another aspect of the sixth chakra is "seeing clearly". Perfectionism may rob them of personal satisfaction, leading to a vicious cycle of not seeing their soul's truth. This chakra involves awareness and clear vision, not only physically but seeing within oneself. Dr. Gerber wrote, "Diseases caused by dysfunction of the brow chakra may be caused by an individual not wanting to see something that is important to their soul growth."[2] The energy of this chakra gets distributed to the nervous and glandular centers in the physical body. Migraine headaches can be triggered when this energy is blocked.

Types of Migraines
Several types of migraines exist:

- Migraines with an aura
- Ophthalmologic migraines
- Carotidynia migraines
- Basilar artery migraines
- Status migraine headaches

Migraines with an aura are those preceded by either an aura of bright shimmering light around objects or zigzag or wavy lines 10 to 30 minutes before the headache. They may cause temporary vision loss. The soul discovery of this headache involves seeing what is happening around one and to one.

Ophthalmologic migraines begin with a headache felt in the eye. As the headache progresses, the eyelid can droop and become paralyzed. This can last for a few days or even weeks. The soul discovery of this headache involves seeing clearly, and releasing intense anger and judgment of oneself.

Carotidynia migraines usually occur in older people. They're characterized by a facial headache that radiates to the jaw and neck, causing swelling and tenderness over the carotid artery. The soul discoveries for these individuals are to feel and express love, and to release the belief that life is one long problem.

Basilar artery migraines involve the basilar artery in the brainstem and occur mostly in young people who consistently received the message that it's not okay to be who they are. The soul discovery is to know that it's perfectly okay to be who you are.

Status migraines usually involve intense pain that last longer than 72 hours and may require hospitalization. With this rare type of headache, there could be a big block to the flow of life, and the soul discovery is to understand the block, release it, and flow with life.

Case History

Lia had severe migraines. When I told her two of the emotional sufferings were abandonment and perfectionism, she said, "Well, I can relate to feeling like I have to be perfect but not the abandonment." So we worked on the former—her perfectionism.

When Lia went home from the session and discussed it with her mother, she told her mom, "Maureen kept asking me if there had been some type of abandonment in my life and I couldn't come up with one." Her mother said, "Honey, remember, you were adopted." Lia had been abandoned at birth and given up for adoption. Her birth mother was very young when she got pregnant. Of course Lia knew that, but it did not cross her mind because her adopted mom was "her mom". She called me later and said, "Oh, boy, was there abandonment. I was given up at birth." We both laughed and she came back for another session.

In her second session, I asked her about other times of abandonment in her life. She had several relationships that had not worked out and had never married.

Lia also could never find the "perfect" combination in her work or relationships. Perfectionists often have problems with procrastination because of the overwhelming feeling that if something can't be done perfectly, why do it at all.

Lia released the abandonment and stopped abandoning herself, fully accepted herself, and released that soul discovery. She is now very happy with a beautiful baby and working in a job she thoroughly enjoys.

I used to have severe migraine headaches and was definitely a perfectionist and felt abandoned. I lived in constant chaos growing up, so keeping things perfect around me helped me feel safe and secure. Because my mother was always putting out fires caused by my father, she didn't have the time to give me the loving acceptance that I so desperately craved.

It also upset me when others were not perfect. Life became one big disappointment. I took this to extremes. For example, if I saw a weed out in the lawn, I would have to pick it immediately. In my immaculate house, everything was always in its place. I needed to get straight A's in school, and when I received a B I felt devastated. I realized I did everything for the approval of others. Once I released the emotional sufferings of migraines using the MO Technique, I not only rid myself of headaches, but life became much more manageable and free.

Yes, I still like to have things neat and tidy, but I'm not obsessive about everything being perfect and I no longer expect that of others. If a regular headache comes on, I know my body is telling me I'm abandoning myself in some way, and that I need to love and accept myself. I figure it out and release it right away using the MO Technique.

The Value of Healthy Mental Pictures

Our bodies are wonderfully obedient to our own words and the mental pictures we feed it. When we feed the body mental pictures of wholeness instilled at the soul level, it builds cells according to that picture. That's why teaching children to pat themselves on the back and value themselves is a simple way to nurture and create an emotionally strong child. We can let them know we approve of who they are, but teach them not to value their accomplishments based on the approval of others. We can regularly tell them we love them, no conditions attached. We can teach them that hard work pays off and help them problem-solve.

The human reality is one of imperfection. Teaching children the principle of healthy striving can prevent migraine headaches and show them how to be there for themselves, no matter what. Once they've instilled their own worth inside, they can reach out to others and be there for them. They can also discern who can be there for themselves and allow the support.

Remember, self-worth is based on approval from oneself, not from others, and it recognizes the authentic soul within. Once we discover our truth and accept our authentic selves, we can then accept others wholeheartedly. This acceptance will create the connection from individual consciousness to family, community, and planetary consciousness, helping us understand that whatever we do to others, we also do to ourselves.

Chapter 26: Multiple Sclerosis

"The voice of our original self is often muffled, overwhelmed, even strangled by the voices of other people's expectations."
– Julia Cameron

The Disease

This disease is marked by patches of hardened tissue in the brain and spinal column. Multiple sclerosis (MS) causes nerve lesions that create electrical conduction disturbances in the central nervous system. Loss of nerve endings result in weakness and lack of coordination associated with partial or complete paralysis and muscular tremors.

The Soul Discovery and MO of Multiple Sclerosis

The soul discovery of MS is to heal the programmed rigidity. What is one way that the rigidity can be set up? The commonality in the MO and programming of many MS clients is an "I have to" pattern of thought. This pattern may set up the rigidity and hardened tissue of the brain and the spinal column. The "have to" is programmed in at a very young age. Not surprisingly, at the end stages of MS, the client's body becomes rigid; the hardened thought process has led to a rigid body. Their soul discovery is to become free and flexible and live in the moment and to learn to *feel* their feelings.

Using the MO Technique can increase a MS person's flexibility and ease of flowing with life, knowing that nothing in life is an absolute "have to".

MS may reflect a programmed rigidity that prevents flexibility of any kind. The brain houses our thoughts; the spinal column holds our bodies upright. Individuals with MS may feel a lack of support in their lives, and that they have to sustain everyone and everything around them. This may cause resentment and their resentment and anger/rage may build in the body over time.

The clients I have seen with MS feel like they "have to" do everything in life. This "have-to" feeling may create a world in which they may not believe they have control. To compensate, they willfully and rigidly try to control everything. Brain problems may result from a conflict between the ego and personal goals—what their souls came to do—their divine intent. Spinal column emotional problems may stem from a feeling that they don't feel supported in life.

The rigid, inflexible attitude and inability to support the life process may have been spawned by being in a family in which they were too young for the responsibility placed on them— something they believed they "had to" take on. This led to feeling responsible and accountable for everything in their lives. At the same time, it restricted what they believed they could and couldn't have, becoming a part of their makeup. They may have also experienced undermining and blame in their families, and taken that on, too.

The Universal Soul Discovery of Multiple Sclerosis
To feel, be free and flexible and live in the moment.

The Emotional Sufferings of Multiple Sclerosis

- Signature emotional suffering—Experiencing programmed rigidity
- Adopting a "I have to" attitude
- Lacking support
- Having difficulty feeling emotions
- Lacking trust
- Feeling abandoned
- Feeling undeserving
- Craving control
- Feeling helpless or a learned helplessness

- Not feeling validated
- Unique emotional suffering
- The Common Thread—resentment, anger/rage, power-lessness, lack of self-love

My first client with MS called for an appointment, not for herself but for her cat. Kali, the cat, had cancerous lesions on the outside of her body. I did some healing work on her cat (well, why not— I love animals!) and left when I was finished.

Two days later, this client called to report that all the lesions on Kali's body had disappeared. Her veterinarian was amazed and pronounced Kali in remission. I told the client that Kali had given me a message for her during the healing. "Do you want to hear it?" I asked. "Of course," she replied. I said, "Kali indicated it's your turn to heal your MS." With that, she got upset and insisted she was doing everything her doctor told her to do. She shouted, "YOU DO NOT HEAL MS!" I got her message and dropped the idea.

Not surprisingly, multiple sclerosis reflects a programmed rigidity and prevents flexibility. The rigidity may harden the tissue in the brain and spinal column, which adds to an already inflexible load. This client witnessed a *miracle* when the cancerous lesions disappeared on her cat, but her programming and MO prevented her from even considering that she might also have a chance to heal.

At the end stages of MS, the body may become as stiff as a board. As noted above, those suffering from MS show an overwhelming fear of being free and flexible, but that may be exactly what their souls signed up to discover. Their symptoms can include fatigue, balance and coordination problems, numbness, tingling or burning, and tremors. MS sufferers may also have vision problems, depression, sexual difficulties, bowel and bladder problems, and memory and reasoning difficulties.

Let's discuss the message of the psychological meaning of these symptoms and what they are trying to convey to MS sufferers.

Fatigue. Usually the first symptom of MS, the fatigued body is saying, "enough already; love me and take care of me enough to give me the energy I need." Lack of support mixed with a sense of inadequacy and incompetence can leave an individual emotionally exhausted. The soul discovery of fatigue is to love and take care of yourself enough and allow downtime to rejuvenate your energy.

Balance and coordination problems. Their bodies may be sick and tired of all the responsibility and accountability. These people may feel they're being thrown off base and that they're wobbly and out of balance, and their bodies are reflecting this. The soul discovery of balance and coordination problems is to bring their responsibility into balance and be accountable to *themselves*.

Numbness, tingling, and burning. Numbness is the body saying it doesn't want to feel anything which may be due to experiencing so much hurt. Painful tingling is the body saying "please feel me" and the burning sensation may reflect anger. The soul discovery is to learn and allow themselves to feel.

Muscular tremors. The psycholgical meaning of muscle problems in general indicate feeling fearful of moving forward in life. Tremors represent a fear for the people afflicted that if they can't control all the issues presented to them, everything will fall apart. The soul discovery is to move forward in life and know that control is an illusion.

Spasms. Opposing groups of muscles contract and relax at the same time, bringing on the spasms. This may reflect a fear of gripping and a belief that letting go will bring on disaster. The soul discovery is to learn to trust and have faith.

Memory and reasoning problems. These sufferers may be undergoing a transformation and healing that requires them to reprogram themselves all the way back to the beginning of their lives. Specifically, as they went through life, they may have had a habit of repressing, denying, or just "forgetting about it" after a traumatic event occurred. This pattern is showing up at this time because of severe stress in their lives, which may create the memory loss and reasoning problems. It may have come from feeling powerless as a child. Remember, the soul discovery is to *remember* their true selves.

Vision problems. They may not want to see issues they need to look at. The soul discovery is to see something that has been suppressed or to learn to handle what they do see.

Bladder and bowel problems. They may feel pissed off and their bodies may be trying to clear out toxins. The emotional cause of bowel problems may reflect a fear of letting go of the past. They may display a rigid, cautious, and controlling approach to life, indicating a deep fear of letting go of the old to take on the new. They may also be afraid of abandonment, wanting frantically to control every situation. The soul discovery is to replace anger with love and compassion and to let go of the past and control.

Depression. This may represent a conflict between their personalities and their divine intent. The soul discovery is to tap into your inner wisdom and discover your divine intent and pursue it.

Paralysis. MS sufferers may not dare move forward due to immobilizing terror mixed with a feeling of helplessness. Ironically, the MS may bring this on at the end of their lives because of the belief that there's no cure for it. The soul discovery is to learn to be flexible and free.

One way to prevent MS is to look at our *modus operandi*—how we operate in life. Most of the time, we can't "see" our own emotional sufferings. Some MS individuals have a learned helplessness. This programming is set up when they are very young and they are not taught how to cope or flow with change. And some individuals who have MS have a hard time letting others help them until their bodies deteriorate to a point that they *must* ask for help. This is a heck of a way to learn our soul discoveries! It's much easier to use the MO Technique, release the emotional sufferings, and learn the soul discoveries ahead of time.

Case History

When Jeff, 45, was diagnosed with MS, his feet and legs were numb all the way to his abdomen. He had trouble with his vision. His overall numbness may have been from not wanting to feel anything arising from the distrust and pain in his life. The numbness in his feet may have indicated a fear of stepping forward in life. For Jeff, this reflected a need to do what he wanted to do instead of "having to" do what he thought was appropriate. The numbness in his legs may have indicated a fear of change, of taking risks, and of moving forward in life (soul discoveries), which our legs help us to do.

During our pre-session interview, Jeff revealed two important facts about himself: his mother became pregnant with him out of wedlock and his father left when he was eight years old. Jeff's whole life was about what he "had to" do—a feeling that could have started in the womb if his mother felt as if she "had to" get married. After his father left, as the oldest child, he believed he "had to" take care of his younger brothers. He "had to" become an adult before he was ready. These beliefs may have evolved into a program of rigidity and restrictions that eventually manifested as MS.

Jeff was brimming with anger that his father had left the family. He felt definite about the idea that if he didn't step in, everything would go to hell. He wanted to be free but had no idea how to get there. The MS may have arrived to tell Jeff to let go of the rigidity so he could feel and be free.

During our first session, Jeff released anger/rage, abandonment, rigidity, and hands-on control. In the second session, he released the idea of being overly responsible, feeling unvalued, undeserving, and not trusting. He also let go of his "had to" belief. In the third session, Jeff let go of feeling trapped and powerless, and his lack of self-love. When he went to the soul level, Jeff saw himself dancing and carefree. He also saw that people wanted to help him. And he saw himself lighten up, trust others, and know that he deserved goodness in his life.

When Jeff imaged freedom, he saw a conflict that presented itself as two people. He called them Ira and Steel. What did Ira need? Jeff said she needed to feel things without being buffered. What did Steel need? Steel needed love. He imaged the two becoming one. He saw that the people in his life wouldn't disassemble or abandon him if he adopted a more conscious lifestyle. Jeff said that from this point forward, every decision he made would come from a base of self-love instead of a "have to" place. Every time he thought of rigidity, he would let go and reprogram his thoughts toward being free.

Jeff's MS stabilized. He went on to get his master's degree and is working for the public sector and in his words, working "for the greater good." And he allowed people to help him. He had a frank talk with his wife about all of the things he felt he "had to" do. She said she could help him with various things so he didn't feel so responsible.

The MO Technique shows people how they were programmed—their MO—and how the disease takes on the characteristics of their programming. Jeff knew what had happened to him but he had no idea that his programming could be the culprit or that it may be one of his soul discoveries. This eye-opening experience made his marriage stronger and his life more flexible and free.

Chapter 27: Parkinson's Disease

"When I grip the wheel too tight I find I lose control."
– Steve Rapson

The Disease
Parkinson's disease is a chronic progressive nervous disease that occurs when the nerve cells slowly die in a small part of the brain called the substantia nigra. This disease is marked by tremors and weakness of resting muscles along with a shuffling gait.

The Soul Discovery and MO of Parkinson's Disease
The commonality and programming of individuals with Parkinson's disease reflect a need to control *every tiny detail* of life because those who have it may have been programmed to lack faith in the Universe. Their soul discovery is that control doesn't exist; it's an illusion. They are here to discover the *freedom* of surrendering, letting go of control, and having faith in the Universe.

Let's look at those in the final stages of Parkinson's disease. They experience physical rigidity, tremors, shuffling gait, and speech difficulty. Because of their desire to control, they may be inflexible in their thinking, which may decrease the dopamine (a neurotransmitter that regulates one's mood) in the substantia nigra (center for control for voluntary movement). When Parkinson's individuals attempt to control people, places, and things, their bodies respond by sending a strong message—it loses control.

Tremors, according to Dr. Michael Lincoln in *Messages from the Body*, result from experiencing an intensely anxious relationship with the Universe. Full of fear, uncertainty, and insecurity, sufferers feel stagnant and unsafe in an uncaring world.

It is a result of a rigid adaption whose family had a very fearfully narrow viewpoint and lifestyle. The individual played the 'family hoist' role, the one who was the pivot of everything behind the scenes. They have an over weaning desire to control everything and everyone about every aspect of every issue, situation and undertaking. They have the complete conviction that all hell will break loose and every-thing will go down the tubes unless they personally hands on determine the purpose, process and outcome of everything.[1]

Using the MO Technique, they'd learn their soul discoveries early: to release the control, become more flexible, and accept that the only things that can be controlled are our thoughts and actions. They would heal their fear of the Universe and being the family hoist. They'd learn to feel divinely safe and protected, and be who they truly are. The body symptoms reveal exactly what needs to change.

Chemically, Parkinson's patients suffer from a dopamine deficiency in the brain. Dopamine produces movement in the body and carries that natural biochemical information of love and joy from one neuron to the next. Because Parkinson's individuals fail to control things, they can experience frequent disappointments. This blocks their pleasure and joy while contin-ually lowering the dopamine produced in the brain.

Parkinson's affects the sixth chakra, which is linked to the master gland of the brain—the pituitary gland along with the pineal, spinal cord, and automatic nervous system. The sixth chakra or brow chakra (third eye) involves seeing clearly. It relates to the search for spiritual fulfillment. Parkinson's disease may also be conveying that it's time to surrender control and become spiritually awake. Mastering this chakra leads to having an open mind and a trust that the Universe will create every situation we need to learn our soul discoveries.

On-Off Phenomenon

There is an "on-off" phenomenon to this disease. In the "on" phase, sufferers are loose and fluid; their minds are clear and movements in control. In the "off" phase, they are rigid and have tremors, loss of balance, and diminished small motor skills. They also suffer from the mask effect. Thinking of a mask reminds me of hiding who they really are. Clearly one of the soul discoveries of Parkinson's is tap into and become who they truly are. Like other diseases, it imitates the emotions going on in the body.

Disappointments also create a high-low or on-off phenomenon; an emotional high occurs, then disappointment causes an emotional low. This happens frequently with those who try to control every detail. As part of their soul discoveries, those with Parkinson's may be programmed for these highs and lows, creating situations in which they experience disappointments many times over because of the control causing the natural dopamine to eventually deplete.

Being who we truly are and living our truth removes the mask and lets in spontaneity. Being able to connect with others and be vulnerable may lead to deep, intimate relationships, thus increasing our happiness and pleasure in life. When we discover our soul intentions, it gives our life meaning and connects us with our divine essence. This is an innate connection of the soul that brings about opportunities of love and miracles that seem too good to be true.

Once released, The Common Thread can be replaced with love, understanding, and the power to heal on every level. In contrast, trying to control details and not succeeding will build the resentment in the body. Eventually, an adverse event that can't be controlled will put a Parkinson's individual over the top and feelings of powerless results. The anger can erupt the disease, and with self-love absent, it can progress. The more the person tries to control the disease, the worse the symptoms may become.

When we learn to trust the Universe, we may find deeper meaning of all the events in our lives and understand there's a purpose for everything we encounter. This we may understand on the conscious level but understanding it at the super conscious level or soul we truly trust and know. It's important to trust that understanding, for trust releases fear, which integrates the physical body with the soul. Then we are able to manifest what we want.

The Universal Soul Discovery of Parkinson's Disease
To trust the Universe, be flexible, and be your soul's truth—who you truly are.

Before discussing how the MO Theory may apply to actor Michael J. Fox, let me emphasize that investigating psychological and spiritual precursors to disease in no way seeks to blame anyone. Rather, we use reflection and compassionate observation to understand the underlying mechanism of disease with an eye toward prevention and healing.

Showing how our programming and MO set us up for a disease is crucial in healing these incurable diseases. This can help prevent them because we can learn our soul discoveries by tuning into our own soundtrack, understanding our MO, and being able to change before disease sets in.

For this discussion, I have taken quotes from Michael J. Fox's book, *Lucky Man: A Memoir,* and applied them to the MO Theory to provide food for thought.

Courageous and pragmatic, actor Michael J. Fox has shown that Parkinson's is not the once-thought "old person's disease". In fact, 40 percent of those diagnosed with this disease are under 60. Michael was only 30 when his onset of Parkinson's developed.

Michael wrote this in his book *Lucky Man:* "I woke up to find the message in my left hand. It had me trembling. It wasn't a fax, telegram, memo or the usual sort of missive bringing disturbing news. In fact, my hand held nothing at all. The trembling was the message."[2] It was his left "pinkie" that was trembling and he couldn't stop it.

According to Dr. Lincoln, the psychological meaning of the left little finger involves issues about connectedness, social acceptance, and expressing one's spiritual side. The left side of the body is the feminine, receptive, and intuitive side. When dysfunction of any part of the left side of the body occurs, the individual may be avoiding his or her intuition, which is an aspect of the third eye chakra. [3]

Our intuition is our innate inner wisdom that knows the soul's contract and how to pursue it. The psychological meaning of tremor, one of the first symptoms of Parkinson's, can be released with the MO Technique. If the soul discoveries are learned, consciousness changes and the physical body responds. If we don't understand the message of the tremor, we can't do anything about it.

The sixth chakra feeds the energy to the brain and central nervous system. When it's blocked, it could be because of this lack of "seeing within" and may produce neurological disorders that lead to Parkinson's. Mastering this chakra leads to having an open mind and a trust that the Universe will create every situation we need to learn the discoveries we signed up for.

Those who develop Parkinson's may have a lifelong pattern of believing they need to uplift others, not only in the family but in the world. Michael may have become the "family hoist" because he became the successful one with worldly fame and fortune as an actor.

An individual that controls their feelings can appear very calm. But inside they may feel insecure and overwhelmed.

Releasing the message of the tremor, the first symptom of the disease, is important because the individual learns the control lesson and addresses any fear of the Universe. Michael was shown both sides of the coin. As he wrote, "My father, the career military man, personified the boundaries of expectation and acceptance of one's limitations, both external and self-imposed."[4] He later stated, "His (father's) view of the world was that happiness and success were not to be trusted. He believed life operated according to an inflexible system of compensation, in which each of life's gains had to be paid for by an equal amount of loss."[5] His father may have modeled the controlling, rigid, non-trusting side of life. In addition to these emotions being modeled for him, they can be handed down through genes.

Another side of the coin was his paternal grandmother, as Michael wrote, "In comparison, Nana, the matriarch and wartime clairvoyant, possessed an essential nature that hinted at the possibility of escape, of transcending life's limits."[6]

The rigid symptoms of Parkinson's can include an over-control of anger and emotional expression, masking one's true personality. Michael wrote, "An actor's burning ambition, when you think about it, is to spend as much time as possible pretending to be somebody else. For those of us lucky (or unstable) enough to become professional performers, the uncertainty about who we really are only increases."[7] Michael wrote, "These two figures, my maternal grandmother and my father, represented two distinct poles of my childhood, two gravitational fields that helped form my character."[8]

Parkinson's disease showed its "on-off" characteristics to Michael. When it's "on", he is loose and fluid, mind clear, movements in control. In the "off" stage, the disease has complete authority over his physical body. The classic symptoms of rigidity, tremors, loss of balance, and diminished small motor skills show up. The small diminished motor skills that causes hypomimia (facial masking) are called the "mask effect" commonly found in Parkinson's patients. Michael wrote, "The impediments to self-expression are not the most painful or debilitating feature of Parkinson's disease, yet they madden me more than even the most teeth-rattling full body tremor."[9]

He had felt secure with the success of the TV sitcom *Family*

Ties and the *Back to the Future* movies. But by the end of summer in 1990, all that changed. *Family Ties* was over and the *Back to the Future* sequels had ended. Michael stated that he didn't feel comfortable finishing any job without another contract in hand, writing about his "keep-your-head-down and-keep-moving mentally, as far back as I can remember, a major part of my personality, my modus operandi. Even as a kid, I lacked the faith required to be still."[10] As he wrote, "No matter how great the acceptance, adulation, and accumulation of wealth, gnawing at you always is the deep-seated belief that you are a fake, a phony—even if you bullshit your way through whatever job you're working on now, you'd better prepare for the likelihood that you're never going to get another. In the face of all evidence to the contrary, this is exactly how I felt about my career in 1990."[11]

Some of Michael's first symptoms were diminished blinking and reduced spontaneity of facial expression. Diminished blinking, according to Dr. Lincoln, indicates a situation that's generating an out-of-control feeling along with dangerous environment feelings.

Symptoms may keep appearing until the person receives the message of the disease and *understands* it, but that information hasn't been readily available. Symptoms that manifest before the disease is diagnosed may be giving the individual the message to open up and be more spontaneous. All of these emotions can hold sufferers captive from knowing who they really are and from loving themselves. It all boils down to self-love.

The Emotional Sufferings of Parkinson's

The following characteristics or emotional sufferings are its precursors.

- Fear and not trusting the Universe, which creates the unsafe feeling

- Signature emotional suffering: The need to control every little tiny detail in life
- Masking who the person truly is
- Need to socially connect and feel, to be vulnerable, and to be accepted
- Need to be spiritually connected or fulfilled
- The Common Thread (lack of self-love, powerlessness, resentment and anger/rage)

These all can be released out of the body using the MO Technique. Through this release, individuals learn that control doesn't exist; it's an illusion. They also need to learn the freedom of surrendering and letting go of control. As they become more flexible, they can release the rigidity of their bodies.

Learning to trust the Universe, we may find a deeper spiritual meaning of all the events in our lives and understand that there's a purpose for everything we encounter. It's important to *trust* that understanding, for trusting releases fear, which integrates the physical body with the soul. Then we're able to manifest what we want. Being who we truly are and living our truth removes the mask and lets in more spontaneity. Being able to connect with others and be vulnerable may lead to more intimate relationships, thus increasing the happiness and pleasure in living.

When we are spiritually fulfilled doing our passion, our soul work, it gives our lives meaning and connects us with our divine essence. Once released, The Common Thread can provide the love, understanding, and power to create our reality and heal ourselves on many levels.

Michael J. Fox, who has become the public face for Parkinson's disease, has raised millions of dollars for PD research. I hope reading this chapter will help millions understand the soul discoveries of this disease. Michael calls this disease, "a gift that keeps on taking." He wrote, "I would never want to go back to that life—a sheltered, narrow existence fueled by fear and made livable by insulation, isolation and self-indulgence."[12] Today, he calls himself a lucky man.

Case History

Phil, age 62 and in the late stages of Parkinson's, came in for a session. His son picked him up out of the car and I watched him shuffle into my office, his wife on one side and his son on the other. He couldn't talk and had severe palsy. His son wiped the drool that continually ran down his chin.

His wife said her husband had been diagnosed after Phil felt he had no control over a certain event. Specifically, Phil had moved his family from New Jersey to New York to accept a new job. No one in his family had wanted to move, but Phil considered it a good opportunity. After working for only a few months at the new job, the company that hired him went bankrupt. Phil had persuaded his family to sell their beloved home in New Jersey and move to New York. Understandably, he believed he'd lost control.

Phil's wife shared with me that her husband's mother had been domineering and controlling, which may have triggered a "no control" response in Phil early on. He overcompensated by proving himself in every possible way and willfully trying to control every aspect of his life. She described him as being over-responsible, the one who always uplifted others around him.

Because Phil couldn't speak, I had him imagine "hands-on-control" out of his body. I didn't know exactly what was happening since he couldn't communicate with me. Nevertheless, I had him release his feelings of powerlessness, anger/rage, lack of self-love, over responsibility, rigidity, and feeling unsafe. I actually did the imaging with him as I asked him to image the suffering, find it in his body, and release it. Although he couldn't respond verbally, I could tell he knew what was going on. This occurred over several sessions.

Happily, Phil did improve. Able to kick up one leg, he could also speak and communicate with his family, and his palsy got a little better. One day in my office, he sang, "I left my heart in San

Francisco." Phil was such a love and I was thrilled with his improvement. But just about the time we were so delighted with his improvement, he got an infection in his lungs that ended his life.

I felt especially good that I was able to educate his son—his wife said that he was so much like his father—on the emotional root cause of Parkinson's. This understanding may help him learn the soul discoveries ahead of time in hopes that he will be spared this devastating disease.

From my experience working with Phil, I believe that if we can catch this disease in the early stages, the psychological meaning of Parkinson's can be released. By catching it at the symptom stage we have a chance to learn the soul discoveries ahead of time.

In the cure for Parkinson's disease, I humbly hope this information helps. The greatest soul discovery that I have shared throughout this entire book is accepting and loving ourselves on every level. The most promising research is discovering why we came to this earth—that is, to do our soul work.

Conclusion: The Opposite of Fear is Love

"You must be the change you wish to see in the world."
– Gandhi

We don't have to wait until an adverse event happens to look for our soul's guidance. We can now understand our soul discoveries by knowing our *modus operandi* and how we've been programmed. With the MO technique we can begin understanding right now.

Why have we come to Planet Earth? To discover what we came to learn—to discover our soul work. Our soul discoveries will lead us to a higher consciousness, our true freedom. The human consciousness can be pain and suffering—the soul consciousness is love, freedom, peace, and unity. As human beings, isn't that what we are really after? Love, freedom, peace, and unity—called euphoria!

Sometimes we have to develop a disease to wake up our soul consciousness.

Yes, we can discover our soul's work before a disease erupts. In fact, we can determine our soul work from conditions at the time of conception, how the pregnancy went, what mother and father we picked, and the way we were birthed. Everything that happens to us is a clue to the puzzle of life, including every symptom, condition, or disease we may develop.

I've come to believe that whatever programmed belief systems we carry factor into the disease or diseases we might develop. In fact, if we understand the dynamics of our soul and recognize how we are programmed, it may be possible to predict the kind of illnesses we will experience in the future.

Disease may motivate us to become *who we truly are* and the MO Technique can set free *who we are not*. We can let go of who we *think* we are—an identity instilled by our programming. We can instill our DNA Power and release our anger and resentment. We can learn to love ourselves as the world's greatest treasure. Mastering The Common Thread of Disease will give us the freedom we yearn for and help us transcend the boundaries of self.

That's the Power of Self-love!

Remember, the opposite of fear is love—the most powerful drug available. Love never masks the lessons we must learn. It lets us release our old programming and instill an MO that operates with love and compassion.

Self-love on a global level will help us transcend the boundaries of self into universal oneness—the love and freedom of all. We can then work on "unconditional love", the Universal Soul Discovery of our planet.

May you enjoy abundant love, health, joy, peace, happiness, and freedom.

Happy Healing!

Maureen

Expressions of Thanks

The following comments come from Maureen's clients regarding their healing sessions.

Regained My Life: After one session with Maureen, I no longer felt my fibromyalgia symptoms. I spent New Year's on the ski slopes and had no symptoms after—a far cry from the last three years when I suffered with severe symptoms after skiing. I've regained my life!
  – *Sue Yesilada*

Joyful Energy Sustained: I felt energized and joyful after my session with Maureen. As I worked with the positive images over 40 days, I sustained what we'd accomplished. This is big news as so often after a healing session, the effects dwindle over time. I still play with the positive images during my meditations.
  – *Lynn-Telford-Sahl, M.A. Psychology with Holistic Specialization, Certified Addiction Counselor, Author of* The Greatest Change of All *and* Intentional JOY: How to Turn Stress, Fear, and Addiction into Freedom.

Healing Session and 40-Day Program Reduced Pain: I am diabetic and I came to see Maureen for severe pain in my feet. After the healing session and 40-day program, I have minimal pain in my feet and can walk without a problem. On a scale of 1–10 my pain was 10 when I met Maureen; now it is a 1. And my A1C test for diabetes dropped, too.
  – *Ron Alexander*

Shifted Key Relationships: Not only did I get relief from back strain after my session with Maureen, but I fully zeroed in on its cause. The resulting insights shifted key relationships and caused me to readily ask for the support I need. That's powerful!

– Barbara Patton

My Eye is Healed: I had used an antibiotic for 45 days with no results. Four days after my session with Maureen, my eye was healed.

– Sara Aragon

Felt Safe and Never Judged: I envisioned all manner of weird and spooky ejaculations from a "healer" with smoke, mirrors, and crystal balls. Maybe I'd saw too many B movies; I found Maureen to be normal, lovely, and gifted. Her work with me was gentle; I felt safe and never judged. The shift was perceptible. Angels do indeed seem to dwell among us.

– Gina Vance, Mind-Body Skills Trainer & Founder, The Integrative Wellness Center

At Ease and Peaceful: I experienced complete confusion going through "the change" plus erratic blood sugar levels that threw me into sweats, weakness, and confusion. I was losing control of my life. I went to the doctor to get a workup and CAT scan to find out what was wrong. When Maureen offered to work with me, I was willing to try anything. In the session, I felt so at ease and peaceful, I had a strong sense of God being with me. My illness hasn't returned and the doctor's tests came back normal.

– Anne Minnehan

A Noticed Difference: I've been doing 40 days of "sinking in" and it has changed the way I look at EVERYTHING.

– Margarete Finn

Goodbye, Stress—Hello, Confidence: I started losing my hair and confidence when I was 16 years old. Going bald wasn't an ideal look for the prom. My mom introduced me to Maureen just before my 17th birthday. Little did I know it would be the greatest gift I received that year. After one session, I felt good about myself, the worry and stress weighing me down felt lifted. The knowledge Maureen gave me continues to improve my life. The real gift was going to my senior prom with self-confidence.

    – Kiernan Rien

Pain Free Six Months Later: The pain in my lower back was so bad, I could barely walk. In my extreme discomfort, I worried about packing up and driving with my three cats from California to Texas. When I left the session, I was completely pain-free! As I packed and lifted, in a fit of "let's get this over with", I threw caution to the wind. No pain. No pain driving. No pain unpacking, either. And six months later, no flare-ups.

    – Chaska Peacock

Works for Everyone, Not Just Those with Disease: What a weight has been lifted from my shoulders! I resolved issues that had not manifested into critical illness. That is the wonder of the MO Technique—it works for everyone, not just those suffering from illness.

    – Paulette Spadini

Life-Changing Results: Maureen has a wonderful way of putting life's problems in perspective. I've learned a new way of thinking that makes it natural to do the right thing and recognize the wrong. I've grown spiritually more than I could have imagined.

    – Bob Howitz

Helped My Hair Grow Back In: I realized I did not have control as a child, so one of my adult survival tools was to have hands-on control. I have crown baldness (which we have no control over). After a session of releasing hands-on control, I noticed my hair growing back in. This work has not only helped my hair grow in, but has helped my life in general.

– *Lazze Jansson*

A Fresh Start, New Lease on Life: My doctor found two irregular moles on my breasts and sent me to a specialist. Then my pap smear had abnormal cells that could lead to cervical cancer. My world was falling apart. I braced myself and called Maureen. She guided me through energy levels and helped me find the problems and release them. She also helped me gain the confidence, power, love, and energy within myself to be healthy. When I went to the breast specialist, he said everything looked fine. Now to beat problem number two. Maureen helped me find disbelief with myself that was causing uncertainties in my health. I experienced amazing things that will always be with me. Good news. The results from biopsy #2 came back fine.

– *Brandi Baugh*

Endnotes

Chapter 1

1   Henahan, Sean, "State of the Heart: The Future of Cardiology,"
     www.accessexcellence.org/WN/NM/rmrob.php.
     Access Excellence (online), 2001.

2   Couric, Katie. *Stand Up To Cancer*. CBS News on YouTube.
     www.youtube.com, (Search Katie Couric, Cancer), 2008.

3   *Webster's New World Dictionary, Third College Edition*. Prentice Hall, 1994.

4   Lipton, Bruce Ph.D. *The Biology of Belief, Unleashing the Power of Consciousness, Matter & Miracles*. Mountain of Love/Elite Books, 2005, p. 162.

5   Narayan-Singh aka Lincoln, Michael J., Ph.D. *Addictions and Cravings: Their Psychological Meaning*. Talking Hearts, rev. 2006, p. 316.

6   Lincoln, Michael J., Ph.D. *Messages from the Body: Their Psychological Meaning*. Talking Hearts, rev. 2006, p. 63.

Chapter 3

1   Krause, Tyra, M.D., Ph.D. "Population-Based Studies on Atrophy in Greenland." Ph.D. Thesis, University of Copenhagen, 2003.

2   Gerber, Richard, MD. *Vibrational Medicine: The #1 Handbook of Subtle-Energy Therapies*. 3rd ed., Bear & Company, Vt., 2001, pp. 386-387.

Chapter 4

1   Gerber, Richard, M.D. *Vibrational Medicine: The #1 Handbook of Subtle-Energy Therapies*. 3rd ed., Bear & Company, Vermont, 2001, p. 378.

2   Braden, Greg. *Walking Between the Worlds, The Science of*

Compassion. Radio Bookstore Press (hardcover), Sacred Spaces/Ancient Wisdom, Bellevue, WA, 1997, p. 95.

3   Lincoln, Michael J., Ph.D. *Messages from the Body: Their Psychological Meaning*. Talking Hearts, rev. 2006, p. 216.

4   Lincoln, Michael J., Ph.D. *Messages from the Body: Their Psychological Meaning*. Talking Hearts, rev. 2006, p. 65.

5   Ibid. p. 373.

Chapter 5

1   Anshara, Sherry. *The Age of Inheritance: The Activation of the 13 Chakras*. QuantumPathicsm Press: Scottsdale, 2004.

Chapter 7

1   Pert, Candace, Ph.D. *Molecules of Emotion: The Science Behind Mind-Body Medicine*. Scribner-New York, 1997. p. 285.

Chapter 9

1   Lincoln, Michael J., Ph.D. *Messages from the Body: Their Psychological Meaning*. Talking Hearts, rev. 2006, p. 146.

Chapter 10

1   "HIV and AIDS in Africa." www.avert.org/africa.htm

2   "HIV/AIDS among Women." Centers for Disease Control and Prevention, U.S. Department of Health and Human Services. www.cdc.gov/hiv/topics/women/resources/fact sheets/ women.htm

3   Centers for Disease Control and Prevention, U.S. Department of Health and Human Services, Office of Minority Health & Health Disparities (OMHD). www.cdc.gov/omhd/default.htm

4   Lincoln, Michael J., Ph.D. *Messages from the Body: Their Psychological Meaning*. Talking Hearts, rev. 2006, p. 41.

5   Hay, Louise L. *Heal Your Body: The Mental Causes for Physical Illness and the Metaphysical Way to Overcome Them*. Hay

House: Calif., 1982, p. 11.

Chapter 11

1   Lincoln, Michael J., Ph.D. *Messages from the Body: Their Psychological Meaning.* Talking Hearts, rev. 2006, p. 79.
2   Hay, Louise L. *Heal Your Body: The Mental Causes for Physical Illness and the Metaphysical Way to Overcome Them.* Hay House: Calif., Expanded/Revised Edition 1988, p. 12.
3   Lincoln, Michael J. *Allergies and Aversions: Their Psychological Meaning.* Talking Hearts, 2000.

Chapter 12

1   Lincoln, Michael J., Ph.D. *Messages from the Body: Their Psychological Meaning.* Vol. I, 2005, p. 32.
2   Hay, Louise L. *Heal Your Body: The Mental Causes for Physical Illness and the Metaphysical Way to Overcome Them.* Hay House: Calif., 1982, p.12.
3   Op. Cit. Lincoln, Vol.II, p. 454.
4   Ibid. Vol.I, pp. 392-393.
5   Op. Cit. Lincoln, Vol. II, P. 568.
6   Ibid. pp. 149-150.
7   Op. Cit. Hay, pp. 22-25.
8   Ibid. p. 53.
9   Op. Cit. Lincoln, Vol. II,p. 426.
10 Ibid. p. 463.
11 Ibid. ,Vol. I, p. 48.
12 Ibid. p. 286.
13 Ibid. p. 305.
14 Ibid. ,Vol. II, p. 624.
15 Op. Cit. Hay, p. 32.
16 Myss, Caroline. *Anatomy of the Spirit: The Seven Stages of Power and Healing.* Three Rivers Press, 1997, p. 265.

Chapter 13

[1] Inhouse Drugstore. "What is Arthritis?" www.inhousedrugstore.co.uk/arthritis/arthritis -information.html

Chapter 14

[1] Braden, Greg. *Walking Between the Worlds, The Science of Compassion.* Radio Bookstore Press (hardcover): Bellevue, Wash., 1997, p. 52.

Chapter 15

[1] American Cancer Society, "What Are the Key Statistics for Breast Cancer?" www.cancer.org/docroot/home/index.asp (Search Breast Cancer)

[2] Motz, Julie. *Hands of Life: Use Your Body's Own Energy Medicine for Healing, Recovery, and Transformation*, Bantam, 2000, p. 153.

[3] "Exercise Can Cut the Risk of Dying from Breast Cancer." *Washington Post* (online), May 25, 2005. www.washintonpost.com/wp-dyn/content/article/2005/05/24A.

Chapter 16

[1] Gerber, Richard, M.D. *A Practical Guide to Vibrational Medicine: Energy Healing and Spiritual Transformation.* Harper Paperbacks, 2001, p. 391.

[2] Lincoln, Michael J., Ph.D. *Messages from the Body: Their Psychological Meaning.* Talking Hearts, rev. 2006, p. 5.

Chapter 17

[1] Lincoln, Michael J., Ph.D. *Messages from the Body: Their Psychological Meaning.* Talking Hearts, rev. 2006, p. 136.

[2] Hay, Louise L. *Heal Your Body: The Mental Causes for Physical Illness and the Metaphysical Way to Overcome Them.* Hay House: Calif., 1982, p. 24.

3   Op. Cit. Lincoln, p. 605.

Chapter 19
1   McNamara, Melissa. *"A Look At Antidepressants."* CBS Evening News, New York. Dec. 13, 2006. *http://cbsnews.com/stories/2006/12/13/fyi/main2255769.shtml*

Chapter 21
1   Janov, Arthur. *The Biology of Love.* Prometheus Books. Amherst, N.Y., 2000, p. 270.
2   Lincoln, Michael J. *Addictions and Cravings: Their Psychological Meaning.* Talking Hearts, revised 2000, p. 316.
3   Gerber, Richard, M.D. *A Practical Guide to Vibrational Medicine: Energy Healing and Spiritual Transformation.* Harper Paperbacks, 2001, p. 62.
4   Lincoln, Michael J., Ph.D. *Messages from the Body: Their Psychological Meaning.* Talking Hearts, rev. 2006, p. 475-476.
5   Lincoln, Michael J. PhD. *Messages from the Body: Their Psychological Meaning.* Vol.I, 2005, p. 309
6   Gerber, Richard, MD. *Vibrational Medicine: The #1 Handbook of Subtle-Energy Therapies.* 3rd ed., Bear & Company: Vt., 2001, p. 399.

Chapter 22
1   Roche Laboratories. "What You Need to Know (about Hep C)." www.hepctherapy.net/need_to_know/need_to_know.asp
2   Hay, Louise L. *Heal Your Body: The Mental Causes for Physical Illness and the Metaphysical Way to Overcome Them.* Hay House: Calif., 1982, p. 47.
3   Motz, Julie. *Hands of Life: Use Your Body's Own Energy Medicine for Healing, Recovery, and Transformation,* Bantam, 2000, p. 72.
4   Gerber, Richard, M.D. *A Practical Guide to Vibrational Medicine: Energy Healing and Spiritual Transformation.* Harper

Paperbacks, 2001, p. 58.

5   Op. Cit. Motz. p. 62.

6   Lincoln, Michael J., Ph.D. *Messages from the Body: Their Psychological Meaning.* Talking Hearts, rev. 2006, p. 573.

7   Schulz, Mona Lisa, M.D., Ph.D. *Awakening Intuition: Using Your Mind-Body Network for Insight and Healing.* Three Rivers Press, N.Y, 1998, p. 219

8   Lincoln, Michael J., Ph.D. aka Narayan-Singh, *Addictions and Cravings: Their Psychological Meaning*—Revised June 2000, p. 269.

9   Boyle, Lydia, P. "Naomi Judd's Voyage of Self Discovery"

10   Boyle, Lydia, P. "Naomi Judd's Voyage of Self Discovery"

11   Judd, Naomi. *Naomi's Breakthrough Guide: 20 Choices to Transform Your Life.* Simon & Schuster, 2004. p. 142.

12   Ibid. p. 262.

Chapter 23

1   Lincoln, Michael J., Ph.D. *Messages from the Body: Their Psychological Meaning.* Talking Hearts, rev. 2006, p. 368-369.

2   Eig, Jonathan. *Luckiest Man: The Life and Death of Lou Gehrig.* Simon & Schuster, N.Y., 2006, p. 12.

3   Ibid. p. 12.

4   Alder, David A. and Terry Widener. *Lou Gehrig: The Luckiest Man.* Gulliver Books (Harcourt Brace and Co.), 1997, p. 2.

5   Ibid. p. 2.

6   Ibid. p. 5.

7   Macht, Norman L. *Lou Gehrig (Baseball Legends).* Chelsea House Pub., 1995, pp. 35-36.

8   Ibid. p. 16.

9   Ibid. p. 34.

10   Ibid. p. 35.

11   Eig, Jonathan. *Luckiest Man: The Life and Death of Lou Gehrig.* Simon & Schuster, N.Y., 2006, pp. 245-236.

12   Ibid. p. 247.

13   Op. Cit. Lincoln, pp. 240-241.

14   Ibid. p. 357-358.
15   Lincoln, Michael J., PhD. *Messages from the Body: Their Psychological Meaning*. Vol.I, 2005,p.378.

Chapter 24
1   Lincoln, Michael J., Ph.D. *Messages from the Body: Their Psychological Meaning*. Talking Hearts, rev. 2006, pp. 77, 569.
2   Ibid. p. 44.
3   Myss, Caroline. *Anatomy of the Spirit: The Seven Stages of Power and Healing*. Three Rivers Press, 1997, pp. 129-130.

Chapter 25
1   Gerber, Richard, M.D. *A Practical Guide to Vibrational Medicine: Energy Healing and Spiritual Transformation*. Harper Paperbacks, 2001, p. 68-69.
2   Gerber, Richard, MD. *Vibrational Medicine: The #1 Handbook of Subtle-Energy Therapies*. 3rd ed., Bear & Company: Vt., 2001, p. 374.

Chapter 27
1   Lincoln, Michael J., Ph.D. *Messages from the Body: Their Psychological Meaning*. Talking Hearts, rev. 2006, pp. 558.
2   Fox, Michael J. *Lucky Man: A Memoir*. Hyperion. N.Y., 2002. p. 1.
3   Op. Cit. Lincoln. p.230-231.
4   Op. Cit. Fox. p. 40.
5   Ibid. p. 138.
6   Ibid. p. 40.
7   Op. Cit. Fox. p. 16.
8   Ibid. pp. 39-40.
9   Ibid. p. 215.
10   Ibid. p. 17.
11   Ibid. p. 16.
12   Ibid. p. 6.

About the Creator of the MO Technique

Maureen meets each client with an open heart and mind and skilled, healing hands. Her desire to help and to heal began with her work as registered nurse more than 37 years ago. After working in emergency room, surgery, oncology, orthopedics, home health care, and hospice care, Maureen turned to learning and teaching holistic and alternative methods of care and healing. Now a Guided Imagery Practitioner, she has devised the MO (Modus Operandi) Technique and has used this technique successfully with clients for the last twelve years. Maureen has continued her education with courses in acupressure, reflexology, polarity, Reiki, emotional anatomy, human behavior, kinesiology and advanced anatomy and physiology. She is a current member of The American Holistic Nurses Association, Associated Body Works and Massage Professionals, Imagery International and The Association For Humanistic Psychology.

The gentle guiding hand of Maureen can help lead you to a greater insight of the issues you face, and at the same time, enhance your inner resources. Through the use of her MO Technique, the meaning behind health challenges can be revealed and understood allowing healing to take place.

Maureen lives and works in the heart of California's Central Valley. In her work, her goal is always to deepen the mind, body, spirit connection. Her web site is *www.MaureenMinnehanJones.com*.

For speaking engagements or healing sessions, contact her at MMJ@MaureenMinnehanJones.com or 209-845-8141.

BOOKS

MySpiritRadio